Travel Agency Accounting Procedures

OTHER BOOKS IN THE TRAVEL MANAGEMENT LIBRARY SERIES

GUIDE TO STARTING AND OPERATING A SUCCESSFUL TRAVEL AGENCY, THIRD EDITION

GROUP TRAVEL OPERATIONS MANUAL

HANDBOOK OF PROFESSIONAL TOUR MANAGEMENT, SECOND EDITION

FOREIGN INDEPENDENT TOURS: PLANNING, PRICING, AND PROCESSING

EFFECTIVE COMMUNICATIONS IN THE TRAVEL INDUSTRY

THE DICTIONARY OF HOSPITALITY, TRAVEL & TOURISM

YOUR CAREER IN TRAVEL, TOURISM, AND HOSPITALITY, SECOND EDITION

TRAVEL AND TOURISM MARKETING TECHNIQUES, SECOND EDITION

COMPLETE GUIDE TO TRAVEL AGENCY AUTOMATION, SECOND EDITION

FINANCIAL MANAGEMENT FOR TRAVEL AGENCIES

TRAVEL AGENCY POLICIES AND PROCEDURES MANUAL

LEGAL ASPECTS OF TRAVEL AGENCY OPERATION, SECOND EDITION

TRAVEL AGENCY GUIDE TO BUSINESS TRAVEL

LEGAL FORMS FOR TRAVEL AGENTS

BUDGETING FOR PROFIT AND MANAGING BY GOALS

GUIDE TO TRAVEL AGENCY SECURITY

THE TRAVEL AGENCY PERSONNEL MANUAL, SECOND EDITION

Travel Agency Accounting Procedures

James Poynter

NOTICE TO THE READER

Publisher does not warrant or guarantee any of the products described herein or perform any independent analysis in connection with any of the product information contained herein. Publisher does not assume, and expressly disclaims, any obligation to obtain and include information other than that provided to it by the manufacturer.

The reader is expressly warned to consider and adopt all safety precautions that might be indicated by the activities described herein and to avoid all potential hazards. By following the instructions contained herein, the reader willingly assumes all risks in connection with such instructions.

The publisher makes no representations or warranties of any kind, including but not limited to, the warranties of fitness for particular purpose or merchantability, nor are any such representations implied with respect to the material set forth herein, and the publisher takes no responsibility with respect to such material. The publisher shall not be liable for any special, consequential, or exemplary damages resulting, in whole or in part, from the readers' use of, or reliance upon, this material.

Delmar Staff:
Sponsoring Editor: Mark Huth
Developmental Editor: Lisa Reale
Project Editor: Carol Micheli
Production Supervisor: Wendy Troeger
Design Coordinator: Karen Kunz Kemp

For information, write:
Delmar Publishers Inc.
2 Computer Drive West, Box 15-015
Albany, NY 12212

Printed in the United States of America
published simultaneously in Canada
by Nelson Canada,
a Division of The Thomson Corporation

10 9 8 7 6 5 4 3 2 1

Library of Congress Cataloging-in-Publication Data

Poynter, James M.
Travel agency accounting procedures / James Poynter.
p. cm.
Includes index.
ISBN 0-8273-3389-7
1. Travel agents—Accounting. I. Title
HF5686.T73P69 1991
657'8—dc20 90-24152
CIP

CONTENTS

DEDICATION

To Sorore Poynter
upon whose
accounting, budgeting, and financial management skills
this author has depended for many years

PREFACE

As the travel agency industry has become more and more competitive, agency management has had to manage both income and expenditures better than in the past. Increasingly, agency owners and executives are learning to emulate management in many other industries by adopting financial management processes, procedures, and programs. However, they have learned that financial management will not work unless good accounting practices are adopted and maintained on a day-by-day and a year-by-year basis.

Fifteen years ago, the average travel agency had an average annual sales level of less than $1 million. Almost all travel agency owners and managers handled the accounting themselves, using a rough manual system. Because agencies were far fewer in number and the natural growth in travel business from year to year was good, the majority of agency owners and managers felt that there was little need to undertake sophisticated accounting and financial management.

Today the picture is totally different. At the end of 1989, the annual revenue per agency, not counting satellite ticket printers, was $2,613,000. The average sales level has approached $3 million, travel agencies have tripled in number, and the competition has increased substantially. Consequently, agency management has found that accurate accounting is needed to produce the financial reports which allow management to undertake ratio analyses, comparative statistical charting, and the multitude of other financial management applications that are vital to success in the marketplace. Increasingly, management is turning to agency staff members and outside personnel seeking (and highly rewarding) accounting specialists, hired to work in the agency on a full-time basis.

Meanwhile, trade schools, two-year colleges, four-year colleges, and universities are producing large numbers of entry-level travel agents. Textbooks have been prepared to train the entry-level agent to be an expert in a wide variety of agent applications. However, no book has been available for students who aspired to work in travel agency accounting. *Travel Agency Accounting Procedures,* though only an introduction to the subject, begins to fill this void. The reader is urged to recognize that, while this book presents a foundation in the basics of travel agency accounting and introduces some financial management applications, it should not be considered anything more than a basic, introductory-level textbook.

Many travel agency accounting systems have been developed. A large number, perhaps most, are based on the *ASTA* (American Society of Travel Agents) system. *Travel Agency Accounting Procedures* is also based on the ASTA accounting system, in the belief that if the student understands the underlying concepts of the ASTA accounting system, he/she should also be able to apply the same principles to the other major manual accounting systems. Although there may be some nuances of other systems that will need to be learned, it can be expected that the basic foundations provided in this book will serve the student well no matter what manual travel agency accounting system the student encounters.

Please also note that this book is based upon a manual accounting system instead of an automated or partially automated system. Just as most academic programs teach students to handwrite airline tickets (even though 95% of all U.S. travel agencies are computerized), so also this textbook presents a manual accounting system in the belief that once a student understands a manual system, he/she will have a good foundation for understanding automated or partially automated systems.

This book is designed to help the student progress from accounting system basics up through the production of standard accounting reports and into budgeting; it then undertakes a brief look at financial management reports. The first few chapters present data that initially may appear to be disorganized one chapter from the next. As the book progresses, however, the student draws increasingly from the knowledge presented in early chapters so that an integration of the knowledge occurs. This integration of knowledge is reinforced through the end-of-chapter and (in later chapters) mid-chapter exercises and learning activities. Even if the instructor does not review or grade the learning activities provided with each chapter, the student is strongly urged to do them so that he/she will be assured of understanding the concepts presented. In the travel industry accounting and financial management courses taught by the author, students are given an opportunity to practice all learning activities. Though reviewed in class they are not graded. Some students, therefore, do not complete the exercises. But there is strong correlation between those who complete the learning activities and ask questions on them, and those who achieve high grades in class and are able to apply what they've learned by performing well in job situations. Reversely, there is a strong correlation between those who fail to complete the learning activities, do not ask questions, and those who make very low grades on examinations.

The learning activities at the end of each chapter have been tested in the classroom over a period of many years. They have been refined and only those that strongly reinforce the chapter's presentations have been included. In most cases, answers are provided on the next page or within the few pages following the exercise. In all cases where answers are not provided in the textbook, the question is intended for classroom review, and the answers are provided in the instructor's manual.

Learning activities vary in nature and purpose. At the beginning of each chapter, students will find a listing of four objectives. Studying these objectives carefully before turning to the chapter itself is strongly suggested. The objectives point out the salient points and the conclusions to be found when studying the chapter.

At the end of each chapter is a series of questions. These are discussion questions intended to provide a review of the chapter. Supplementing the objectives and the discussion questions are exercises providing an opportunity for students to apply what they've learned. Most chapters have one exercise at the end, but a few of the later chapters have several.

The student may proceed in any of several ways. Many will go through the book in a logical progression of reading and reviewing one page at a time. Studying the book in this manner allows one to encounter the overall objectives first, study the chapter while looking for those objectives, review the chapter by answering the discussion questions, and reinforce the understanding of the major points by completing the exercise(s). This approach works well for many people.

An alternative approach is to start with the objectives, but before reading the chapter, review the discussion questions and the exercise. The student might even attempt to answer the discussion questions and think about how to perform the exercise. Then, he/she can read the chapter while looking for the answers to the discussion questions and the knowledge necessary to complete the exercise(s). If necessary, go back and reread the chapter, keeping all of these learning activities in mind. After reading the chapter once or twice, go back over the objectives and determine whether or not they have been achieved. If not, go back and review appropriate sections of the chapter. Next, go through the discussion questions, attempting to answer them yourself. If you have difficulty in doing so, review appropriate sections in the chapter. Finally, tackle the exercise. If you run into difficulties, go back to the chapter. After rereading an appropriate section or two, try the exercise again. If you still have problems, write down as precisely and accurately as you can the nature of the problem you encounter. Bring this to the attention of your instructor so that the instructor can help you develop the correct answer by going through the reasoning or the approaches behind the exercise.

Whatever approach is taken, it is important that the student understand each chapter, because subsequent learning activities are built upon an understanding of the material that was presented previously. Also, when examinations are given, they are generally based upon the learning that is provided in each chapter as one progresses from one chapter to the next.

Though for most students accounting has never been easy or fun, it can be interesting and rewarding. This book is designed to take the accounting student, one step at a time, from the introduction to travel agency accounting up to a high level of ability to perform well in an entry-level travel agency accounting position. By following the study procedures recommended here, students should be able to complete the course and develop a solid foundation in travel agency accounting sufficient enough to provide them with the ability to offer travel agency employers one more, very important skill level. Having an understanding and knowledge of travel agency accounting will serve students well whether they work as travel agency accountants or bookkeepers, if they are employed as agents or lead agents, or if they are promoted into supervisory or management positions. In all three capacities, an understanding of travel agency accounting is of vital importance and can be of considerable benefit to the student in his/her professional career.

ACKNOWLEDGEMENTS

The author extends thanks to Linda Bell, an independent travel industry accounting and financial management consultant; and to Bill Heath of National College for having contributed the text and/or advised on both its adherence to standard accounting practices and its accuracy when variations customary to the travel industry are noted. I thank Nader Koupal, accounting executive with Travel Inc., for reviewing all chapters and for his suggested changes—all of which made the book much more understandable for the student. I also thank executives of the following travel agencies for having provided a review of selected chapters or for providing reference materials: The Travel Society, Master Travel, Thomas Cook Travel, IVI Travel, Azumano Travel, and Uniglobe Travel.

Special thanks goes to the American Society of Travel Agents, which has contributed a substantial amount of material. Their accounting system is the basis of much of the accounting data presented in the text. Also special thanks goes to the Institute of Certified Travel Agents. Not only did the Institute of Certified Travel Agents and the American Society of Travel Agents contribute substantially to the field of accounting for travel agents, especially in its early development, but ICTA was the publisher (in their certification manual) of my first article on the travel agency budgeting process. This was the foundation on which much of the last several chapters of this book was based.

Special thanks also goes to those reviewers whose comments and recommendations were of great importance to the final development of this textbook—Ron Bernthal, Sullivan County Community College; Anne M. Ranczuch, Monroe Community College; Sherry A. Getz, York Technical Institute; Becky Emerson, Parks Jr. College; Elizabeth Van Dyke, University of New Haven; Rose Silverman, West Los Angeles Community College; and Steve Roy, Spencer School of Business.

Finally, a very sincere thanks goes to Dr. Donald Madden of the University of Kentucky. Dr. Madden developed the first Uniform Classification of Accounts for travel agents and published the first book in the field of accounting for travel agents.

It is impossible to provide sufficient thanks to one's family for their patience and understanding during the writing of a textbook. My fondest appreciation is expressed to Sorore, Lewis, Robert, and Michael for their unending patience.

ABOUT THE AUTHOR

Jim Poynter has worked in the travel industry for nearly thirty years. He has worked in almost every segment of the industry, in ten countries on four continents. Mr. Poynter received both his B.A. and his M.A. from George Washington University in Washington, D.C. He has taught with the Florida State University Hotel School, National College, Tallahassee Community College, and Metropolitan State College of Denver, where he currently directs the Travel Administration program in the Hospitality, Meeting, Travel Administration Department of the School of Professional Studies. Mr. Poynter has conducted seminars for three national travel associations, at twelve universities and colleges, and for a wide range of private institutions. He serves as a Board Member of the Society of Travel and Tourism Educators and is the only honorary member ever selected by the Institute of Certified Travel Agents and the Rocky Mountain Business Travel Association. Mr. Poynter is the author of two books.

INTRODUCTION TO STANDARD BASIC ACCOUNTING

OBJECTIVES

Upon completion of this chapter, the student will be able to:

- ❑ Explain the importance of accounting and financial management to business and industry
- ❑ Demonstrate a working knowledge of basic travel agency accounting terms
- ❑ Describe the petty cash record keeping and replenishment process
- ❑ Complete a simple petty cash report

INTRODUCTION

The purpose of accounting in a travel agency is to provide records and data that will give management the information needed to run the agency financially. Accounting data also serves the needs of other audiences, primarily vendors and clients. Accounting data meets government reporting requirements as well, especially those of the Internal Revenue Service.

For small travel agencies, i.e., those with under $1 million per year of sales ($20,000 average weekly sales), accounting is normally handled by a manager or a working owner and is not the full-time job of any one person in the agency. Frequently, the bookkeeping tasks, such as the daily recording of financial data and the preparation of the ARC Report, are handled by an executive in the agency. The more difficult tasks of preparing end-of-month, quarterly, and annual reports and tax filing are undertaken by hired accountants. Agencies handling sales volumes exceeding $1 million per year frequently employ a part-time bookkeeper/accountant. If the sales volume increases to $4 or $5 million per year, the agency will employ one or more full-time accounting/bookkeeping staff members. Most travel agencies in the United States are small, and so the majority do not hire part-time employees, but relegate bookkeeping/accounting responsibilities to an ancillary task performed by a staff member whose primary job is travel sales. Therefore it is essential that everyone planning to work in the travel agency field understand the basics of travel agency accounting, even if they do not plan to work as accountants or bookkeepers. In addition, all staff members should understand basic accounting and bookkeeping, since these principles determine financial management decisions that affect the livelihood, income, and work patterns of all travel agency staff members.

One of the first introductions a newcomer to a travel agency hears is the term *ARC Report* (Airline Reporting Corporation). Frequently, reference to this report is the only introduction to accounting and financial management a new travel agency employee receives. Newcomers to the industry often reach the conclusion that travel agency accounting and financial management and the ARC Report are synonomous. In a few travel agencies this is true; but the ARC Report, prepared weekly, mainly provides air carriers with agency air sales data. Its stated chief purpose is to provide financial information needed by air carriers rather than the agencies. Although the ARC Report may be the center around which many travel agency accounting and financial management systems are based, it is not an accounting system in and of itself. It omits most of the financial reporting or financial management guidelines needed to operate a travel agency efficiently and profitably. The ARC Report is important however, and an entire chapter (chapter 8) of this book has been devoted to it.

VOCABULARY

To be able to understand accounting and financial management in a travel agency, specific words, terms, and acronyms must be learned. These constitute the vernacular in which agency accountants work, and frequently they are used so extensively that an outsider listening to agency accountants talk might almost believe they are speaking a foreign language. The more important words, terms, and acronyms are defined below. It is suggested that these definitions be reviewed as the words, terms, and acronyms are encountered, so that the reader can enter into the lesson with the degree of comfort brought about by understanding the definitions of seemingly strange vocabulary.

This book draws upon terms used by the American Society of Travel Agents (ASTA) accounting system. Although there are many travel agency accounting systems, most are based on one or more aspects of the ASTA accounting system. Because this textbook is also patterned on the ASTA accounting system, most of the accounting terms are defined in a way that is similar to the definitions found in the *ASTA Travel Agency Accounting and Information System.*

Accounting Period — Specific units of time during which the entire accounting cycle occurs. For purposes of this (book) the examples are based on a year consisting of thirteen four-week periods. An alternative approach is a year divided into four quarters each consisting of two four-week and one five-week periods. (This will tend to more closely approximate the calendar months.)

Accounts Payable — Amounts on a reporting or regular billing basis to carriers and suppliers for services rendered (e.g., Rail, Insurance, Auto Rental Vouchers, Traveler's Checks). *Chapter 1, page 3.*

Accounts Receivable — All transactions representing funds advanced or agency indebtedness incurred (e.g., airline tickets issued) on behalf of a client. *Chapter 1, page 3.*

ARC — Airline Reporting Corporation (An organization formed by and for most major domestic and some international air carriers).

ARC Report — A report required weekly from appointed travel agencies by the Airline Reporting Corporation to track airline ticket sales and to identify fund transfer needs.

Assets — Resources owned by the agency for use in satisfying client requests for services. *Chapter 1, page 3.*

Assets, Current — Resources expected to be used in the near future. *Chapter 1, page 3.*

Assets, Long Term — Resources whose life is greater than one year. *Chapter 1, page 3.*

Balance Sheet — Financial statement showing the assets, liabilities, and capital position of the agency at a given point in time. This statement reflects the concept that total assets are always equal to the sum of total liabilities and capital. *Chapter 1, page 3.*

Capital — Amounts invested in the business by its owners, partners, or proprietor as a basis for operations. *Chapter 1, page 3.*

Capital Account — Reflects the total of capital invested, retained, earned or lost (Profit and Loss), and paid out (dividend or withdrawal). *Chapter 1, page 3.*

Commission or Commission Income — The amount that is available for use in operations after payments to carriers and suppliers are made from gross revenues. *Chapter 1, page 3.*

Credit — An entry on the right-hand side of an account.

Debit — An entry on the left-hand side of an account.

Debits and Credits — Offsetting entries reflecting the rule that the two must always equal each other. *Chapter 1, page 3.*

Expenses — Amounts expended while offering services to customers to earn income. *Chapter 1, page 3.*

Income Statement — Summary of the financial results of operations — revenues, commission income, operating expenses, and net income — for a period of time. *Chapter 1, page 4.*

Modified Accrual System — Revenues and expenses are recognized as they occur (i.e., documented) while receivables and payables for other than expense items are periodically accumulated. *Chapter 1, page 4.*

Net Income — The 'bottom line' difference between commission income and all operating expenses for a period of time. *Chapter 1, page 4.*

Net Loss — When commission income is less than operating expenses. *Chapter 1, page 4.*

Profit and Loss — Income statement. *Chapter 1, page 4.*

CASH DISBURSEMENT

Most businesses have special concerns when it comes to the handling of cash. The potential for both loss and theft is greater when dealing with cash than with checks or credit cards. Most retail businesses attempt to limit the amount of cash held on the premises so that in case there is a robbery, the loss will be small. Therefore, travel agencies normally make daily deposits of cash and checks into their bank account(s) or they make a deposit whenever cash reaches a certain level ($500, for example).

Although the desire to keep only a minimum of cash on the premises is justified, all businesses need to have some cash available for working purposes. A client paying for a ticket or other trip arrangement(s) in cash may need to receive change, which the agency must be able to provide. In addition, it is common for the travel agency to receive items for which payment is required upon receipt. This is especially true for new agencies, when the business has not yet established widespread financial credit. Many agencies purchase rolls of stamps and other small items on an "as needed" basis. Although some vendors accept checks for such purchases (as the post office does), others do not, and sometimes it is necessary or just easier to pay by cash. Therefore most travel agencies establish *petty cash* funds (a small amount of "on-hand" funds to pay for daily small expenses and to utilize in order to make change) and make most cash disbursements from them. These transactions are usually handled in the following manner:

1) An agency policy is set regarding the amount of petty cash funds that will be kept on hand. It is decided that this amount not exceed $100, for example. An initial check is written for $100 to establish the fund.

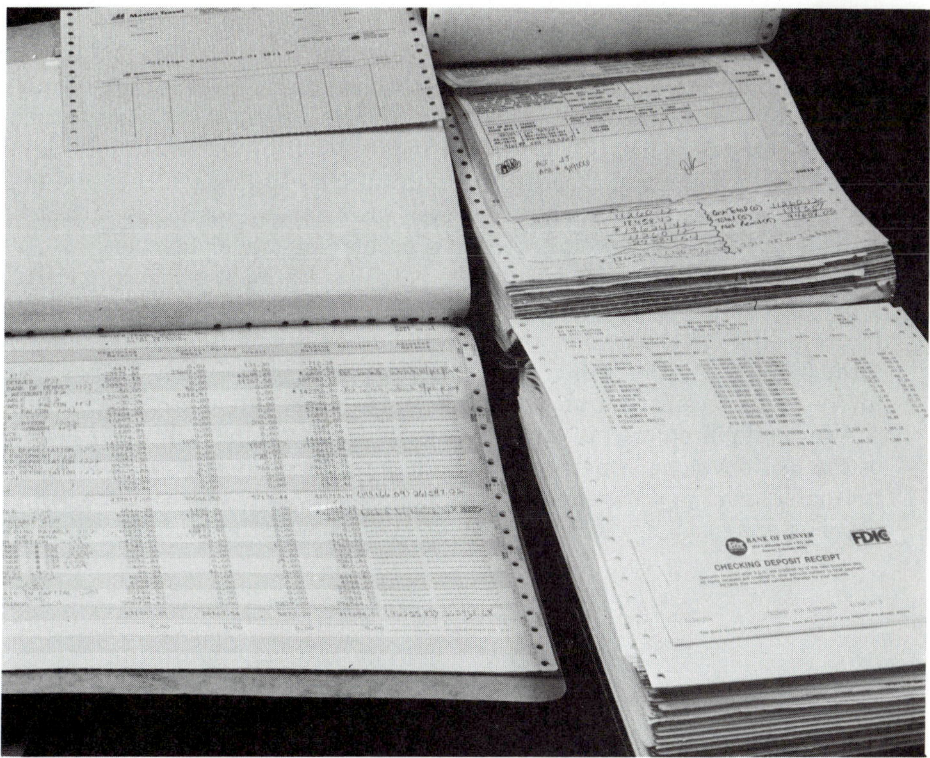

Figure 1–1 Accounting books, logs, and journals (Courtesy of Master Travel, Denver, CO)

2) Petty cash money is normally kept in a money change box that can be locked. Usually smaller bills are kept, if at all possible, in a drawer for each denomination (similar to a cash register drawer).
3) The petty cash box will normally hold a pad of petty cash receipts. Standard petty cash receipts can be purchased from office supply houses or the agency can devise its own form and have copies made.
4) Whenever there is a cash expenditure, a petty cash receipt is filled out, showing the reason(s) for the expenditure; and a vendor receipt is attached (if one has been obtained).
5) Cash on hand, i.e. petty cash, must be balanced regularly. Therefore, either at the beginning or the end of each business day, the accountant *balances* the petty cash. Balancing means that the accountant counts all of the cash in the petty cash box and reviews all of the receipts. The sum of the receipts plus the amount of cash should always equal the original petty cash starting figure ($100, in this example). If there is a

discrepancy, and there is less cash in the petty cash box than there should be, probably one of the employees forgot to put a receipt into the box for an expenditure. If petty cash is balanced daily, the accountant can ask employees if they have any outstanding receipts or if they forgot to complete a petty cash form, and the discrepancy can be readily resolved. If unresolved discrepancies occur continually, and especially if they are major discrepancies, limitations on access to the petty cash box should be considered. This, however, is seldom a problem in travel agencies.

6) When the total amount of cash in the petty cash fund has been reduced to a predetermined level (to $70 from $100, for example), a check is written for the difference between the current amount and the predesignated total ($100). At the same time, all completed petty cash forms, with appropriate receipts stapled to them, are taken out of the petty cash drawer and placed into an envelope marked with the period from the date of the last envelope of petty cash receipts to the current date. These are normally kept in an envelope file box and filed by date in case tax or other reviews are needed. Retention of petty cash records is determined by

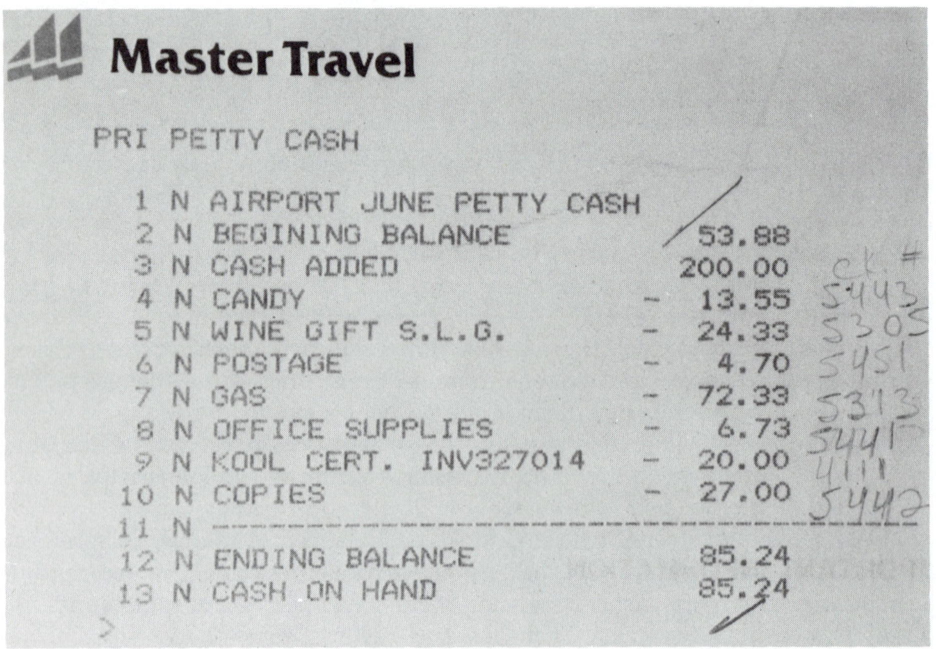

Master Travel

PRI PETTY CASH

					ck. #
1	N	AIRPORT JUNE PETTY CASH			
2	N	BEGINING BALANCE		53.88	
3	N	CASH ADDED		200.00	
4	N	CANDY	-	13.55	5443
5	N	WINE GIFT S.L.G.	-	24.33	5305
6	N	POSTAGE	-	4.70	5451
7	N	GAS	-	72.33	5313
8	N	OFFICE SUPPLIES	-	6.73	5441
9	N	KOOL CERT. INV327014	-	20.00	4111
10	N	COPIES	-	27.00	5442
11	N	--			
12	N	ENDING BALANCE		85.24	
13	N	CASH ON HAND		85.24	

Figure 1–2 Sample completed petty cash report (Courtesy of Master Travel, Denver, CO)

space availability and tax considerations. Most agencies retain these records for a minimum of five years.

In addition to petty cash expenditures, most agencies will maintain a *cash disbursements journal,* which is simply a listing of cash expenditures that are made from funds other than petty cash. Although it is unusual, some agencies do at times make cash expenditures in larger amounts than the amount available in petty cash. The cash disbursements journal is usually very small and can normally be kept on an annual basis, since it is rare for agencies to make such major cash payments.

GENERAL JOURNAL

The basic concept of accounting is that all monies brought into the business and all monies spent for debts incurred by the business are *accounted* for. These transactions are normally recorded first in *journals.* There are a number of different types of journals, but a *general journal* is one that usually shows all expenditures and income.

Perhaps the bane of the new accounting student is the concept of debits and credits. Although these can certainly be confusing from time to time, the basic concept is that whenever there is an expenditure of money, a balancing process takes place. This balancing process is a recording of the transaction on a *T account.* The term *T account* is utilized because it looks just like a very large T. T accounts are named according to each income or expenditure category utilized by the travel agency. When a transaction takes place, an *accounting entry* (sometimes referred to as simply *entry*) takes place. An entry that is made on the left-hand side of the T account is called a debit, while an entry that is made on the right-hand side of the T account is called a credit. The result looks like the following:

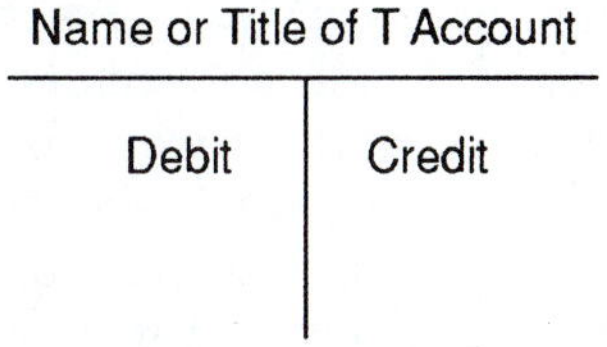

Name or Title of T Account	
Debit	Credit

Debits and credits balance out to one another, and the idea is that all accounts will be in balance at all times. The *general journal* is a book in which all income and expenditures are recorded, thereby reflecting the debit and credit transactions occurring and the T account debit and credit entries.

General journals can come in all styles and sizes. Usually they are larger than standard size paper, and they come as bound books. They have sections for each major type of income and expenditure. Usually entries are made on a date basis, recording the date on which the income is received or the expenditure is incurred. Sometimes they are recorded by actual date and time (although the time of day is seldom recorded), but more often income/expenditures are recorded sequentially by invoice, receipt, or invoice/receipt number.

EXPENSE JOURNAL

Although many travel agencies will show every receipt and every expenditure in the general journal, some travel agencies maintain a separate *expense journal.* When this is done, the expense journal can be maintained in two different ways. Perhaps the more common approach is to simply list expenditures as they occur. If an agency uses checks only and maintains a policy that expenditures other than petty cash (for small emergency needs) be made by check only, then the agency checkbook serves as an expense journal. This is usually the case for small agencies. However, because of the regulations of the Airline Reporting Corporation, even small agencies frequently maintain two or more checking accounts. When this is done, an expense journal is frequently kept to obtain a daily balance in all checking, savings, and other accounts. The expense journal normally shows a record of the check number, the vendor, the reason for the expense (what was purchased), and the amount of the expense. Many also have a decreasing column showing the balance in the specific account after the expenditure is deducted (similar to the way in which a checkbook register is kept).

CASH RECEIPT JOURNAL

Possibly the way in which internal theft is most likely to occur is with cash receipts. When a client pays cash for a travel purchase, it is easy for an agent to pocket the money. Unless accounting records and documentation are kept, there is a real danger of high potential loss. Tracking cash receipts can also be a concern in a travel agency. The *cash receipts journal* provides a central location for reporting all monies received when payment was made in cash. This journal can be totalled at the end of each day and provides a balance against which the cash deposit slip(s) is compared. The cash receipts journal normally lists the amount of cash received in payment, notes whether each receipt was a deposit or a final payment, reflects the name of the payor and the name of the client (if they are different), and briefly describes the purchase, such as domestic air ticket or cruise deposit. As noted in later chapters, there are other counter balances and safeguards against theft as well. Most feel that having multiple safeguards built into the system is the best way to discourage internal theft.

GENERAL LEDGER

In many ways the *general ledger* is similar to the general journal. It normally reflects two entries for every transaction. It displays a T account for each account kept by the agency. In many cases, instead of showing a large number of accounts, the general ledger will simply show "Sales Revenue" and "Expense" accounts, or it may show as few as three or four overall accounts. The important concept is that whenever there is a transaction, some account in the general ledger is debited and another credited. The general ledger, therefore, must show balanced accounts at all times.

ACCOUNTING REPORTS

There are literally hundreds of accounting reports that a travel agency might obtain that could be of use in managing its financial affairs. Many of the largest travel agencies prepare a large number of accounting reports on daily, weekly, and monthly bases. In addition to preparing accounting reports for their own use, many agencies that specialize in corporate and group travel prepare reports for their major clients as well. Some of these specialized reports are discussed later in this book. However, there are several standard reports that all travel agencies should consider developing on a regular basis. Almost all travel agencies do prepare weekly, monthly, and annual reports, such as an Airline Reporting Corporation weekly report, an income statement, a monthly balance sheet, and an annual balance sheet.

Daily and Weekly ARC Report

The ARC Report is required by the Airline Reporting Corporation from all *appointed* travel agencies. Appointment by the Airline Reporting Corporation means that the travel agency is authorized to sell tickets on major domestic and some international air carriers. Although the requirement is that the report must be filed weekly, a few agencies have requested permission to file the report daily; other filing arrangements have been negotiated by a very few agencies around the country.

Most travel agencies prepare the material for the ARC Report on a daily basis, but submit the report on a weekly basis. The reason for this is that although the standard reporting period is the week, it is often easier for the agency bookkeeper or accountant to prepare daily reports, which are then merged into a weekly report. The ARC Report is discussed in detail in chapter 8. However, it is important to understand some of the highlights of the ARC Report and the reasons for it. Many travel agencies consider the ARC Report to be their most important weekly report. Since well over 50 percent of the income derived by most travel agencies comes from the sale of domestic airline tickets, and since the ARC Report is the easiest way of being able to measure and track basic accounting data, agencies look for ratios in the ARC Report and address concerns that identify themselves in the report.

Basically, the ARC Report consists of sending to the air carriers a copy of every air ticket issued that week, together with a summary of the total air ticket sales made during the week. Sales are broken down into two categories, labeled "CASH" and "CREDIT CARD." Those tickets that are paid for by check and those tickets that are billed to clients (but not yet paid for) are listed as cash sales, which are treated as cash paid-for items by the air carriers. Individual ticket commissions and tax amounts (as well as total commission levels for the week) are also reflected in the ARC Report. Commissions are paid on base fares only, meaning the fare after payment of all taxes, and, in some cases, service charges.

Travel agencies frequently identify sales levels (and whether or not they are meeting sales goals) by ARC Report totals. A rough formula utilized in the industry is that $20,000 of ARC reported weekly sales on an average basis is the equivalent of $1 million in annual sales. Many agencies work with formulas based on total sales, and knowledge of ARC sales levels helps an agency identify where it stands each week in relation to its goals.

Income Statement

The *income statement* is more commonly referred to in the industry as a *Receipts and Disbursements Statement.* It is a monthly report that shows both the income received and the expenses incurred by the agency. Every income item and every expenditure is placed in its own account. Most income statements show comparison data with the expenses incurred and income received during the same month in the previous year. The income statement also has a year-to-date column for earnings and expenditures in each account. By comparing the income received during a given month of one year with the income received during the same month in the previous year (in any category of income—domestic air sales, international air sales, cruise sales, etc.), the agency can readily identify any problems affecting sales. Expenditures can be compared in the same way, and with such categories as rent, telephone charges, or office supplies, the agency can determine any unusually large expenditures and again readily identify any problem areas.

The income statement is normally prepared at the same time that the monthly balance sheet is prepared. Most travel agencies attempt to complete these reports by the tenth of each month, so as to show all financial activity during the previous month. If they are prepared late (especially if they are prepared several months after the close of a particular month's financial activities), trends will still show, but it may be too late to take action to correct problems that might have been revealed. A problem may then become too serious and much more expensive to correct than if the financial reports were completed on time.

Monthly Balance Sheet

"The balance sheet is the detailed breakdown of assets (what is owned by the agency), liabilities (what is owed by the agency), and capital (the difference between assets and liabilities at the balance sheet date)" (*ASTA Travel Agency Accounting and Information System.* Chapter 11, page 3.) In other words, the balance sheet compares the values of the agency with the amount of money it owes and shows a current profit or loss. The balance sheet divides the value of the agency into current assets and other assets and divides the debts of the agency into liabilities and capital.

For most agencies, current assets will consist of cash currently in the bank, petty cash money on hand, accounts receivable (the amount of money owed to the agency by its accounts), investments, and notes owed to the agency (notes receivable). These are considered to be the current assets because they represent funds that can be converted to cash immediately or over a very short period of time (normally within one year). Other assets may include automobiles, office equipment, and other items owned by the agency that could be sold, if necessary.

Balanced against the assets are the liabilities and the capital. Liabilities normally consist of monies owed by the travel agency. Normally, the largest amount of liabilities is divided between two categories. The first category is money owed to the airlines and to suppliers. Because of the mechanisms of the Airline Reporting Corporation payment system, travel agencies at any given time owe the airlines money for tickets that the agencies have issued. The amount of this account payable to the Airline Reporting Corporation can be quite substantial. It is normally listed as a separate item under liabilities. Liabilities can also be owed to other suppliers, such as insurance companies for travel insurance sold, car rental companies for car rental vouchers sold, cruise lines for cruise payments due. There may also be notes payable to investors or to vendors.

The second major category of liabilities is taxes. Taxes are normally paid monthly, quarterly, or annually, depending upon the type of tax. Frequently, they are accrued and paid on periodic dates. For many agencies the largest amount of tax is the federal income tax, which is withheld from employees' salaries. However, there can also be state taxes, city taxes, county taxes, unemployment compensation taxes, and other taxes.

Capital is shown as a liability, since it is money that was invested by stockholders to provide the initial funds for the agency. Usually, the largest item in capital is invested capital, that is, money that was put into the agency in the beginning and left over a period of time. Capital can be put into the agency from time to time, as needed, or it can be taken out of the agency by selling stock back to the agency. Therefore, the total amount of "invested" capital can and often does change over time for many travel agencies. Another item of capital is retained earnings. This is money that was earned as profit and carried over from previous years. Finally, the profit or loss for the current year is shown in this section.

The monthly balance sheet and the annual balance sheet consist of the same items and appear to be the same. However, the annual balance sheet reflects the agency's financial position at the end of the fiscal year. This statement is circulated to the stockholders. Frequently, it is verified by a C.P.A. (Certified Public Accountant) or at least another accountant, since major decisions regarding the management of the agency are based on the agency's condition as reflected by the balance sheet.

SUMMARY

Many who are new to the travel agency industry hear about an ARC Report. They assume that the preparation of a weekly ARC Report is synonymous with travel agency accounting and financial management. This is incorrect. The ARC Report provides some useful data, but it is only one of a number of accounting and financial reports needed for travel agency accounting, reports that give management the information it needs to financially manage the agency and produce a profit. Since most agencies are small businesses with limited budgets, individuals who perform accounting tasks usually handle them as only a part of their responsibilities and are not full-time bookkeepers or accountants. Therefore, it is important that not only managers and owners understand the basics of travel agency accounting and financial management, but that all employees understand them as well.

In order to understand the basics of accounting and financial management, it is important to understand accounting terms. Several have been listed in this chapter, and it is recommended that the student become thoroughly familiar with them.

In addition to encountering new terms, the student also has encountered several instruments and books used in accounting and financial management. Perhaps the accounting book most often worked with is the general journal. This is a central source recording of all transactions that occur in a travel agency. Every expenditure and every income item is listed in the general journal.

The expense journal centralizes a record of expenses and lists them by category or type. Some travel agencies use their checkbook as an expense journal, while others keep a separate journal for this purpose.

Most travel agencies keep a cash receipts journal, and it is in this book that all cash monies brought into the agency are recorded. Cash, in this case, refers to checks as well as cash. Most agencies balance checkbook deposit receipts with the cash receipts journal.

Most travel agencies also keep a general ledger. This is a T account, which shows two balancing entries for each transaction.

The handling of cash is of special importance in any small business because of its high liquidity and the ease with which it can be lost or stolen. Therefore most agencies keep a small amount of cash on hand and maintain a petty cash control system. This system involves keeping a running balance of a small amount of money (often $100), and it requires that receipts documenting each expenditure be completed and recorded. The person handling the accounting function usually reviews the petty cash books daily or every other day, balances out the amount of cash on hand with the receipts, and resupplies the petty cash fund, if necessary.

While there are many optional accounting reports available that may help in the financial management of an agency, a few of the mandatory accounting reports include a weekly ARC Report (an accounting to the airlines of all tickets sold and the form of payment received for each ticket); an income statement (often referred to as a receipts and disbursements statement), which provides a monthly and an annual breakdown of income and expenses by type; and monthly and annual balance sheets, which provide an overall financial picture of the travel agency at the end of each month and at the end of each year.

❑ DISCUSSION QUESTIONS

1. What is the purpose of accounting?
2. In what ways does the general journal differ from specialized journals?
3. How is cash managed in a travel agency?
4. What are the most important monthly and weekly accounting reports and what functions does each fulfill?
5. What does the ARC Report consist of and what information does it provide to air carriers and to travel agencies?
6. Compare the Cash Disbursement Journal with the General Journal.
7. Why do even small travel agencies often maintain more than one checking account and how does this relate to the need to have an expense journal?
8. What types of transactions are reported as cash sales on the weekly ARC Report?
9. Why is the income statement often referred to as a receipts and disbursements statement, and what kinds of comparison data can be found on the income statement?

10. What types of data are reflected in the Total Liabilities and Capital section of the balance sheet?

❑ *ROLE-PLAYING EXERCISE*

Two students can participate in this role-playing exercise either as an out-of-class, fun way to review basic accounting, or as an in-class exercise. One student plays the senior level student, who has already completed several accounting courses. The other plays the entry-level student. Please read the script and then pick up the conversation in your own words.

Entry-level Student: It seems like there are a lot of books, logs, and reports a person has to keep and prepare to be able to do a good job in travel agency accounting.

Senior-level Student: It can seem overwhelming at first, but there really aren't a lot of logs and reports that need to be done everyday. It is like a building block approach. You do the day-by-day work well and the weekly, monthly, and yearly reports are built on your good daily work foundation.

Entry-level Student: That doesn't sound so bad. Which reports, logs, and books should be prepared daily, and which ones should be completed weekly and annually?

Senior-level Student: The person who handles the daily accounting and bookkeeping work in a travel agency usually starts by. . .

CONTINUE ON YOUR OWN

❑ *CHAPTER ONE EXERCISE*

INSTRUCTIONS: You are preparing a weekly petty cash balance report. Your agency's policy is to maintain $100 as a Tuesday morning start-up for petty cash each week. It is currently Monday afternoon. You are preparing the petty cash report and writing a check, which will be cashed this afternoon so that the petty cash drawer will start out tomorrow morning with a full $100. Reflect the following petty cash voucher expenditures on your report and fill in the amount for the check request in the designated block on the report form.

The expenses from the previous week are as follows:

Tuesday:	Post offict receipt for mailing ARC Report	$3.10
	Manager parking reimbursement	.20
	Grocery store cellophane tape purchase	2.28
Wednesday:	Insufficient postage collection	$ .43
	Sales person public phone call charge	.50
Thursday:	Morning breakfast meeting coffee & rolls	$6.18
	Postage	3.10
Friday:	Tip to snow removal firm for removing ice from front window of the agency	$4.00
	Postage	2.20
	Cruise videotape rental from video store	3.80
Monday:	No petty cash expenditures.	

Fill in the following petty cash report form.

WEEKLY PETTY CASH REPORT

For the week of Tuesday, (Month) __________ (Day) __________
through Monday, (Month) __________ (Day) __________
(Year) __________

Starting weekly balance Tuesday morning: $100.00

EXPENDITURES

Postage: ______

Office expenses: ______

Automobile expense reimbursements: ______

Other (explain): ______

____

____

Total expenses past week: ______

Petty cash check request amount: ______

GOAL SETTING

OBJECTIVES

Upon completion of this chapter, the student will be able to:

- ❑ Discuss the reasons why travel agency bookkeepers and accountants should be involved in the agency's goal setting process
- ❑ Identify basic goals and complete an elementary goal-setting objective form
- ❑ List the criteria that must be met by well-written objectives
- ❑ Identify at least one financial goal, one travel agency marketing goal, one personnel goal, and one equipment goal.

INTRODUCTION

A basic tool of management, utilized successfully by industry for many years, is goal setting. Goal setting and effective management to attain goals provides a company with an instrument that helps the company make and maintain consistent progress. Goals must meet several criteria if the goal-setting system is to work. Goals should be realistic, attainable, and challenging. Goal setters are challenged to set goals that are well-defined, clearly understood, and easily measureable.

Goals can be of several different types. Many are financial and relate directly to accounting and financial management. Other goals, though not directly related to financial management, have financial implications. Some of these goals, which are discussed in this chapter, include marketing goals, equipment goals, and personnel goals. Each has financial implications and therefore each relates to both accounting and financial management.

THE RELATIONSHIP BETWEEN GOAL SETTING AND BUDGETING

The financial aspects of goal attainment are sometimes overlooked when setting goals. There is a correlation between expenditures and activity increases.

Since all goals include some type of activity, then almost all goals involve some type of financial expenditure. Therefore, goal setting needs to be undertaken at the same time the annual budget is prepared, so that the goals will not outstrip the budget and the financial resources will be available to meet the required expenditures.

An example of failure to consider financial resources when setting goals occurred when an airline set a goal of increasing its flights to a particular new city. The airline's marketing strategies worked, a large number of new passengers were convinced that they should fly with that air carrier, and the increase in flights was substantial. In other words, the goal was reached. However, the equipment budget for the destination airport was not considered when setting the marketing goals. Consequently, the airline found itself in the position of having several flights landing at almost the same time while having only one set of stairs by which passengers could embark or disembark. Passengers had to wait for as long as an hour to board or deplane and substantial flight delays resulted. In addition, there was a considerable loss among the new ridership that the marketing department had spent so much of its resources attracting. It is essential, therefore, when setting goals, to review the expenses involved in reaching the goals and to make certain that funds will be available not only to attain the goal, but also to maintain it.

Financial Goals

Some goals appear to be purely financial in nature. For example, a financial goal might be to increase profits by a certain percentage. Another financial goal might be to reduce expenditures by a certain dollar figure or by a certain percentage. Although these goals appear to be purely financial in nature, the mechanics of reaching them may not be. An error that many companies make in establishing purely financial goals is to look at only the financial aspects and not at the other ramifications. For example, a travel agency might establish a goal of reducing expenses by 1 percent during the next fiscal year. In order to do this, management reviews expenditures from the previous year and may arbitrarily reduce the percentage of dollar budgets in various areas. These dollar reductions may result in a loss of clientele because of a reduction in service or a reduction in sales and marketing activity. This loss of clientele is accompanied, in this case, by a loss in sales and revenues (income). The result is that, at the end of the year, the travel agency has less money with which to operate than it had planned to have. The cost cutting goal may have been reached, but the financial picture may be much worse than it was when the budget and cost cutting decisions were originally made. Therefore, goals appearing to be purely financial in nature need to be reviewed for their implications outside the financial area. This does not suggest that the goal of reducing expenditures is a bad one. It simply means that the goal should be managed in such a way that the results are positive rather than negative.

Marketing Goals and Financial Implications

Generally, marketing goals are oriented toward increasing the number of clients, the number of sales, and/or the dollar volume per transaction of sales. In each case, there are financial implications, in that there are costs involved in increasing any of the marketing factors. If, for example, concentration is given to increasing the number of clients, then a system must be put in place by which clients are attracted to the travel agency. This involves expenditures of some type, such as expenditures for direct mail pieces, salaries and commissions for sales staff, salaries and commissions for telemarketers, additional equipment and offices for marketing personnel, proposal development expenses, and a wide range of other necessities. Obviously, a relationship needs to be developed that will result in a realistic cost per additional dollar of income from marketing expenses.

GOAL SETTING OBJECTIVE FORM

OBJECTIVE: To increase annual car rental commissions by the end of the next fiscal year (199__) by 5 percent

SUB-OBJECTIVES OR TASKS	CHECK DATES	DEADLINE
1) To reduce car rental vendors represented to only those which pay commissions of 10 percent or more		
2) To identify car rental company franchisees from which a large number of cars were rented during the last fiscal year		
3) To negotiate larger commissions from favored-vendor franchisees		

COSTS: 1) No cost involved
2) $200 for record search
3) $800 for phone, letter, and personal visit negotiations

TOTAL COST: $1,000

A few years ago, a travel agency brought in a consultant to help identify its problems and concluded that its major problem was marketing. The agency undertook a very expensive but effective marketing program. The agency hired top quality sales people and purchased expensive, quality prospective client lists. They employed telemarketers to set up sales appointments based on responses to telephone calls made using the lists. The result was extremely good. Although in the first year there was a loss because of the high marketing costs, it had been expected and budgeted. The program was continued because the increase in clients was so considerable. However, they stopped tracking costs versus income because it was so time-consuming, and everyone felt that the increase in income from the additional bookings of new clients would soon more than offset the continuing expenses of the high marketing costs. Within an additional six months, corporate financial officers realized that the company was rapidly running out of money. The cost of obtaining new clients, it seemed, exceeded the commission income received from the new client bookings. This marketing-finances relationship must always be considered if a travel agency is to remain competitive and profitable.

Personnel Goals and Financial Implications

Like marketing goals, personnel goals usually also carry with them financial commitments. One personnel goal might be to hire additional specialized staff in order to attract more clients or to more efficiently handle current clients. Or a personnel goal may be to meet or to beat competitors in personnel compensation so that there will be less turnover and a better quality of staff. Another personnel goal may be to increase productivity by rewarding personnel with bonuses or financial incentives when the agency meets its productivity goals. There are many other possible personnel goals, as well. Almost all goals, including personnel goals, require expenditures if they are to be achieved. Whenever personnel goals are established, the expense inherent in reaching the goals needs to be carefully estimated. One way of doing this is to consider the current versus the projected personnel return on investment. Each agent making bookings and handling travel arrangements for clients brings revenue to the travel agency. Executives or managers setting personnel goals should always keep in mind the relationship between revenue income generated by each agent and the cost of the agent and/or other staff members.

Equipment Goals and Financial Implications

Perhaps more than with financial, marketing, and personnel goals, the financial implications of equipment goals can be easily seen. It is always best to work with good or new equipment, but most important, equipment is necessary to be able to adequately serve accounts at all. Without proper equipment it is impossible to provide the service necessary to keep accounts. However, it is important to clearly identify equipment costs and the return on investment that can be realized on the purchase, lease, or rental of equipment. The ramifications are several. The major equipment cost in most travel agencies is computer reservations equipment. Whenever a new CRT or a new printer is added, the agency enters into a new five-year contract for the entire computer reservation system, not just for the new CRT or printer. This means that the owner makes a commitment to pay monthly for the duration of the new contract (currently, vendors have set it at five years) for the entire reservations system.

The five-year commitment should never be taken lightly. Such a commitment can mean an owner's personal financial ruin if the travel agency goes into bankruptcy and he/she has signed a personal guarantee for the purchase. (Vendors usually require one.) A five-year commitment can also make it difficult to change computer reservation vendors. However, it can be especially dangerous when a substantial amount of new equipment is ordered in order to serve a new account. If that account is lost during the five-year period, the agency will still have to continue paying for the equipment. Therefore, setting equipment goals should be considered very carefully. The key consideration is to estimate the potential return on investment of each new piece of equipment and to weigh that potential return against the risk involved.

Other Goals and Financial Implications

There are several other areas in which goals may be set and for which there could be major financial ramifications. Consider rent and utilities. If the agency grows, it may find its current quarters too small. Work facilities should be evaluated regularly for an agency that is undergoing rapid growth.

Utilities may or may not be a part of rental costs. In some cases they are included in the base rent. In other cases there is a required utilities fee, which is either a percentage of the rent or a flat fee added to the rent. In still other cases, utilities are paid monthly by the renter directly to the utilities company. In whatever arrangement utilities have been set up as it relates to rent, there is a close relationship between the cost for rent and the cost for utilities. Therefore, these two expenditures are often considered together for planning purposes.

When moving to a new office, an agency encounters a number of expenses besides a possible higher rent payment. These expenses can include the costs of reconditioning the offices; construction of walls; painting; electrical wiring; computer and telephone lines and hookups; and decorations. Therefore, it is often wise to review the possibility of reconfiguring current office space rather than moving to new quarters. Frequently, better space utilization is a much less expensive alternative.

Telephone equipment and utilization goals also carry financial implications. Telephone system hardware must be purchased and there are line charges. As in the case of rent and utilities, telephone services for clients versus hardware and line costs should be analyzed carefully when setting telephone goals.

Other areas for which specific goals will probably be set are organizational membership fees and educational expenses. As with the other goals, both of these require considerable planning, because additional expenditures, whether substantial or very small, are involved.

SUMMARY

Goal setting is a basic tool of management, and goals are needed in all areas of operation. The goals, however, need to be realistic, attainable, and measureable. While some of the goals are purely financial, most are related to other aspects of management but have financial ramifications. Therefore, it is necessary to consider the financial ramifications when establishing goals in any area.

This chapter pointed out some real problems encountered by not coordinating expenses so that a smooth-running operation results. Problems can also occur when large commitments are made for expensive projects which provide less than needed return on investment. The return-on-investment consideration, and specific ways to measure the return, should always be planned when setting goals. Some specific areas where financial implications of goal setting need to be carefully considered include marketing, personnel, equipment, rent, utilities, the telephone system, organization membership fees, and educational expenses.

❑ DISCUSSION QUESTIONS

1. What criteria must goals meet and why?
2. What are some types of goals that may have financial implications?
3. What kinds of problems can occur when goal setting and expenditure planning is not coordinated throughout all aspects of the business operation?
4. Why might a goal of reducing expenditures result in a loss of income and a lower end-of-year profit?

5. Why is return on investment a major consideration when setting marketing goals? Provide an example where a problem regarding marketing return on investment might occur.
6. What should always be kept in mind when establishing personnel goals and why?
7. What type of financial problem might occur when adding substantial computer reservation equipment in order to provide service for a major new account and why is this problem considered significant? What are some potential financial ramifications of this problem for the business and its owner?
8. Why is reconfiguring current office space an option that is often wise to review prior to undertaking a move?
9. What financial implications and considerations need to be considered when setting telephone system goals?
10. Why does the setting of specific goals for organizational membership fees and educational expenses require considerable planning?

❑ *ROLE-PLAYING EXERCISE*

Two students can participate in this role-playing exercise either as an out-of-class, fun way to review goal setting, or as an in-class exercise. One student plays the role of an experienced travel agency bookkeeper. The other plays a new (recently hired) travel agency bookkeeper. Please read the script and then pick up the conversation in your own words.

Experienced Agency Bookkeeper: As you know, my spouse took a position in another city and we are leaving shortly. However, I am delighted to have this opportunity to brief you on the agency's bookkeeping processes and procedures. You have had an opportunity to look at some of the overall objectives. How do you feel about them?

New Agency Bookkeeper: The goals for next year seem ambitious. I expect they can be attained, however. What concerns me is that there are some places where they don't seem to fit with one another.

Experienced Agency Bookkeeper: Management and an absentee-owner do the initial goal-setting work, but they expect the bookkeeper to bring to their attention objectives that may have been missed, objectives that are probably unrealistic and cannot be met, or objectives that don't seem to fit with one another. Of course they want us to provide them with accounting and financial reasons and justifications for any changes suggested, but we all suffer if the objectives are unattainable or unrealistic. Management expects everybody in the agency, especially the bookkeeper, to contribute to the goal-setting process. What specific points did you find where it appears goals do not seem to mesh?

New Agency Bookkeeper: Well, let's start by looking at the goal of increasing sales by 4 percent. While this may be realistic, the very small increase in personnel expenditures will probably result in. . .

CONTINUE ON YOUR OWN

❑ *CHAPTER TWO EXERCISE*

INSTRUCTIONS: Complete the goal setting objective form on the next page, filling in all pertinent blanks based on the following information. The objective will be to increase the average air commission override by one-half of one percent. One step to be taken to reach this objective will include negotiation by agency executives with favored-vendor air carriers. They will work out an agreement to increase override commissions based upon the agency's attainment of a specific higher volume of ticket sales for the carrier in each quarter of the next fiscal year. Another step will be the establishment of a bonus incentive for agents. The purpose is to encourage agency staffers to promote favored-vendor air carriers by applying the bonus only after the agent reaches established favored-vendor air ticket sales goals each month. A third step will be the utilization of a quality control process whereby a senior agent will review all airline reservations made prior to ticketing and convert them to favored-vendor carriers when the conversion will not be harmful to the client. The negotiation activity deadline will be November 1 of the current year with check dates on October 1 and October 15. The deadline for the development and initiation of the bonus plan will be January 1 of next year. Check dates should be scheduled on a monthly basis after implementation. The same schedule will apply to the development of the quality control program.

Budgeted costs include $1,200 for the negotiation meetings with favored-vendor air carrier representatives. The budget for bonuses is $4,300 (total figure for all agents and for all months during the next fiscal year). For the quality control program, no additional cost beyond the currently projected salary of the quality control specialist is budgeted, since this will be an add-on responsibility for the quality control specialist.

GOAL SETTING OBJECTIVE FORM

OBJECTIVE:		
SUB-OBJECTIVES OR TASKS	CHECK DATES	DEADLINE
COSTS:		

ACCOUNTING SYSTEM DIFFERENCES

OBJECTIVES

Upon completion of this chapter, the student will be able to:

- ❑ Discuss the basic reasons for the differences between accounting practices utilized in the travel agency industry and those utilized by most other small businesses
- ❑ Identify the benefits and the drawbacks of the ASTA accounting system
- ❑ Explain the historical development of the ASTA accounting system
- ❑ List the major reasons why travel agency accounting systems utilize a modified accrual accounting system

INTRODUCTION

Often when accountants work with travel agencies, they become upset about the way in which books are handled. Many accountants say that the systems are all wrong because travel agency accounting systems do not follow standard accounting rules and processes in significant ways. Standard industry accounting systems, however, have been designed to meet the needs of most accountants.

System differences stem from several sources or reasons. A major one goes back to the ARC Report. The airlines require some payments immediately while other payments are actually transferred to the air carriers at a later time. Therefore the agency must show on its books (1) current payments made to the agency and to the vendor; (2) payments made to the agency, but not to the vendor; and (3) payments made to the vendor, but not to the agency. Accountants say that businesses should keep their books on either a cash basis or on an accrual basis, and that travel agencies claim they acceptably utilize a combination of both methods. Accountants are correct regarding both statements. However, with airline regulation of travel agency payment systems, agencies are forced into a situation of operating in a way different than those in which most small businesses operate.

NON-INVENTORY ACCOUNTING

Travel agencies have no inventory. There are those who say that ticket stock is inventory and it certainly is a financially valuable supply of documents kept under lock and key. However, blank tickets, as pieces of paper, carry no value until they are filled out and there is no cost to the travel agency in holding a supply of ticket stock. This, therefore, is a major departure from the inventory costs of most small businesses. Most pay at least a deposit, if not full payment, for an inventory of goods purchased from a wholesaler and resold to the general public. In some ways this is better for the travel agent, but there is no mark up, little or no control over profit potential, and therefore little control over agency income for the sale of specific items.

DIFFERENCES RESULTING FROM ARC REPORTING

As noted earlier, ARC Reports require weekly settlements with the air carriers for tickets sold. For those tickets for which payment is by credit card, from the standpoint of the travel agency there is an immediate settlement of payment to the airlines. The agency deducts its commissions for credit card sales from the cash amount they owe airlines for weekly cash or check sales. They then send the credit card charge forms directly to the area bank for air carrier settlement. For agency accounting purposes, the travel agency has been paid for these transactions.

For cash payment and check payment transactions, however, a report of the level of sales is made to the airlines and the air carrier deducts all but the commissions from those sales through an automatic deduction of the travel agency's account approximately twelve days later. Although for the travel agency this may be a cash sale, it represents a delayed payment to the vendor. Airlines look at ticket sales by travel agencies as being completed sales for which payment is due to them. So if a travel agency receives payment from its client (normally a business) thirty, sixty, or more days after the ticket was issued, the agency must still submit a report of the sale of that ticket on a weekly basis and must pay the air carrier for that ticket approximately twelve days after the report is submitted. In this case, what appears to be a cash sale for the air carrier represents an amount to be received (income owed to the agency, but not yet received) for the travel agency.

Once accountants understand these differences and the reasons why there is a difference between the actual distribution of cash and receipt of income for transactions in a travel agency, then the books can be kept accordingly. However, the accountant must understand that agencies have no choice in this process and must adhere to the requirements mandated by the airlines since for most travel agencies air travel sales constitute such a considerable portion of total sales.

HISTORY AND DEVELOPMENT OF THE ASTA ACCOUNTING SYSTEM

In the late 1960s, the Institute of Certified Travel Agents, recognizing the concerns expressed by several in both the retail and the wholesale ends of the travel business (travel agents and tour operators), offered a comprehensive financial management seminar at Michigan State University. This five-day program featured Dr. Donald Madden (then of Michigan State University; now associated with the University of Kentucky). In preparing his presentations, Dr. Madden did research on the travel industry and found several accounting problems in the industry as a whole. Primary among these problems was a lack of a uniform system of accounts. This created an inability to make national comparisons in terms of both expenses and income. Since most income was earned as a result of commissions paid on air, hotel, and cruise travel sales, however, national comparisons based on income could be fairly accurate if one took the data from suppliers. But national comparisons based on expenses were impossible to project because everyone in the business was classifying expenses in a different manner. Preparing and presenting this seminar (and subsequent efforts for the Institute of Certified Travel Agents), preparing several chapters of a book sponsored by Pan American World Airways, and undertaking research for presentations for the American Society of Travel Agents all helped Dr. Madden determine the parameters of the problem. ASTA recognized the accounting concerns in general and the comparative data concerns in specific. It established a committee to work with Dr. Madden, initially in the design of a uniform classification of accounts and ultimately in the design of an accounting system tailored specifically for travel agencies.

Overview of Benefits and Drawbacks of the System

Although the initial system was somewhat cumbersome, it has been streamlined and several major changes to it have been made over the years. Fortunately, key individuals (such as the late Nancy Stewart, CTC, and both Doris Davidoff, CTC and Phillip Davidoff, CTC) have worked with the project either from its inception (in the case of Nancy Stewart, CTC) or almost from its inception. This longevity, highlighted by the fact that these individuals had and have their own travel agencies with different areas of specialization, has given the ASTA accounting system a reality foundation which makes it a very practical and beneficial program for travel agencies.

System Cost Reduction

The ASTA accounting system has a purposefully simplistic approach, specifically planned so that travel agents who have no background whatsoever in accounting and financial management can implement the system and make it work. Plus the cost of the system has been kept down in three ways. First, ASTA has done all the design work in-house or on contract and has not passed on a substantial portion of that design work in the cost of the system. Second, since the forms that are key to the program have also been designed in-house and printed in bulk, the ongoing monthly accounting charges are very small as they compare to the cost of many other accounting systems. Most importantly, because the system is simple, requiring less complicated and less time-consuming steps than many accounting systems, the personnel costs of maintaining an accounting system are reduced considerably since in many small travel agencies all bookkeeping and accounting functions can be and are undertaken by the owner, owner/manager, or a senior agent.

System Benefits

Although the major benefits of the ASTA accounting system are its simplicity and ease of application, there are a number of other benefits as well. Although there are many different forms serving several accounting purposes, there are few key forms (only three data-input forms, for example) which can be understood with just a few minutes of reading the manual and which capture all essential data. Since the key forms serve multiple purposes, much of the need to copy data several times or to prepare several different forms is eliminated. In addition to capturing all essential data, the key forms provide a foundation on which sophisticated financial management approaches for a travel agency can be based.

Criticisms

There are some who criticize the ASTA accounting system and emphasize its drawbacks. These drawbacks should be recognized. The system is designed for a small travel agency. The system was originally designed when there were only a very few travel agencies in the United States that had a total gross sales level of over $1 million. In fact, in those days prior to deregulation, there was a publication that annually listed all travel agencies in the United States that had over $1 million in gross sales because that was considered to be such a major accomplishment. The ASTA accounting system served almost all travel agencies very well at the time of its design since there were so few agencies that had sales of such an amount that the volume of sales outstripped the capacity of the accounting system to efficiently handle an agency's accounting needs.

Today, the average travel agency is selling more than $1 million in gross sales annually. Many agencies exceed $5 million annually. Most would agree that the ASTA accounting system works best for travel agencies that are selling up to about $3 or $4 million in gross sales. A more streamlined system is needed when an agency exceeds this level. There is some consideration of automating the ASTA accounting system and this may well serve as a next-step system for agencies with large sales volumes. However, the ASTA accounting system still meets the needs of the vast majority of travel agencies in existence today since agencies selling $3 million or more in gross sales are a minority of the total travel agency population.

A second criticism of the ASTA accounting system is that it is not a system that has double entry documentation. This is true. However, as the *ASTA Accounting Manual* states, "Nevertheless, this system is designed to insure that every measure is treated in precisely the same manner as would occur if ledgers were used" (page 2 of An Overview of Key Considerations section of the *ASTA Travel Agency Accounting and Information System*). The *drop system* utilized in travel agencies with the ASTA accounting system is considered cumbersome by many accountants and is not considered to be as precise as double entry bookkeeping. This was considered by the committee at each step in the design of the accounting system. The drop system, which is document-driven, was adopted instead of double entry bookkeeping because it can provide the same degree of accuracy, but it eliminates the need for trained (usually expensive) bookkeepers and/or accountants to be on staff recording transactions in ledgers on a daily basis. As the ASTA accounting manual states, a "professional is (still) capable of reducing each component in the input forms into a double-entry frame of reference" (page 2 of An Overview of Key Considerations section of the *ASTA Travel Agency Accounting and Information System*).

A third criticism is that the ASTA accounting system does not operate on either a cash basis or on an accrual basis. Traditional bookkeepers/accountants frequently mandate that one must maintain either a cash basis system or an accrual basis system, but that they cannot be combined. As noted earlier, commissions are not earned on air sales until the ARC Report has been cleared. Therefore, the ASTA accounting system operates on a modified accrual basis. According to the *ASTA Accounting Manual*, "Weekly Air Reports rather than daily ticket issuances thus serve as the primary basis for recording Commission Income. Technically, air commissions are 'booked' when the ARC liability is paid. This modification is acceptable because of 'Generally Accepted Accounting Principles' because the resulting commission measure is objective and verifiable" (page 3 of An Overview of Key Considerations section of the *ASTA Travel Agency Accounting and Information System*).

A final major criticism of the ASTA accounting system deals with focus. Although most retail businesses focus accounting on gross and unit sales, the ASTA system in general and its chart of accounts in specific focus on commission income. This is an elected focus, but because commission is the only earning vehicle for most travel agencies, as the *ASTA Accounting Manual* states, "this measure best reflects the monetary resources that can be used to sustain operations during each accounting period" (page 3 of An Overview of Key Considerations section of the *ASTA Travel Agency Accounting and Information System*). Although it is not the most common focus used in accounting, as noted above, the focus on the measurement of commission income rather than on total sales is nevertheless consistent with Generally Accepted Accounting Principles.

The ASTA System as a Foundation System

Having recognized both the major strengths and the criticisms of the system, it is good to also recognize that the ASTA accounting system has served as a foundation against which many other systems have been developed in the industry. In fact, it is fair to say that most in the industry who have developed automated accounting systems and automated accounting interface systems have based many of the principal foundations of those systems on the ASTA accounting system. This also has its strengths and its drawbacks. The strengths result in classifications of accounts that are closer to one another than one would expect if there were no foundation system on which to base other accounting systems. However, at the same time, there has been perhaps less innovation in development or specific design to meet the exact needs of specialized travel agencies when it comes to considering a classification of accounts. The same is true when one considers vouchers and other documents used within the industry. Many have been patterned after the ASTA documents. While this has provided a foundation, it can be hypothesized that it may also have reduced the innovative development which might have occurred had a foundation system not been available. Nevertheless, once the ASTA accounting system was developed, the travel industry went on to develop, in a very short period of time, many other and many more sophisticated accounting systems designed specifically for travel agencies. Therefore, a debt of gratitude is owed to those individuals noted earlier and others in the industry who were instrumental in designing the first ASTA accounting system and keeping it up-to-date. It remains perhaps the most often used accounting system in the travel agency industry today.

SUMMARY

Major differences between travel agency accounting and the accounting undertaken by most small businesses can be seen in the lack of an inventory (and the problems that are associated with accounting for an inventory) and in the fact that travel agency accounting is undertaken utilizing a combination of both cash basis accounting and accrual basis accounting. While most accountants do not like keeping books on both a cash and an accrual basis, most understand when airline payment regulations and procedures are explained to them.

The ASTA accounting system was developed in the 1960s starting with the design of a uniform system of accounts by Dr. Donald Madden. It is a manual drop system tailored to meet the needs of small and medium sized travel agencies. It operates on a modified accrual basis and meets Generally Accepted Accounting Principles. Many other industry accounting systems have been designed based on the ASTA system and this has produced both benefits and drawbacks for the travel agency industry.

❑ DISCUSSION QUESTIONS

1. How does the ARC and its reporting requirements affect travel agency accounting?
2. Why do some consider travel agencies as inventory maintainers?
3. Why do travel agencies maintain their books on both a cash and an accrual basis?
4. What role did Dr. Madden play in the development of the ASTA accounting system?
5. Why is the ASTA accounting system described as a drop system?
6. What is a "Uniform System of Accounts" and why is it important?
7. In what ways has the cost of the ASTA accounting system been kept down?
8. What are the benefits of the ASTA accounting system?
9. What are the drawbacks of the ASTA accounting system?
10. What is the focus of the ASTA accounting system and why?

❑ ROLE-PLAYING EXERCISE

Two students may participate in this role-playing exercise either as an out-of-class, fun way to review accounting system differences, or as an in-class exercise. One student plays the New Agency Bookkeeper, a bookkeeper who has worked in other industries and is new to the travel industry. The other plays the Experienced Agency Bookkeeper, a bookkeeper who has worked with travel agencies for many years. Please read the script and then pick up the conversation in your own words.

New Agency Bookkeeper: I don't know how you manage with this travel agency accounting. It just seems very different to me from the bookkeeping I have done in other businesses.

Experienced Agency Bookkeeper: There are some differences, but in reality the differences are relatively small. You are working with a drop system rather than a system of recording debits and credits, aren't you?

New Agency Bookkeeper: Yes, and I don't understand it. Why does travel agency accounting differ from standard accounting in its practices?

Experienced Agency Bookkeeper: It really doesn't differ that much. However, there are some reasons for the differences. Probably the most important factor to consider is that. . .

CONTINUE ON YOUR OWN

❑ CHAPTER THREE EXERCISE

INSTRUCTIONS: Complete the Pros and Cons chart below. It is designed to summarize the benefits and the drawbacks of the ASTA accounting system. In ten words or less list three or four benefits of the ASTA accounting system and three or four drawbacks of the system.

ASTA ACCOUNTING SYSTEM PROS AND CONS

PROS	CONS
1) ____________	1) ____________
2) ____________	2) ____________
3) ____________	3) ____________
4) ____________	4) ____________

THE INVOICE/RECEIPT FORM

OBJECTIVES

Upon completion of this chapter, the student will be able to:

- ❑ Complete the recording of a simple airline ticket charge and payment by any of the three standard forms of payment on an invoice/receipt form
- ❑ Describe what credit card data goes on the "Credit Card" line of an invoice/receipt
- ❑ List the circumstances under which invoice reference numbers are recorded on invoice/receipts
- ❑ Describe the distribution of invoice/receipt copies and explain why each copy goes where it is designed to go

INTRODUCTION: THE DESIGN OF THE INVOICE/RECEIPT FORM

Form managers and form designers sometimes get excited about forms when, on that rare occasion, they encounter a form that remains clear, concise, easy-to-utilize, and yet provides considerable information and serves a multitude of purposes. Such a form is the accounting system's *Invoice/Receipt* form. It is quite simply a masterpiece of design. It captures on one side of one piece of paper all the data needed to provide a complete invoice to a client, a complete receipt for payment, and a complete historical tracking of the accounting/financial transactions inherent in a travel booking/sale. Prior to the development of the accounting system invoice/receipt form, many in the industry thought it impossible to do all of this on one piece of paper.

AN OVERVIEW EXAMPLE

To understand the invoice/receipt preparation process better, look at the examples. Figure 4–1 shows a blank invoice/receipt form. Figure 4–2 shows a

INVOICE/RECEIPT FORM

Client Name ______________________________ Client # ____________

Client Phone ______________________________

Client Address ______________________________

Passenger Name ______________________________ Phone ____________

Trans-action #	Product or Service	Ticket/ Doc. #	Date of Trip	City Pair	Cost	Total Cost

TOTAL INVOICE .... $________

PREVIOUS PAYMENT .... $________

BALANCE .... $________

AMOUNT RECEIVED __ CASH __CHECK #257 $________

CREDIT CARD (NAME, NO., & EXP. DATE)

________ ______________ ________ $________

REMARKS

REFUND $(________)

I/R REFERENCE NUMBER ________ TOTAL CREDITS $________

BALANCE DUE $________

INSIDE SALESPERSON ____________

OUTSIDE SALESPERSON ____________

RECEIVED BY____________

Figure 4–1

INVOICE/RECEIPT FORM

Client Name *Xerox Corporation* Client # *F 01*

Client Phone *(303) 597-4581*

Client Address *123 State Street, Denver, CO 33333*

Passenger Name *Parker, Mr. & Mrs. John* Phone *B (303) 597-4581*

Trans-action #	Product or Service	Ticket/ Doc. #	Date of Trip	City Pair	Cost	Total Cost
596	*Air Tkt John Parker*	*RT0078402970274*	*12 Jan*	*DenLAX*	*$375.00*	
597	*Air Tkt Mrs. Parker*	*RT0078402970275*	*12 Jan*	*DenLAX*	*$375.00*	
598	*Hertz Car LAX BLLCN08593*		*12 Jan*		*$ 75.00*	
						$825.00

TOTAL INVOICE .... $ *825.00*

PREVIOUS PAYMENT .... $ *—0—*

BALANCE .... $ *825.00*

AMOUNT RECEIVED __ CASH *X* CHECK #257 $ *800.00*

CREDIT CARD (NAME, NO., & EXP. DATE)

______ ______ ______ $______

REMARKS

REFUND $(______)

I/R REFERENCE NUMBER ______

TOTAL CREDITS $ *800.00*

BALANCE DUE $ *25.00*

INSIDE SALESPERSON *JP*

OUTSIDE SALESPERSON ______

RECEIVED BY ______

Figure 4–2

sample completed invoice/receipt form. Study both forms in order to understand the sorting and distribution of information on the invoice/receipt form.

Before studying the invoice/receipt form line-by-line, a brief review of figure 4–2 will help familiarize the students with the components of the form. The sample invoice/receipt form is made out to the Xerox Corporation. The address is that of the company, not of the traveler. The invoice/receipt is for air tickets for two travelers, Mr. and Mrs. John Parker. (It is presumed that Mr. Parker is working for the company and Mrs. Parker is accompanying him, although it may be the other way around.) Since the company is the client, the company requested two tickets and will be paying for both. (It is the company's decision whether or not the Parkers will pay for the spouse's ticket.) There is a client number, which relates back to the company. There is a business and/or home phone number for the traveler, as well.

In the next section, Mr. Parker's ticket number is listed first and below that the ticket number for Mrs. Parker. The routing is also provided, noting that it is round-trip. The ticket prices are added together to obtain the amount reflected in the "Total Cost" column.

There is also a car rental involved and the agency expects pre-payment for the car by the client. The Hertz reservation number is shown, as well as the $75 pre-payment charge. That figure is carried to the right and included in the "Total Cost" column.

By adding the ticket and car rental amounts together, one determines the Total Invoice amount. There were no previous payments, so the balance is the same as the total invoice.

The company paid this invoice by check at the time the tickets and documents were delivered. Therefore, the check line is marked, the check number (257) is recorded, and the amount paid ($800) is listed. That figure ($800) is carried down to the "Total Credits" line. The Total Credits ($800) is deducted from the balance ($825) and the difference ($25) is recorded in the "Balance Due" block. Finally, the initials of the salesperson are shown on the "Inside Salesperson" line.

The Invoice/Receipt Sections

The invoice/receipts form is designed to give the basic data needed to prepare accounting and financial reports, especially the budget. This form is completed whenever there is a financial transaction and whenever there is an exchange of money—especially as it relates to a client. In other words, when a client owes money to a travel agency, this form is completed. When a client pays money to a travel agency, this form is completed.

The first part of the form is basic data relating to the client and the traveler. The second part of the form is that section which is considered to be the *INVOICE*. It takes up the bulk (almost half) of the form. The third part of the form is the *RECEIPT*. There is then a small amount of additional information at the very bottom.

Header Data. The top of the invoice/receipt form is completed first. This section is frequently referred to as the *header data*. It includes much of the client and accounting data that can be of benefit in both marketing management and financial management. It is frequently used in tracking analyses. The header data is completed whether the form is used as an invoice, as a receipt, or as an invoice and a receipt.

The header data is basic data information. At the top right hand corner one may enter a sequential number. Though this is not an accountable document as far as the airlines are concerned, it may be sequentially numbered. It is very important to keep up with what happens to each invoice/receipt, much like one does with tickets, but there are no penalties to pay to the airlines if one is lost.

The first data entry is the name of the client. This is the top line on the left-hand side of the form. It is stressed that the name of the client is often not the same as the name of the passenger. For most corporate accounts, the client will be the business, whereas the passenger will be an employee taking a business trip. On the other hand, if it is a leisure account (e.g., someone taking a vacation), the client and the passenger will probably be the same, since the individual traveler is most likely paying for his/her own vacation.

On the right side of the form, opposite the section for client name, is client number. Many travel agencies will assign numbers to all of their accounts, to their better corporate accounts, or to their better leisure accounts. Many of these numbering systems classify accounts by type. In other words, one alpha-numeric system may apply to corporate accounts; another alpha-numeric system may apply to cruise clients; still another alpha-numeric system may apply to tour clients. These systems help to track financial and marketing data. Most travel agencies, however, use no client numbering system whatsoever, and when this is the case, the client number block on the invoice/receipt should be left blank.

The next line of header data is for phone. This is the phone number of the client. It is important to include the area code.

The next line relates to city, state, and zip code. This data is self-explanatory.

The last line of header data is for passenger name(s). The names of all passengers whose accounting data is reflected on the specific invoice/receipt should be listed here. In some cases this will be several business travelers, all of whom have different last names and are not related in any way except that they all work for the same company. In other cases it may be several members of the same family who may or may not be traveling together. It is not wise to combine passengers who do not have some natural point of relationship (e.g., working for the same company; or members of the same family).

Opposite the passenger name line is a line for the passenger's phone number. One of the major complaints that travel agency marketing executives express is the lack of tracking data, and that includes phone numbers. Although many agents do not record the phone number of the passenger on the invoice/receipt, it is wise to do so since this will assist in tracking marketing data. It will also be very helpful if debit notices or other problems come up with the account at a later time. Remember that the phone number will be eliminated from the reservation computer records once the passenger has completed the trip. The invoice/receipt form may be the only reference in the travel agency where accounting and marketing executives can track and match past clients and/or passengers with their phone numbers. It is wise to enter both home and business phone numbers whenever possible. By simply using either the initial *B* (business) or the initial *H* (home) before the phone number, the invoice/receipt reader can rapidly distinguish whether the number listed is a business or a home phone number.

The Invoice Section. The next section of the invoice/receipt form immediately following the header data, is the invoice section. The invoice part of the form is used to record the financial data relating to the type of travel purchased. Historically, the data entered in this section has changed somewhat as the form itself has been revised over the years. Therefore, although current usage will be discussed here, agents may find themselves working in agencies where agency management learned the system several years ago and still follows an older pattern of data entry. (If this is the case, the pattern utilized in the agency should be followed rather than that which is described here, since all persons working in a travel agency should follow the same data entry system.)

For each transaction (an airline ticket, a tour order, a hotel confirmation, a car rental confirmation number), a number identification is entered in the far-left column. This is followed by a description of the product or service rendered, then the costs. The information recorded in these columns needs to include more than just a document information number. It is beneficial, for example, if information relating to the name of each passenger is included when the invoice/receipt covers trips made by several passengers. In addition, if several trips for the same passenger have been arranged and are billed on the invoice, it is beneficial to show the routing (the city pairs) of the trips (or some other identifying data) so that the client and/or passenger can rapidly identify the billing line that applies to each trip.

As noted, on each line where an entry is to be made (only enter line information if there is a billing transaction), one puts trip identification information. This identifying information will usually be ticket numbers. If one invoice is being prepared for more than one passenger, the line information needs to identify the passenger to whom the trip information on each line relates. The total cost is then entered to the right and on the same line. Once this has been done for each transaction for each traveler or each current transaction of a trip being billed to the client, the total amount of each transaction listed is brought down and across to the line marked "Total Invoice" and the total is entered in that line.

Total and Previous Payments Sections. There are three blocks that appear beneath the invoice documentation section of the invoice/receipt. These are lines for Total Invoice, Previous Payments, and Balance.

Everything entered in the invoice section is totaled and the figure entered in the "Total Invoice" block. If there have been any previous payments made on the bill, the amount of those payments is entered in the "Previous Payment" block. The "Balance" block is filled in after calculating a balance (deduct Previous Payment from Total Invoice).

The "Total Invoice" line amount is for the total amount of the invoice calculated by totaling all items in the invoice section of the form. The "Previous Payments" line is for listing the amount of any previous payments received from clients for charges recorded in the invoice section. Therefore, if previous payments were made, the amount is recorded on the previous line and the previous invoice/receipt numbers are recorded on the "Invoice Reference Number" line at the bottom of the receipt section of the form. The "Balance" block, which is the last block in the invoice section, usually reflects a figure that is the same amount as that recorded in the "Total Invoice" block. However, if previous payment(s) have been made, they are deducted from the total invoice to provide the amount recorded in the "Balance" block.

The "Remarks" section is a block in which notes to clients may be made. This section is for any remarks the agent completing the invoice/receipt may wish to make. Many will put in a generic note to clients, such as, "Have a good trip." Some travel agencies have a policy of stamping a note in this block indicating that payment is due upon receipt or within fifteen days, thirty days, or some other specified period of time. Other agencies do not have a set policy, thereby allowing agents who so desire to include appropriate notes to clients. Such notes could say "It was a pleasure working with you; please return again" or "Thanks for using our travel agency." In many cases, however, agents leave this block blank.

The Receipts Section. The next section of the form is the receipt section. It constitutes the bottom part of the form. It is utilized to record payments received from a client. If payment is received at the same time the invoice is prepared, only one invoice/receipt will be needed to record both the charges and the payment for those charges. However, in many cases, payment is received at a time later than when the invoice is rendered. If this is the case, the invoice section is completed at the time the charges occurred, and the first two copies of the invoice/receipt are given to the client. Total Credits in the receipt section will show zero and a Balance Due will be shown as being exactly the same as the balance in the invoice section. When payment is received, a new invoice/receipt will be prepared with only the receipt section filled in. In the "Invoice Reference Number" block, the number of the previous invoice/receipt is shown. The receipt section will be completed showing a credit for the amount paid (normally the full amount due), and the balance due (normally zero). Since the invoice reference number for the invoice/receipt reflecting the amount due can be balanced by the accountant to the invoice/receipt completed showing the payment received, the travel agency accountant can balance out both the charge and the payment by reviewing both invoice/receipts.

The receipt section has two short lines on the left-hand side to show form of payment. The options available are, on the first full line, check or cash; and on the second full line, Credit Card. If the client paid the amount due by check or by cash, the appropriate short line should be checked and the amount entered in the section to the right, figure 4–2. Many travel agencies will ask the agent to enter the client's check number next to the word "Check." This allows the travel agency to track invoice/receipts and balance these against a daily check of payments versus invoice/receipts. This is especially important when a client pays for several invoices with a single check.

Credit Card Payment. There is one line on which to enter credit card payments. On this line the credit card being used should be identified. The credit card number and the expiration date should be shown on the same line. To the right, one should show the amount of the charge. Many people will enter a credit card approval code number as well. Since the approval code number appears on computer-generated tickets and on the credit card charge form, it is not mandatory that it also appear on the invoice/receipt. However, for tracking purposes it is more convenient for the agency's accountant if the approval code does show on the invoice/receipt. Again, the amount of the charge to the credit card should appear on the line across from the word "Credit Card."

"Total Credit" and "Balance Due" Lines. Whatever the form of payment, the total amount of money paid should be carried down to and entered on the "Total Credits" line, figure 4–2. Usually the amount appearing on the "Total Credits" line will be the same as and will be equal to the amount appearing on the "Balance" line. If so, then the "Balance Due" line will show $0.00 or a line will be drawn above it indicating that there is nothing due. If, however, the amount on the "Balance" line exceeds the amount on the "Total Credits" line, the total credits will be subtracted from the balance and the resulting figure will be placed on the "Balance Due" line, figure 4–2. On the other hand, if the amount appearing on the "Balance" line is less than the amount appearing on the "Total Credits" line, the difference between the two figures will also appear on the "Balance Due" line, but in this case it will have brackets at both ends indicating a negative balance due, i.e., the travel agency owes the client some money. This would probably result from the client paying too much.

Refunds. There are some additional lines on the form for unique situations. For example, if a refund has been received from a supplier and that refund is owed to the client (not to the agency), an explanation of that refund should appear on the "Refund" line in the receipts section. The amount of the refund should be shown on the line immediately across from and on the same line as the word "Refund." That same amount should also be shown in the "Total Credits" block. Since in this case there would probably be no money owed by the client, the amount shown as a refund in the "Total Credits" section of the receipt will have nothing to balance against on the "Balance" line of the invoice. Therefore the amount shown on the "Total Credits" line of the receipt will be owed to the client by the travel agency. As noted earlier, this is reflected by showing an amount of money in parentheses on the "Balance Due" line of the receipt. The parentheses indicate a debit, or an amount to be paid by the travel agency to the client.

When a refund is received from a supplier and credited back to the client, the amount will be entered in the "Amount" column and carried over to the "Total Credits" column. Often, when such a circumstance occurs, the refund is the only item showing on the invoice/receipt. Therefore, the amount of the refund will be carried down from the "Total Credits" line to the "Balance Due" line and shown in brackets to indicate that the amount is owed to the client. Later, when the client is paid the refund, the payment out is indicated, a reference back to the invoice on which the credit is showing is made, and the two invoice/receipts balance themselves out creating a completed transaction.

Invoice Reference Number. Whenever there are refunds or partial payments made and when there are several payments required by vendors, one will normally encounter a situation where an invoice reference to one or more previous invoices will be necessary. The *invoice reference number* is the number of one or more previous invoices showing an accounting flow relating to the current transaction. The earlier invoice which has been referenced may be for a deposit, a refund, a cancellation credit, or any other type of transaction with a direct bearing on the present transaction.

Salesperson Lines. The very bottom section of the invoice/receipt form is to be completed showing the name of the salesperson in the travel agency. The purpose of completing these lines is to identify the productivity of salespeople. Therefore, it is important that agency personnel responsible for completing the sale and handling the transaction be identified clearly by having the name(s) typed or hand-printed fully on the appropriate "Salesperson" line of the invoice/receipt. In some cases, however, while one agent may handle the entire transaction, the ticket may be picked up by the client at a time when the agent who handled the transaction is out to lunch, on vacation, or otherwise not available. In such a circumstance, the initials of the person who gave all documents to the client can be entered in the section immediately to the left of the words "Inside Salesperson." This identifies the person who last handled the transaction in the travel agency, in case there is a question at a later time.

In some agencies, *outside* sales representatives, who are working on a commission basis, may be responsible for initiating a transaction with a client, but in many cases they turn over the processing of that transaction to an *inside* agent. In other words, the inside agent obtains the flights, hotels, car rentals, and other services; issues the tickets; and prepares the tickets for delivery or pick up by the client. Since both the outside sales representative and the inside agent worked on the same transaction, both should get some productivity credit for the transaction. Most travel agencies identify this split productivity arrangement by entering the name of the outside sales representative on the "Outside Salesperson" line and the name of the inside agent on the "Inside Salesperson" line. This tells the accountant and the manager of the agency that both individuals have been responsible for some degree of productivity in the transaction.

The "Rec'd By" Line. The "Rec'd By" line is to show who in the travel agency received the payment for which credit on the invoice/receipt form is shown. In some travel agencies all monies, checks, and credit card payment forms are given to the agency accountant who remains responsible for all forms of payment. When this is the case, the agency accountant normally places his/her initials or name on the "Received By" line to indicate that the payment has been received. This transfers responsibility for that payment from the agent to the agency accountant. This line is also used when the agent of record (the person handling the transaction) is unavailable for some reason and someone else in the travel agency accepts payment.

INVOICE/RECEIPT DISTRIBUTION

The invoice/receipt form is a standard form with multiple copies. The client receives the first (white) copy. If the client is paying at the same time that he/she receives the invoice, then the client is given only the first (white) copy. If the client will be paying for the invoice at a later time, perhaps at the end of the month, then the client receives both the original (white) copy and a second (green) copy. The green copy is designed to accompany payment. When the payment arrives into the travel agency, the green copy accompanying the check (in the case of figure 4–2, from the Xerox Company) provided as payment should balance out to the total amount of the check. This should be the same as the total amount due for the period covered by the check (usually a one month or a two week period), as documented by the invoice/receipts mailed out to the client or given to traveler(s). Having the green copy(ies) is an easy way to be able to balance payment(s) against actual charges, so that when the green copy comes in, the agency accountant knows what the check was for. If there are several green copies coming together with a check, the accountant knows that the combination of all of these should offset the appropriate invoices and that the check from the client company was meant to cover these charges.

There are also other copies of the invoice/receipt. One is the numerical (yellow) copy. This copy goes into a standard numerical file. Most travel agency accountants and financial management executives insist that this be kept on a long-term basis, very much like the ticket file. Then, if anyone questions a transaction at a later time, the agency accountant can go back to the numerical copy and find out exactly what occurred.

There is also a red accounts receivable copy. This is so that accounts receivable can be handled on a *drop file* basis. The way this works is that whenever a client owes money to the travel agency for a transaction for which an invoice/receipt was rendered, the invoice/receipt copy reflecting that bill is dropped into the drop file. When payment is received, the accounts receivable copy is taken out of the accounts receivable drop file and either thrown away or attached to the green copy that was received with the payment. Therefore, by simply reviewing the drop file the accountant is able to determine all amounts owed to the travel agency at any particular point in time. At the end of the month, an aged accounts receivable list is easy to put together since the accounts receivable copies of the invoice/receipt form can simply be put into stacks based upon the amount of time (number of days) that each has been outstanding. Any invoice/receipt that is in the accounts receivable drop file should be an amount currently owed to the travel agency.

The last copy of the invoice/receipt (this one is beige in color) goes into the file of the agent who conducted the transaction. The reason for this is to measure productivity. By reviewing all the invoice/receipt copies in files that have accumulated over a month's time, the manager of the agency is able to determine the total sales of each agent. If two people were responsible for a sale, such as an outside sales representative and an inside agent, a photocopy of the agent copy of the invoice/receipt should be made so that a copy can go into each person's file. Again, this is a drop file and it is therefore easy for the accountant or bookkeeper to review the invoice/receipts in each agent's monthly file to determine whether or not productivity quotas have been met.

OTHER INVOICE AND RECEIPT FORMS AND SYSTEMS

The system works well for most agencies that are using it and a large number of travel agencies utilize some version of this system. This, however, is only one system. It is much more time consuming than a totally automated system. However, it is also less expensive. Although there are many other systems, none are utilized in the industry to the extent that the invoice/receipt system is and many were founded on the invoice/receipt system.

SUMMARY

It is on the invoice/receipt system that many travel agency accounting systems have been built. In addition, the invoice/receipt form is the foundation document for tracking money coming into or owed to the travel agency. This form, in turn, is used in conjunction with other forms that track differently. Perhaps of greatest value, invoice/receipts help in the development of a more global financial picture of the travel agency which is received on a monthly basis in the form of an "Income" statement (perhaps better known in the industry as a monthly Receipts and Disbursements Report). But the Receipts and Disbursements Statement receives data from the invoice/receipt which needs to be balanced or checked in the traditional checks-and-balances system of accounting.

❑ *DISCUSSION QUESTIONS*

1. What is there about the accounting system's invoice/receipt form that might make form designers get excited?
2. What information is included in the Header Data?

3. There is one central data part of the invoice/receipt form. What sales data is entered into this part of the form?
4. Why should agents make a concerted effort to be sure that the phone number is listed in the Header Data?
5. What are examples of some remarks that might appear in the Remarks section of the invoice/receipt?
6. What information is recorded in the Receipts section of the invoice/receipt?
7. Under what circumstances might a refund be the only item showing on an invoice/receipt?
8. Why is the recording of invoice reference numbers important and under what circumstances might invoice reference numbers be recorded on an invoice/receipt?
9. In what way might invoice/receipts be utilized to measure the productivity of salespeople?
10. How many copies of an invoice/receipt are there and how are they distributed?

❑ *ROLE-PLAYING EXERCISE*

Two students may participate in this role-playing exercise either as an out-of-class, fun way to review how an invoice/receipt form is completed, or as an in-class exercise. One student plays the travel agency bookkeeper. The other plays the new agent who has recently begun working at the agency. Please read the script and then pick up the conversation in your own words.

New Agent: I understand that we need to keep good financial records whenever there is a sale. But, I really don't understand how to fill out this invoice/receipt form.

Bookkeeper: It is a fairly simple form. The header data is basic information on the client and the travelers. The invoice section lists all of the charges. The receipts section is where you record the form of payment and the amount paid. You simply balance out the invoice and receipt. Most of the time it will result in a zero balance.

New Agent: It sounds simple, but tell me in greater detail. For example, Mary Jackson will be coming in this afternoon to get her ticket to Chicago. The cost is $250 for the round-trip ticket and she is going to be paying by check. What do I put on each of these lines?

Bookkeeper: The header data is pretty self-explanatory. Take that information directly from your PNR (Passenger Name Record). If Mary is working for a company and the company is paying for the ticket, you will need to enter the company name on the client line. If she has a client number, you will need to identify and enter it. But let me explain what you enter in the invoice section and then we will talk about the receipt section and the lines below the receipt section. You start by. . .

CONTINUE ON YOUR OWN

CHAPTER FOUR EXERCISE

INSTRUCTIONS: Complete the invoice/receipt form on the next page for a ticket issued for Jack Ford. The ticket number is 8402 970 281. It has been validated on American Airlines and their airline code is 001. The ticket is from Dallas to Houston round trip and the gross fare is $200. This is a business trip. Jack's company, Brakes Unlimited, will be paying for the ticket. Jack's client number is BU-29. Jack has requested that the ticket be delivered to his office which is located at 297 Williams Street in Dallas. The zip code is 75230. Jack will be departing for Houston the morning of the first day of next month and he will be returning the same evening. His telephone number at Brakes Unlimited is (214) 698-7751. The ticket will be charged to the company's American Express Card, number 3361 215490 80125. The card expires in March of next year. The approval code received from American Express is 5936. Please be sure to show your name as the inside salesperson. Janet Greenspan, the agency's bookkeeper, will receive the financial documents.

INVOICE/RECEIPT FORM

Client Name ______________________________ Client # ______________

Client Phone ______________________________

Client Address ______________________________

Passenger Name ______________________________ Phone ______________

Trans-action #	Product or Service	Ticket/ Doc. #	Date of Trip	City Pair	Cost	Total Cost

TOTAL INVOICE .... $__________

PREVIOUS PAYMENT .... $__________

BALANCE .... $__________

AMOUNT RECEIVED __ CASH __CHECK #257 $__________

CREDIT CARD (NAME, NO., & EXP. DATE)

__________ __________________ __________ $__________

REMARKS

REFUND $(__________)

I/R REFERENCE NUMBER __________ TOTAL CREDITS $__________

BALANCE DUE $__________

INSIDE SALESPERSON ______________

OUTSIDE SALESPERSON ______________

RECEIVED BY______________________

5

THE VOUCHER CHECK

OBJECTIVES

Upon completion of this chapter, the student will be able to:

- ❑ Complete a voucher check reflecting a simple travel payment transaction
- ❑ List the points of distribution of each of the five copies of the voucher check
- ❑ Compare the information which appears on a voucher check utilized in a travel agency and the information which appears on standard business checks
- ❑ Identify the major categories of chart-of-accounts numbers which appear in the detachable section of the voucher check

INTRODUCTION

While the invoice/receipt form is the key document tracking incoming funds (income), the voucher check is the key document utilized in tracking, managing, and controlling outgoing funds (expenses). Both are key documents in that, if used properly, they provide the starting point for tracking and controlling financial transactions.

TOP OF CHECK

The standard industry voucher check comes in five copies. As can be seen in figure 5–1, the top part of the check is the same as any standard check: the name and address of the travel agency in the top left-hand corner, a sequential check number in the top right-hand corner, a date line, an amount payable line, a dollar payable line, a signature authorization line, and a block in which the name and address of the payee can be entered.

VOUCHER CHECK

5309

Date ______________

PAY ____ Dollars $______________

To the order of

____
Authorized Signature

INCOME CREDITS		ACCT RCVBLE DEBITS		OTHER DEBITS	
301 AIR COMM	$___	101 A/R HOTELS	$___	501 AGT SAL	$___
302 HOTEL "	$___	104 A/R CRUISES	$___	502 MKT SAL	$___
303 CAR "	$___	105 A/R RAIL	$___	503 SUP SAL	$___
304 CRUISE "	$___	106 A/R TOUR	$___	504 ADM SAL	$___
305 RAIL "	$___	107 A/R OTHER	$___	505 TAXES	$___
306 TOUR "	$___	108 A/R OTHER	$___	506 BENEFITS	$___
307 OTHER "	$___	109 A/R OTHER	$___	507 OTHER	$___
ACCTS PAY DEBITS		**OTHER DEBITS**			
901 FED WITH	$___	601 ACCOUNTING	$___	602 AUTOMA	$___
902 STAT TAX	$___	603 DUES	$___	604 EDUCATN	$___
903 FICA TAX	$___	605 FEES	$___	606 INSURNC	$___
904 LOCL TAX	$___	607 LEGAL	$___	608 OFF EQU	$___
905 CITY TAX	$___	609 OFF REPRS	$___	610 OFF SUP	$___
906 OTHR TAX	$___	611 PRINT (NM)	$___	612 RENT	$___
907 OTHR TAX	$___	613 SUBSCRIP	$___	614 PHONE	$___
910 ARC	$___	615 OTHER	$___	616 OTHER	$___
		MARKETING DEBITS			
401 AUTO TKT	$___	402 AUTO OTHR	$___	403 PRNT MKT	$___
404 O/S COMM	$___	405 ADVERTISG	$___	406 PROMOTIN	$___
407 OTHER	$___	408 OTHER	$___	409 OTHER	$___

Figure 5–1

DETACHABLE SECTION

The largest section of the voucher check is a detachable section. This constitutes over half of the voucher check form. This section provides accounting data that allows the travel agency bookkeeper/accountant to rapidly allocate check-paid expenses to appropriate accounts.

CHART-OF-ACCOUNTS NUMBER BLOCKS

The detachable bottom portion of the check relates to accounting lines (chart-of-accounts number blocks). This allows the writer of the check to indicate which account(s) should be charged for the amount of the check. It is possible to charge more than one account from a single check. For example, materials for a promotional effort are purchased at an office supply house and other materials for general office use are purchased from the same source. If one check is issued to the office supply house for payment of the monthly bill, it would be possible for the bookkeeper/accountant to break out the amount of the monies spent for promotional campaign matter and the amount spent for general office supplies. By breaking down the total amount of the bill into allocations appropriate for each of the expense areas, it will be easier for the manager and/or owner to prepare a budget for the following year that will accurately reflect expenses in each category. If these breakdowns were not possible, one might budget considerably more (or less) expense for office supplies than needed for the next year; or, one might budget considerably (more or) less monies for promotional campaigns than needed. The allocation of expense categories corresponds with the chart-of-accounts numbers. These are listed by expense or credit headings as follows: income credits, accounts payable debits, accounts receivable debits, marketing debits, and other debits.

VOUCHER CHECK COPY DISTRIBUTION

The first copy of the check (the original) is normally broken down by sending the check itself to its intended recipient. The bottom part of the original check (copy one) can serve several purposes. It is especially important for clarifying to employees what the breakdown is on payroll checks. If the check is written for a vendor expense, this section of the original can be attached to the bill received from the vendor in order to show both the check number and date when the bill was paid.

The second copy of the check receipt is a full-page copy, showing both the check and the lower section. This is the numerical copy and, like the numerical invoice/receipt file, the numerical voucher check file provides the travel agency with a permanent record, in numerical order, of all checks written. This aids in security. It also helps to track when there is a question as to whether or not a payment has been made or a question relating to the details of a payment.

As with the invoice/receipt accounts receivable file, there is also a voucher check accounts receivable file (copy three). Although one does not normally associate the payment of a check with accounts receivable, when a check is rendered for a service for which reimbursement will be received from a client, the rendering of a check creates an account receivable.

Copy four of the voucher check, a full-page copy showing the check and the voucher expense allocation section, is the client file copy. As with the invoice/receipt client file, this copy goes directly into the client file so that a permanent record of all expenses associated with the client can be kept. Also, any monies owed by the client (because of the writing of the check to a supplier, or for any other reason) can be kept together so that an appropriate bill can be prepared and rendered.

The fifth copy of the voucher check is also a full-page copy. It is utilized for a payment summarization and is usually helpful for completing the bank reconciliation.

BALANCING TRAVEL PURCHASE INVOICE/RECEIPTS AND CHECKS

The system allows a flow through, a balancing of financial documentation in keeping with the natural flow of financial transactions. When a client purchases a travel product (e.g., a tour), the agent issues an invoice/receipt billing the client. The invoice section of the invoice/receipt is completed, providing a bill to the client. When the client either makes a deposit or gives full payment to the travel agency, based upon the invoice, a new invoice/receipt is prepared. However, if payment is rendered at the time the invoice is given to the client, the same invoice/receipt is used. In such a case the receipt portion of the invoice/receipt is completed balancing out or offsetting the invoice charge to the client. A check is then issued by the travel agency to the tour operator to pay for the tour. This payment is recorded on a ledger that corresponds with the appropriate allocation-of-expense category at the bottom of the check voucher form. The ledger entry will be balanced by showing an earned commission and a payment for the rest of the incoming funds (the client's check) to the tour operator. To ensure that the funds are allocated to appropriate expense categories and that the income is recorded on the appropriate ledger, the chart of accounts is utilized.

SUMMARY

The voucher check for expenditures, like the invoice/receipt for income, is used to control and track travel agency expenses. The check comes in five copies. The top part of the check is similar to that of any standard business check. The bottom part of the check, which is the largest section of the check, is detachable. It provides a location for filling in chart-of-accounts line item numbers and titles within five broad categories. These are: 1) income credits, 2) accounts payable debits, 3) accounts receivable debits, 4) marketing debits, and 5) other debits. This type of organization allows the person writing the check to allocate the expenses directly on the check to appropriate chart-of-accounts line items.

The distribution of checks is similar to the distribution of invoice/receipts. The original check is given to the supplier or to the client, as appropriate. The bottom part of the check can either be given to the employee (if it is a payroll check) or attached to the vendor bill. The second copy of the check is the numerical file copy and it is kept on file numerically. The third check copy is an accounts receivable file copy. The fourth copy of the check is the client file copy. The fifth voucher check copy is used to prepare a payment summarization.

Because the invoice/receipt and the voucher check provide account numbers, it is possible to utilize both documents to develop a check and balance system so that errors are minimized, the possibilities of loss and theft are reduced, and accounts can be balanced.

It should be kept in mind that the voucher check discussed in this chapter is a standard industry voucher check. While this is no doubt the most frequently used type of voucher check in the travel agency industry, there are many other forms of checks and voucher checks that are utilized.

❑ DISCUSSION QUESTIONS

1. Together with the invoice/receipt, the voucher check provides the starting point for what process?
2. What information appears on the voucher check itself and in what ways does the check resemble any standard business check?
3. The voucher check comes in how many copies and how are these copies distributed?
4. What are the major categories of chart-of-accounts numbers that appear in the detachable section of the voucher check?

5. In what way does the organizational arrangement of the voucher check lend itself to tracking exact expenses so that agency accountants and managers will be able to more accurately project expenses?
6. Under what circumstance might the payment of a check be considered an accounts receivable?
7. If the agency purchased promotional materials and general office materials from an office supply house, how might the bookkeeper/accountant break out these expenses on the voucher check when making payment utilizing only one check?
8. In what way does the utilization of a voucher check make it easier for a manager and/or owner to prepare a budget for the following year?
9. What information for employees is sometimes provided on the bottom part of the original check (copy one)?

❑ *ROLE-PLAYING EXERCISE*

Two students may participate in this role-playing exercise either as an out-of-class, fun way to review travel agency use of voucher checks, or as an in-class exercise. One student plays the travel agency's bookkeeper. The other plays a new travel agent who has just begun working for the travel agency. Please read the script and then pick up the conversation in your own words.

New Agent: I have never worked with a voucher check before. The top of it looks like a regular check, so I don't think I will have any problem with that. But what do I do with the rest of it?

Agency Bookkeeper: Just fill in the appropriate line or lines in the appropriate sections at the bottom.

New Agent: That sounds easy. I'm not sure though that I understand what you mean by "appropriate line" or "appropriate section." What happens when I pay Kankara Cruises $3,000 for the balance due on Mr. and Mrs. Blake's cruise through the Panama Canal? The total cost includes both the cruise and the air. How do I separate out the amounts and put them on the appropriate lines? Or do I even need to do that?

Agency Bookkeeper: It sounds more complicated than it is. First you. . .

CONTINUE ON YOUR OWN

❏ *CHAPTER FIVE EXERCISE*

INSTRUCTIONS: Complete the voucher check on the next page, drawing from the following information. Beth Hathaway has booked the Johnson and Rheingold Tour Company's ten day "Grand Europe" tour (I T number JRTC 986) departing next Thursday. She has made full payment to your travel agency and left the agency about an hour ago. The cost of the tour is $2,850, land only. Beth is a leisure client. Because the agency does not assign client numbers to leisure clients, there is no client number for Beth. The Johnson and Rheingold tour company pays 10 percent commission off of the entire price of their tours and they allow travel agencies to deduct their commissions prior to sending payment to them. The address of the Johnson and Rheingold Tour Company is 597 Kallex Avenue, Newbergh, Iowa 82610.

Make sure you show your commission on the appropriate income credits line. Of course you will need to show a debit on the appropriate accounts receivable debits line. Note that the total of the amount shown in your income credit as the commission plus the amount of the check itself should equal the amount of the accounts receivable debits.

VOUCHER CHECK

5309

Date ______________

PAY ________________________________ Dollars $______________

To the order of

____
Authorized Signature

INCOME CREDITS		ACCT RCVBLE DEBITS		OTHER DEBITS	
301 AIR COMM	$___	101 A/R HOTELS	$___	501 AGT SAL	$___
302 HOTEL "	$___	104 A/R CRUISES	$___	502 MKT SAL	$___
303 CAR "	$___	105 A/R RAIL	$___	503 SUP SAL	$___
304 CRUISE "	$___	106 A/R TOUR	$___	504 ADM SAL	$___
305 RAIL "	$___	107 A/R OTHER	$___	505 TAXES	$___
306 TOUR "	$___	108 A/R OTHER	$___	506 BENEFITS	$___
307 OTHER "	$___	109 A/R OTHER	$___	507 OTHER	$___
ACCTS PAY DEBITS		OTHER DEBITS			
901 FED WITH	$___	601 ACCOUNTING	$___	602 AUTOMA	$___
902 STAT TAX	$___	603 DUES	$___	604 EDUCATN	$___
903 FICA TAX	$___	605 FEES	$___	606 INSURNC	$___
904 LOCL TAX	$___	607 LEGAL	$___	608 OFF EQU	$___
905 CITY TAX	$___	609 OFF REPRS	$___	610 OFF SUP	$___
906 OTHR TAX	$___	611 PRINT (NM)	$___	612 RENT	$___
907 OTHR TAX	$___	613 SUBSCRIP	$___	614 PHONE	$___
910 ARC	$___	615 OTHER	$___	616 OTHER	$___
		MARKETING DEBITS			
401 AUTO TKT	$___	402 AUTO OTHR	$___	403 PRNT MKT	$___
404 O/S COMM	$___	405 ADVERTISG	$___	406 PROMOTIN	$___
407 OTHER	$___	408 OTHER	$___	409 OTHER	$___

6

THE CHART OF ACCOUNTS

OBJECTIVES

Upon completion of this chapter, the student will be able to:

- ❑ Correlate simple direct check expenses to appropriate chart-of-accounts lines
- ❑ Verbally evaluate the pros and cons of a travel agency industry chart of accounts
- ❑ Identify the purpose of each digit in a multidigit chart-of accounts system
- ❑ Explain the benefits to the travel industry of having a uniform classification of accounts

INTRODUCTION

As noted in the discussion of the ASTA accounting system, the system itself resulted from a problem in not having a uniform classification of accounts or, perhaps more correctly put, a chart of accounts on which a large number or all travel agencies agreed. A chart of accounts is basically a labeling system to categorize sources of incoming monies (receipts) and outgoing monies (expenditures). Having a clear labeling system that is strictly adhered to by all who work in the agency makes it possible to track both income and expenses, to measure income and expenses by category, and to manage the travel agency's finances. The key here is uniformity. In other words, if all follow the same labeling system, it can be presumed that data will be accurate. Therefore, forecasts and plans based upon past data will have some reasonable expectation of being met, since past financial activities provide some indication of possible future activity. However, in individual agencies if labeling is imprecise, if a system exists but no one in the agency is required to follow it, or if each person labels income and expenses according to titles they like best, serious consequences will develop. It will not be possible to group income and expense categories, plans based upon the data will not have an accurate foundation, and projections will probably be inaccurate.

Some will argue that it does not matter how the income category or the expense category is labeled as long as there is uniformity in labeling. That is, the same income item is labeled the same way each time it occurs and the same expense item is labeled the same way each time it occurs. Indeed, some very large travel agencies, with a wide range of income sources and an equally wide (or wider) range of expenses, frequently use a strictly numerical coding system for their chart of accounts rather than a clear-cut multiword label. Such a coding system lends itself to computerization better than multiword lengthy titles.

THE NEED FOR A LONGER, MORE DETAILED CHART OF ACCOUNTS

When the ASTA accounting system was developed, a simple and short chart of accounts was developed. This provided a substantially better labeling system and a more uniform chart of accounts for those ASTA agencies adopting the system. For most, it was a good system that worked well. However, as the travel agency business changed over the years and as deregulation affected both income and expenditure categories to a considerable degree, many have found that a longer chart of accounts with a number of additional categories for both income and expenditures is needed. For example, with the original ASTA chart of accounts there was no allocation for automation or computer expenses. Today, many agencies break down automation expenses into two broad categories—expenses for hardware and software. Under these two broad categories there are as many as five to fifteen different subcategories of expenses. Obviously, at the time that the first ASTA accounting system was developed, there was little or no automation in the travel agency industry. Today, almost all travel agencies have computer reservation systems and many agencies have automated interface systems and stand-alone automation systems serving a wide range of needs.

CURRENT INDUSTRY CHART-OF-ACCOUNTS SYSTEMS

Current industry chart-of-accounts systems break down accounts into five broad categories: (1) assets, (2) liabilities, and (3) capital (for the balance sheet) and (4) revenues and (5) expenses (for the income statement). Each category may have its own range of account numbers and account titles. The balance sheet assets are often divided into current assets (with account numbers ranging from 100 to 199, for example) and other assets with a separate

BALANCE SHEET

FOR: ____________ 19__

CURRENT ASSETS

Increase/ Decrease			Account	Balance	
			120 Cash in Bank—ARC Acct		
			121 Cash in Bank—Other Acct		
			122 Cash in Bank—Other Acct		
			123 Petty Cash		
			124 Other:		
			125 Other:		
			110 Accounts Receivable		
			111 Notes Receivable		
			112 Investment:		
			113 Investment:		
			114 Other:		
			199 TOTAL CURRENT ASSETS		
			OTHER ASSETS		
			200 Automation Equipment		
			201 Less Depreciation		
			202 Office Equipment		
			203 Less Depreciation		
			204 Automobile		
			205 Less Depreciation		
			206 Other:		
			207 Less Depreciation		
			299 TOTAL OTHER ASSETS		
			TOTAL ASSETS		

Figure 6–1

BALANCE SHEET

FOR: ____________ 19__

LIABILITIES AND CAPITAL

Increase/ Decrease			Account	Balance	
			LIABILITIES		
			910 Accounts Payable—ARC		
			911 Accounts Payable—Hotels		
			912 Accounts Payable—Car Rental		
			913 Accounts Payable—Cruises		
			914 Accounts Payable—Rail		
			915 Accounts Payable—Tours		
			916 Accounts Payable—Automation		
			917 Accounts Payable—Other:		
			920 Notes Payable		
			901 Federal Income Tax Withheld		
			902 State Income Tax Withheld		
			904 Local Income Tax Withheld		
			905 City Income Tax Withheld		
			903 FICA Tax Withheld		
			999 TOTAL LIABILITIES		
			CAPITAL		
			800 Invested Capital		
			801 Retained Earnings		
			810 Withdrawals		
			820 PROFIT OR LOSS (THIS YEAR)		
			830 NET CAPITAL		
			TOTAL LIABILITIES AND CAPITAL		

Figure 6–1 (Continued)

INCOME STATEMENT

FOR MONTH OF ____________, 19__

INCOME

ACCT. NO.	INCOME/EXPENSE FOR MONTH		ACCOUNT	INCOME/EXPENSE YEAR-TO-DATE	
301			Air Commissions		
302			Hotel Commissions		
303			Car Rental Commissions		
304			Cruise Commissions		
305			Rail Commissions		
306			Package Tour Commissions		
307			Other:		
308			Other:		
			TOTAL INCOME		
			EXPENSES		
			MARKETING EXPENSES		
401			Auto—Ticket Delivery		
402			Auto—Other		
403			Printing (Marketing)		
404			Outside Sales Commissions		
405			Advertising		
406			Promotional Programs		
407			Other:		
408			Other:		
			TOTAL MARKETING EXPENSES		
			PERSONNEL EXPENSES		
501			Inside Agent Salaries		
502			Marketing Staff Salaries		
503			Support Staff Salaries		
504			Admin./Exec. Salaries		
505			Taxes		
506			Employee Benefits		
507			Other:		
508			Other:		
			TOTAL PERSONNEL EXPENSES		

Figure 6–2

INCOME STATEMENT

FOR MONTH OF ____________, 19__

EXPENSES

ACCT. NO.	INCOME/EXPENSE FOR MONTH		ACCOUNT	INCOME/EXPENSE YEAR-TO-DATE	
			ADMINISTRATIVE/OFFICE EXPENSES		
601			Accounting		
602			Automation Costs		
603			Dues		
604			Educational Expenses		
605			Fees		
606			Insurance		
607			Legal		
608			Office Equip & Furn		
609			Office Repairs & Maint		
610			Office Supplies		
611			Printing (Non Mktg)		
612			Rent		
613			Subscriptions		
614			Telephone/Telex/Fax		
615			Other:		
616			Other:		
			TOTAL ADMIN/OFFICE EXP.		
			SUMMARY		
			TOTAL MARKETING EXPENSES		
			TOTAL PERSONNEL EXPENSES		
			TOTAL ADMIN/OFFICE EXPENSES		
			TOTAL EXPENSES		
			NET PROFIT (OR LOSS)		

Figure 6–2 (Continued)

series of account numbers (for example, ranging from 200 to 299). Balance sheet liabilities usually have account numbers as well. These might range from 900 to 999. Balance sheet capital categories might have account numbers ranging from 800 to 899. The income statement categories are for revenues and usually have their account numbers (ranging from 300 to 399 for example) and various types of expenses (with account numbers which might range from 400 to 699). These chart-of-accounts numbers are reflected in figure 6–1 (for the balance sheet) and figure 6–2 (for the income statement).

As can be seen, each account number is a three-digit number. Each digit identifies a specific factor. The first digit classifies the type of account, the second digit identifies a specific category, and the third digit narrows that into a specific division. A further narrowing is possible by using a decimal point system and additional digits. Another way in which a further narrowing is possible is the allocation of open account numbers. This provides an opportunity for a travel agency to identify and appropriately label specific categories of income or expenses unique to itself.

MAJOR ACCOUNTS ON CHECKS AND THE INCOME STATEMENT

Glance at the sample voucher check in the chapter on voucher checks. Note that major sections of the chart of accounts are reproduced on the voucher check so that at the time the check is written an allocation of expenses to the appropriate account can be made. Chart-of-accounts items on the voucher check are broken down into five categories. Since most checks represent debits from travel agency accounts, four of these categories are debit categories: 1) accounts payable debits (account numbers 901–910, representing monies due to ARC and tax monies that have been withheld and are due to one or more government entities); 2) accounts receivable debits (account numbers 100–110, representing monies owed to an accounts receivable); 3) other debits (account numbers 501–616, representing other debits); and 4) marketing debits (account numbers 401–409). The check voucher also lists income credits, since some payments by check constitute income credits for the travel agency. The chart-of-accounts items listed under income credits are numbered from 301 to 308 and relate to commission income credits. Major chart-of-accounts items are summarized on the income statement as well. Note that chart-of-accounts items are grouped into related categories, figure 6–3. This allows the income statement to show comparisons of both income and expenses in all major categories on month-by-month and year-to-date bases.

INCOME STATEMENT

FOR MONTH OF ____________, 19__

INCOME

Acct. No.	Income/Expense For Month		Account	Income/Expense Year-To-Date	
301			Air Commissions		
302			Hotel Commissions		
303			Car Rental Commissions		
304			Cruise Commissions		
305			Rail Commissions		
306			Package Tour Commissions		
307			Other:		
308			Other:		
			TOTAL INCOME		
			EXPENSES		
			MARKETING EXPENSES		
401			Auto—Ticket Delivery		
402			Auto—Other		
403			Printing (Marketing)		
404			Outside Sales Commissions		
405			Advertising		
406			Promotional Programs		
407			Other:		
408			Other:		
			TOTAL MARKETING EXPENSES		
			PERSONNEL EXPENSES		
501			Inside Agent Salaries		
502			Marketing Staff Salaries		
503			Support Staff Salaries		
504			Admin./Exec. Salaries		
505			Taxes		
506			Employee Benefits		
507			Other:		
508			Other:		
			TOTAL PERSONNEL EXPENSES		

Figure 6–3

INCOME STATEMENT

FOR MONTH OF ____________, 19__

EXPENSES

Acct. No.	Income/Expense For Month		Account	Income/Expense Year-To-Date	
			ADMINISTRATIVE/OFFICE EXPENSES		
601			Accounting		
602			Automation Costs		
603			Dues		
604			Educational Expenses		
605			Fees		
606			Insurance		
607			Legal		
608			Office Equip & Furn		
609			Office Repairs & Maint		
610			Office Supplies		
611			Printing (Non Mktg)		
612			Rent		
613			Subscriptions		
614			Telephone/Telex/Fax		
615			Other:		
616			Other:		
			TOTAL ADMIN/OFFICE EXP.		
			SUMMARY		
			TOTAL MARKETING EXPENSES		
			TOTAL PERSONNEL EXPENSES		
			TOTAL ADMIN/OFFICE EXPENSES		
			TOTAL EXPENSES		
			NET PROFIT (OR LOSS)		

Figure 6–3 (Continued)

The first section relates to income, with account numbers from 301 through 306. In addition, space is left for listing other income accounts which may be unique to a particular agency. Expenses are broken down into three categories. These are marketing expenses, personnel expenses, and administrative/office expenses. The marketing expenses relate to all chart-of-accounts items reflecting marketing, promotion, and sales efforts. These are numbered from 401 through 408. Personnel expenses list costs relating to salaries and benefits. These are numbered from 501 through 508. Administrative/office expenses reflect those costs incurred for all other expenses and are numbered from 601 to 616. As with income items, space is left for adding chart-of-accounts lines for expenses unique to a particular travel agency. There are also summary chart-of-accounts lines.

As can be seen, the chart of accounts provides a place to record all income and expenditures of the travel agency in a uniform manner so that all documents will categorize income and expenses in the same way.

SUMMARY

The standard industry chart of accounts is a coding and labeling system that allows all travel agency personnel to classify types of payments and types of income consistently in the same way. This enables the agency to measure types of income and types of expenditures over periods of time. Based upon these measurements, forecasts for future income and future expenditures in each category can be made.

The standard industry chart of accounts is based on a three-digit number system with each digit providing a more specific classification of accounts. For those who want an even more detailed breakdown, a decimal point system is also possible.

The more important categories of expenses are shown on the voucher check system and a breakdown of the major account classifications is provided on the monthly income statement. By following the guidelines provided by the chart of accounts, it is possible for agency management to consistently identify income and expenditure categories. With this data, agency management has a key tool needed in preparing to undertake budgeting. The use of this information for the budgeting process is detailed to a greater degree in later chapters regarding budgeting.

❑ DISCUSSION QUESTIONS

1. What led to the development of the ASTA accounting system?
2. Why is it considered important to have a labeling system (for categorizing income and expenses) that is strictly adhered to by all who work in an agency?
3. Why do some feel that a longer chart of accounts with additional categories for both income and expenditures is needed?
4. What is the range of account numbers on the balance sheet and in what order are they organized?
5. Each account number is a several-digit number. How many digits are in the number?
6. Why are major sections of the chart of accounts reproduced on the voucher check?
7. Why are lines left blank on the income statement?
8. Why might automated accounting systems utilize numerical system codes rather than multiword lengthy titles for their charts of accounts?
9. What major sections of the chart of accounts are reproduced on the income statement?
10. What major sections of the chart of accounts are reproduced on the voucher check?

❑ ROLE-PLAYING EXERCISE

Two students may participate in this role-playing exercise either as an out-of-class, fun way to review the importance of charts of accounts, or as an in-class exercise. One student plays a travel agent who does not understand the importance of having a chart of accounts or of working with one. The other plays the travel agency's bookkeeper. Please read the script and then pick up the conversation in your own words.

Agent: No matter what our income or expenditure, you insist that we allocate the money to some three-digit number. Life in the travel agency is busy enough without having to waste time giving arbitrary numbers to each bit of money we receive or spend.

Agency Bookkeeper: I understand that you are busy, but without some type of an allocation system, it would be very difficult to complete the bookkeeping tasks required by management.

Agent: I suppose there are reasons for this classification process, but I don't understand them. Why do we have to go through assigning numbers for every expense and every income?

Agency Bookkeeper: The system is called a chart of accounts. Let me explain the process and the benefits of the system. The system starts with. . .

CONTINUE ON YOUR OWN

❑ *CHAPTER SIX EXERCISE*

INSTRUCTIONS: Utilizing the chart of accounts shown on the balance sheet (figure 6–1), the income statement (figure 6–2), and the voucher check (figure 5–1), assign a chart-of-accounts classification number to each expense noted below.

#	Chart of Accounts #	Cost	Item Purchased
1)		$39.50	Three-year subscription to *Travel Weekly*
2)		$24.30	Business cards for agency manager
3)		$261.60	Payroll tax payment
4)		$422.95	Payment to tour operator for FAM trip for F.I.T. specialist
5)		$21.19	Bimonthly payment to copy center for photocopies
6)		$10.50	Federal Express charge for A.J. Johnson ticket overnight delivery
7)		$220.00	Annual membership in Chamber of Commerce
8)		$42.00	Newspaper bill for cruise tag ad—Sunday edition
9)		$81.00	Bus driver tip for Senior Citizens' weekend trip
10)		$21.80	Reimbursement for long-distance calls made by outside sales rep

PROFITABILITY PERFORMANCE MEASURES AND COST COMPARISONS

OBJECTIVES

Upon completion of this chapter, the student will be able to:

- ❑ Apply equity build-up approaches and principles to a simple equity position determination application
- ❑ Calculate a return on equity percentage utilizing given figures for net income after taxes and for owner's equity
- ❑ Calculate a return on assets percentage when given the net income after taxes and the total assets of a travel agency
- ❑ Explain a travel agency's comparative dollar profit per sales employee pattern based on business mix and dollar volume of business

INTRODUCTION

Profitability indicators, performance measures, long range decision ratios, cost comparison data, and three major financial analyses will be introduced in this chapter. These are all financial management applications to financial data. They allow the travel agency's accountant to provide the executives with the data they need to make sound decisions relating to the future direction of the agency. They affect staffing decisions, marketing directions, investment considerations, and in fact, most major executive moves relating to the ongoing sound management of a travel agency.

PROFITABILITY INDICATORS

Obviously, travel agency investors and agency executives have an ongoing concern about the agency's profitability (or, as it is usually addressed, with the agency's level of profitability). After all, this is why most businesses are in business, i.e., to make a profit—preferably a good profit. Therefore, travel agency accountants are usually expected to provide profitability indicator data to management on a regular basis.

RETURN ON EQUITY

Perhaps the profitability indicator that is of paramount importance to investors is the agency's *return on equity*. Equity in a new business is the money the owners put in to make the business run. Equity refers to the money that is invested in a business. It is a combination of initial capitalization (the original investment to establish the business), any additional funds put into the business over the years by the owners to keep it going, and any retained profits (profits that normally would be paid out to owners, but which they choose to leave in the business). Ultimately equity can also be profits that have been put back into the agency. It can be additional monies the owners may have invested in the agency in early years or at times when the agency lost money and needed extra capital with which to work. This, of course, is in addition to the money originally invested to start the company. If an owner puts his/her money in the bank, the owner knows that, at no risk (within government financial institution insurance limitations), a certain amount of money will be earned as interest.

EQUITY

Because equity can be considered money belonging to owners, and because business people who have invested money in a business expect to receive a return on investment, owners tend to consider equity as that which belongs to them. Many owners guard it jealously. However, equity is seldom tangible cash that an owner can put his hands on right away.

Equity can be looked at in two ways. One is a flat dollar amount and the other is a percentage, figure 7–1.

THE RETURN ON EQUITY FORMULA

$$\frac{\text{NET INCOME AFTER TAXES}}{\text{OWNER'S EQUITY}}$$

or, for example

$$\frac{\$4{,}500 = \text{Net Income After Taxes}}{\$80{,}000 = \text{Owner's Equity}}$$

Therefore, the Return on Equity Equals a Rounded Off 6%

Figure 7–1

RISK AND RETURN

The usual justification for people to put money into a business is to get more money back than they would if they put the same amount into a secured investment. The reason they expect to get more back is that there is risk involved. Theoretically speaking, the greater the risk, the greater the potential (ideally, the real) return on investment.

There are choices. If a person wants little risk and is willing to accept a small return, money can be put into straight savings. It can be taken out whenever needed and is often backed by a government guarantee protecting the bank and its funds, normally up to $100,000 per investor. There is virtually no risk.

But that money could be put into a different kind of an account and earn more interest—a money market account, for example. While the return on investment may be better, the risk is greater. It may not be much of a risk, but it is some risk—more than in a government guaranteed savings account.

A third choice is to invest the money in a business. The investor's expectation is that there will be a higher return on investment. Some travel agencies, of course, do produce a very good return on investment. Others return very little on the investment. Still others lose money. Before putting money into a business, it behooves an investor to consider what the return on investment might be. In this case, what is considered is return on equity, equity most often meaning the investment. As pointed out earlier, however, equity can be more than just the initial investment. It could be additional monies put into the business at a later time to keep the business open or it could be rolled over profits.

THE RETURN ON EQUITY FORMULA

The formula for return on equity is to divide net income after taxes by owner's equity, figure 7–1. What does this term "owner's equity" mean? There are some nuances of meaning that need to be considered when discussing financial management. For example, what is meant in terms of profit when the term "profit" is used? Another term to be considered is "net income after taxes." Some people in the industry interpret net income after taxes as being profit. What they are basically saying is that the amount of money remaining after paying expenses and after paying taxes is profit. Others say that profit is what remains after paying all expenses, taxes, and a predetermined amount for return on investment. Profit, therefore, can be interpreted several ways. The easiest way to identify return on equity is to point out how it is calculated, namely, the net income after paying taxes. Net, in this case, means money remaining after all expenses are paid. There is a problem that is unique to the travel industry because the industry talks in terms of "net" as being commission. Commission is a net figure when one considers what the agency keeps after paying the airlines or other suppliers. But in this case, when net income is referred to, it means the amount of money that remains after paying all expenses including taxes, but not including those expenses incurred in giving some type of return on investment to the owners.

Return on Equity Example

For a better understanding of how the formula actually works, it is beneficial to consider specific examples using figures based on regional and national statistics. Based on the 1988 averaging of sales of travel agencies by a major metropolitan area broker who specializes in agency sales, the average agency sold for a figure that rounded off to 8.5 percent of the annual gross sales of the business. For an example that shows ROE (Return on Equity), see figure 7–2. The sample agency had an annual gross sales level of $2.2 million. If that agency had sold for a price based on 8.5 percent of annual gross sales, the total agency sale price would have been $187,000.

For this metropolitan broker the average down payment was 28 percent. This meant that the purchaser of the $2.2 million travel agency made a down payment of $52,360. The purchaser therefore, had an initial equity of $52,360 at the moment the check was given to the previous owner and the contract was signed for transfer of ownership, figure 7–3.

CALCULATION OF PURCHASE PRICE OF A $2.2 MILLION GROSS AGENCY

$2,200,000	(Agency's Annual Gross Sales)
× .085	(1988 Average Percent of Gross Sales for which Agencies were Purchased)
$ 187,000	(Purchase Price of Sample Travel Agency)

Figure 7–2

CALCULATION OF DOWN PAYMENT AND INITIAL EQUITY OF AGENCY INVESTOR

$187,000	(Purchase Price of Sample Travel Agency)
× .085	(Average Down Payment for Purchased Travel Agencies)
$ 52,360	(Down Payment Made and Initial Equity of Investor)

Figure 7–3

CALCULATION OF EQUITY AT THE END OF THE FIRST YEAR OF AGENCY OWNERSHIP ONLY BASED ON INITIAL DOWN PAYMENT AND INTEREST PAYMENTS—NOT INCLUDING ANY RETAINED EARNINGS

$52,360.00	(Down Payment and Initial Equity)
+$14,810.40	(Interest Payments—Additional Equity)
$67,170.40	(Investor Equity at the End of the First Year of Ownership)

Figure 7–4

However, the new owner was expected to pay interest annually on the balance owed ($134,640). Interest is normally pegged to the prime rate, and average rounded interest rate on contracts signed for agencies purchased from this broker during 1988 was 11 percent. Based upon this figure, by the end of the first year of ownership of the $2.2 million gross sales agency the new owner paid approximately 11 percent of $134,640.00 or $14,810.40 in interest. This meant that at the end of the first year of ownership (presuming that there were no principal payments due until the start of the second year), the new owner had an equity or an investment of approximately $67,170.40, figure 7–4.

The second part of the return on equity formula relates to profit. Based on a 1988 ASTA study, one- and two-outlet travel agencies that had an annual gross sales volume of $2 million or more had an average net profit before principal remuneration of $80,211.00. Taking this average figure as the annual profit earned by this hypothetical new owner and plugging it into the profit portion of the formula, there is now an equity of $147,381.40 ($67,170.40 plus $80,211.00), figure 7–5.

CALCULATION OF EQUITY AT THE END OF THE FIRST YEAR OF AGENCY OWNERSHIP BASED ON INITIAL DOWN PAYMENT, INTEREST PAYMENTS, AND RETAINED EARNINGS WHEN RETAINED EARNINGS ARE THE SAME AS PROFITS

$52,360.00	(Down Payment and Initial Equity)
+$14,810.40	(Interest Payments—Additional Equity)
+$80,211.00	(Net Profits Rolled Over to Retained Earnings—Additional Equity)
$147,381.40	(Investor Equity at the End of the First Year of Ownership)

Figure 7–5

WHAT IS A GOOD RETURN ON EQUITY?

Obviously, many business people would like to get an average return on equity in excess of 100 percent. To determine a reasonable return on equity, one must compare the amount of money that can be earned when investing. Generally, the expected return on investment will vary greatly, but there is a strong relationship to the amount of risk involved. In the example shown in figures 7-2 through 7-5, the return on equity is very good when compared to the maximum of 10 or 11 percent one might earn in a relatively secure investment. It is even better when one considers that during that same year, 1988, some of the most secure investments (government bonds, certificates of deposit, and federally insured bank savings accounts) paid return on investment figures between 7 and 9 percent.

However, there are other figures and other factors that need to be taken into consideration. Obviously, the risk of investing in a new business, even if that business is substantially profitable at the time of the purchase, is much greater than an investment where there is a government backed guarantee of paying interest. With the history of small business losses and bankruptcies, one must consider that the risk involved in investing in any small business can be considerable. In addition, there are factors in the example just given that need to be looked at more closely.

First, the ASTA statistics, based on average net profit, exclude principal remuneration. If the investor bought the travel agency and is working in the agency on a full-time basis, these figures on net profit no longer look as good as they did initially. The reason is that no salary or benefits have been taken out to pay the owner(s).

Although statistics relating to average owner compensation have not been found in the research of the literature, the October 1987 Census Report found that the average American with a four-year college degree and fifteen years of experience has an annual income of $16,652. A 1988 study by Davidoff of compensation for all travel agency employees revealed that employees with five years of experience in the average travel agency earned $16,000 per year and that the average employee working in a corporate-oriented travel agency with five years of experience earned $20,800.

Based on these findings, a somewhat average figure of $17,000 per year is allocated to the owner of our hypothetical travel agency. If this $17,000 annual compensation is deducted from the $80,211 profit, the real profit is reduced to $63,211 and the return on equity is reduced to slightly less than 100 percent. This is still considered to be an excellent return on equity, but obviously not as good a return on equity as the one calculated prior to figuring in the payment of remuneration to principals (compensation to owners).

If the owners do not work in the travel agency, the higher return on equity would apply. However, one would expect that the owner would have to spend a considerable amount of time managing the investment of the travel agency. This time would be spent without compensation if the high return on equity figure is expected. Whether the owner takes the money as a return on equity, reinvests the money in the business to build up equity, takes a salary, or splits the money by taking some combination of profit, reinvestment into equity, and/or salary, depends upon the needs of the owner and applicable tax considerations.

One factor to be considered is there is the new owner's ongoing obligation to pay the previous owner an annual interest plus additional capital payments until the agency is fully paid for. If profits are paid to the new owner each year and the new owner in turn pays money directly to the previous owner for a percentage of the balance of principal and the interest on the balance of principal until the agency is fully paid for, the equity position of the new owner becomes substantially greater each year. Concurrently, the return on equity becomes much smaller each year (presuming that profit remains the same). However, if annual payments to the previous owner and interest on the balance due are paid by the business from what would otherwise be profits, but before profits are declared, the annual profit figure will be reduced each year. Equity will stay the same. Although the return on equity will be lower than that calculated in the initial year, it can be expected that if the ASTA average profit statistics remain the same or close to the same, the return on equity for the investor will still be quite good.

In the long run what is considered to be a good return on equity varies considerably—often from year to year. Usually what owners will do is to look at what the going bank rate is (there are several bank rates, of course). One way is to look at an established rate banks are paying for straight savings accounts in one's community and average it out. Another is to look at the lending rate. There is a lending rate called a *preferred lending rate* that is published by financial publications on a regular basis. For example, the *Wall Street Journal* publishes a preferred lending rate for an averaging of New York City banks every day. Whatever one determines to be a comparative rate in terms of presumably safe investments, the return on equity is normally two or three points (i.e., percent) higher than for those standard "safe" investments. It should be this way. Otherwise there is no incentive for an investor to take money out of a bank and put it into a business or to leave it in a business. In fact, there is a disincentive to leave money in a business if the return on equity is less than what the investor would have if the money were put into a bank savings account. Therefore, "good return on equity" varies from month to month and from year to year.

The requirement of constantly earning a good return on equity is frequently more theory than fact. The reality is that a travel business that is making very little money and providing very little return on equity may not be in a position to liquidate and immediately return the owner's investment. It may not be easy for investors to say that the bank is paying more than the travel agency and therefore the equity paid into the agency will be immediately drawn out and reinvested in a bank account. The investor must wait until someone buys the agency (or his/her stock in the agency) before being able to reinvest the equity money. It could be a long wait and the buyer may pay more or less than the equity amount for the agency. It is probable that he/she will not pay an amount equal to the equity.

Return on equity therefore makes a difference in the attraction or rejection of relatively sophisticated investors. These people may say, "Yes, the risk looks reasonable enough to take money out of the bank" or "No, the risk does not look reasonable enough to do that." Therefore, to some degree return on equity helps to determine the number of travel entities that a community, city, or state has.

For example, several years ago when airline competition was severe, there was considerable price cutting. The average ticket price was extremely low—as low as $78 in some communities. Travel agencies sold for very small amounts of money and no potential investors rushed to open new agencies because the return on equity was a negative figure. On the other hand, as average ticket prices have gone up substantially, the average commission earned by travel agencies has increased dramatically. Now many more agencies are being purchased and opened because the return on equity for many is very good, compared with putting the money into other investments. Therefore, there is a strong positive correlation between the amount of travel agencies in existence and return on equity.

RETURN ON EQUITY TAX RAMIFICATIONS

It should be kept in mind that tax ramifications can be considerable. When the new owner of the travel agency retires and wishes to sell the agency, generally speaking the money that was invested in the agency is not subject to tax when payment is received from the sale of the agency. Therefore, if monthly payments to the first owner by the second owner have come from travel agency profits earned regularly by the second owner, and if taxes are paid on profits earned each year, then a substantial amount of tax-free equity can be built up into the business. When selling the agency at the time of retirement, the second owner could well have a substantial amount of tax-free money on which to retire.

But this annual contribution to equity comes at a price. Because profits were paid to the owner by the company, the profits are taxable to the owner as income. In other words, equity is built with after-tax income.

On the other hand, if the first owner is paid from pre-profit money directly by the company, the second owner is left out of the financial loop and does not have a tax liability on the money paid to the first owner. Nor does he/she have additional equity.

Both scenarios have advantages and disadvantages. Therefore it is wise to seek sound advice from trusted tax consultants. How monthly payments are made can result in considerable differences in the return on equity position for the company.

RETURN ON ASSETS

Another figure to be considered in terms of profitability indicators is *return on assets.* The return on assets is an indicator of managerial performance. This is calculated by dividing net income after taxes by the total assets of the business, figure 7–6. The return on assets, though a somewhat arbitrary figure, should be a positive figure. Many people value good will, meaning the value the agency places on its customers (often both a nebulous and arbitrary figure). Good will is an intangible asset. Business managers and owners often place a very high value on good will in order to give themselves a return on assets that looks good, but is inflated.

There are a number of other profitability indicators and some will be considered later in the book. However, for travel agencies, those disucssed here are the major ones.

THE RETURN ON ASSETS FORMULA

$$\frac{\text{NET INCOME AFTER TAXES}}{\text{TOTAL ASSETS}}$$

or, for example

$$\frac{\$4,500 = \text{Net Income After Taxes}}{\$300,000 = \text{Total Assets}}$$

Therefore, the Return on Assets Equals a Rounded Off 1%

Figure 7–6

PERFORMANCE MEASURES

The single most important performance measure has already been discussed: personnel costs. What is done in any kind of performance measure is to take

THE PERSONNEL COST PERFORMANCE MEASURE

$$\frac{\text{PERSONNEL COST}}{\text{COMMISSION INCOME}}$$

or, for example

$$\frac{\$148{,}000 = \text{Personnel Costs}}{\$300{,}000 = \text{Commission Income}}$$

Therefore, Personnel Cost is 49% of Commission Income

Figure 7–7

a percentage of commission income for the cost that is involved. As has been seen, personnel costs constitute by far the largest percentage of total costs for a travel agency. Therefore, travel agency executives are most concerned about this single performance measure.

If this is the case, how does one determine personnel costs as a percentage of commission income? Personnel costs are divided by total commission income, figure 7–7. What kind of percentage are agency executives looking for? Industry studies indicate that personnel costs constitute approximately 50 percent of all costs. Agency executives strive for a level of personnel costs as a percentage of commission income that is under 50 percent, or better than average. The goal is to reduce personnel costs so that the agency can have profit.

It should be remembered that there are only two ways to make money in a business. One is to reduce costs and the other is to increase sales. Therefore, the more the costs—especially personnel costs—can be reduced, the more likely that profit will be attained. But the agency must provide enough services to keep clients. There is a constant struggle to find out how to reduce costs while maintaining satisfied clients. If the agency can get down to between 40 and 45 percent and still provide good service, it stands a very good chance of making a profit. But this will vary to a great extent depending upon the type of agency, the type of business conducted, and other factors.

As pointed out, a performance measure can be a relationship between any cost factor and commissionable income. In addition to personnel cost, the agency's executives are usually concerned about all other major costs (some lesser ones as well). Two of these are rent and computers. The cost of office space, or square footage, is one agency management should be very careful about. Sometimes agencies spend much more in rent than the agency can justify. All areas of automation can also escalate costs. This is not just hardware, but also software expenses. Agency executives expect their accountants to identify ideal or certainly industry average costs in all major expense areas and to continually compare these ideal or industry average costs against the agency's own costs. Many agency owners and executives expect their accountants to flag problem cost areas early and consistently so that real and/or potential problems can be addresed before serious danger occurs.

LONG-RANGE DECISION RATIOS

One aspect of *long-range decision ratios* has to do with the relationship between account types and commission income over time. One of the concerns that agency executives have is the degree of reliance on particular accounts. The agency wants to avoid a potential problem of relying too much on single accounts. If the agency finds, for example, that over a period of time one account constitutes 50–60 percent of the agency's business, the agency has a major potential problem and a risky situation. One agency marketing executive advises his salespeople not to pursue major accounts even when they think they may be able to get them. The reason is that if they get such an account, it could be too risky for the agency. To be able to get and service such an account, they would have to hire additional staff, bring in additional computer equipment, and reorganize the agency. It may represent a strong potential for additional money, but when an agency has one account that constitutes 60 percent or more of its total business, what happens if that account moves to some other agency?

An example will help emphasize the point. A travel agency in the Midwest landed a major account several years ago. The agency signed a five-year contract for additional office space so that it could expand to handle the account. They signed a five-year contract for additional automation equipment. They hired additional staff. Within three months that major business account (a very large company) had been purchased by a large firm that owned many different types of businesses. One of the other businesses owned by the parent company was a national travel agency chain. The parent company mandated that all of its companies had to use its travel agency chain. Needless to say, the agency that three months ago had patted itself on the back for landing such a big account now faced major problems. Committed to a long-term space rental contract and a long-term automation equipment lease contract, they immediately started an effort to downsize the agency. The cost of doing so hurt their reputation in the community, hindered their ability to attract quality staff members later on, and almost sent the agency into bankruptcy. New big accounts are risky. A travel agency can move from profitability to nonprofitability in a matter of just a few months. Nevertheless, the temptation is great.

What percentage figure should travel agencies aim toward to prevent this type of problem? It varies, but many travel executives agree that they should work toward a figure that will not exceed 40 percent. In other words, the amount of business provided to the travel agency by any single account should not exceed 40 percent of that agency's total business. However, many agency owners are uncomfortable with the 40 percent level and mandate that no account can exceed 20, 15, or even as low as 10 percent of the agency's total business. Again, most executives turn to the agency's accountant(s) to watch this relationship. They expect their accountants to warn them if it appears that any single account will create a strong dependence or place them in a position of meeting or exceeding the designated percentage of total business.

Another long-term relationshp that travel agencies watch is the *long-term debt to total equity ratio.* This is a relationship that one needs to be very careful about. The example provided in figure 7-8 shows a ratio of approximately one to two. A debt of approximately $21,000 is divided by total equity of $44,000 providing approximately a one to two ratio.

What ratio should a travel agency be striving for when considering the relationship of long-term debt to total equity? This depends upon what is being considered. This standard relationship is often reviewed when a travel agency attempts to get a loan from banks or other financial institutions. Usually one of the first questions asked by these institutions concerns the debt (both short-term and long-term) to equity ratio. Usually the long-term debt to equity ratio is of major concern. Simply, if the debt exceeds equity, the owners are usually getting nothing back from their investment. Of course, the agency could be paying only interest on the debt and not principal. On paper at least, the value of the stock or of ownership of the business is either zero or a negative value.

LONG-TERM DEBT TO EQUITY RATIO

$$\frac{\text{LONG-TERM DEBT}}{\text{TOTAL EQUITY}}$$

or, for example

$$\frac{\$21{,}000 = \text{Long-Term Debt}}{\$44{,}000 = \text{Total Equity}}$$

Therefore, the Long-Term Debt to Equity Ratio is Approximately One to Two Expressed as 1:2

Figure 7–8

On the other hand, if the travel agency's debt to equity ratio is as low as one to five or one to six, many financial institutions will at least consider making a loan to the business. This ratio is considered not too bad in the industry.

The one to two (approximate) ratio shown in figure 7–1 is not a ratio that most agencies would like to have. It means that 50 percent of the equity is committed—not just to the business, but to some type of financial lending institution. Most conservative travel executives try to keep the long-term debt to equity ratio very low. However, that is not always possible.

COMPARISON STUDIES

Having considered some of the more important profitability indicators, performance measures, and long-range decision ratios that are of concern to travel agency accountants, comparison data showing the importance of financial measures will now be considered. Most of the comparison data that will be reviewed comes from a study conducted by the American Society of Travel Agents. This study was completed in late 1988 or early 1989. The statistics developed from the study were produced and published by ASTA in months that range from March 1989 through late 1989 and early 1990.

What will be considered are comparative data relating to commission income, profits, and expenses. Expenses will be considered first. The first study compares booking volume (total amount of travel booked) in an annual year by travel agencies with specific expenses, figure 7–9. This will provide an indication of the differences between large, average, and small travel agencies. It has already been noted that personnel costs average approximately 50 percent of total costs for the average agency. To calculate total personnel costs other costs, in addition to salaries, must be considered. Therefore, the first two lines of this study are reviewed. It can be seen that employee salaries and other employee costs are provided. To determine the figure for total employee costs, these two figures are added. So for travel agencies with a booking volume of less than $1 million ($700,000 or less per year, in this case) employee costs ran approximately 42 percent. However, keep in mind that this is 42 percent of an average of $70,000 (working with an average 10 percent commission). This is a substantial portion of the total amount of money the agency has. This will come close to $32,000 annually and will leave a balance of only about $38,000 to pay all other expenses. This percentage for personnel costs is below the 50 percent level and would initially appear to be good. However, considering the actual amount spent out of what is coming in and the amount left to pay all the remaining costs, this a very difficult situation with which to work.

EXPENSE ALLOCATIONS PER ANNUAL RETAIL BOOKING VOLUME

Expense	Booking Volume				
	Under $700,000	$700,000 to $999,999	$1 million to $1.19 million	$1.2 million to $1.99 million	$2 million or more
Employee Salaries	34.8%	37.7%	40.7%	41.0%	42.8%
Other employee costs	5.4	6.4	7.1	7.8	7.2
Rent/Utilities	16.2	13.8	12.7	12.0	10.6
Automated reserverations	10.4	9.8	8.6	7.0	5.3
Automated accounting	1.1	1.2	1.4	1.6	1.8
Advertising/Promotion	6.1	6.3	6.1	5.2	4.9
Communications	7.6	7.2	7.0	6.5	6.4
Office supplies/Postage	4.7	5.0	4.4	4.8	5.3
Travel/Entertainment	4.3	3.9	3.7	3.8	3.6
Other expenses/Depreciation, etc.	9.2	8.6	8.2	10.3	12.1

Figure 7–9 (Courtesy of ASTA)

Next look at the travel agencies that are in the $700,000 to $1,000,000 range, figure 7–9. Here the employee salary costs constitute 37.7 percent and other employee costs constitute 6.4 percent, for a total of 34.1 percent (or slightly higher). When considering this situation, one is looking at a much greater amount of money left over to pay nonemployee expenses. There will be approximately $56,000 for these expenses. This is considerably more than was available for the smaller travel agencies. Even though the agency is spending a larger percentage for personnel, there is still much more money left over at the end to pay all remaining agency expenses. Now one starts to understand why a travel agency needs a reasonable amount of volume to be able to stay in business at all.

We now consider those travel agencies with an annual volume of $2 million or more, figure 7–9. At this level exactly 50 percent of the income is spent on personnel costs. At a 10 percent commission level the agency has $200,000 of annual income with which to pay all operating costs, profits, returns on investment, and so forth. Half of this $200,000 is used to pay personnel costs. This leaves the agency with $100,000 for all other costs, profit, and R.O.I. There is a substantial difference in what the agency can pay for personnel and what it can spend on other services. The larger agency spends three times as much on personnel than does the small agency. Almost three times as much money remains to pay for all other costs as well, compared to the travel agency doing under $700,000. Therefore, even though the percentage spent on personnel increases with the volume of business done, the dollar amount remaining to pay additional costs increases to a much greater degree with the volume of business being done. This is a far greater percentage increase than the amount of additional dollars spent on personnel. This, of course, means that if one is considering buying a travel agency, one may want to evaluate what one has if a small agency is purchased rather than a large one.

Please note that these figures do not agree with those quoted earlier in terms of an average travel agency having approximately 50 percent spent on personnel costs. The main reason is that these figures are based on the 1988 ASTA Profitability Study and these figures are skewed in two ways. First, only responding ASTA member travel agencies are reflected in these studies. Some say, probably with justification, that ASTA member agencies are better than average agencies in terms of their ability and skills in financial management. Probably a larger reason for the skew, however, is the fact that the ASTA study left out owner and agency principal remuneration from its consideration of salaries, benefits, and all other costs. When figuring in owner/principal compensation, it can be expected that the 48–50 percent average salary and benefits statistic would apply. It should be remembered that every study undertaken will probably be slightly different. Some studies will look at "other employee costs" differently. For example, some studies may not include payroll taxes in employee compensation, while others will.

Some may be surprised to see that expenses for staff in larger agencies comprise a similar percentage of total expenses as compared to smaller agencies. One may question where the *economies of scale* come in. There are two factors that account for this similar percentage of personnel costs carrying over to larger travel agencies in spite of the economies of scale that do apply. One, of course, is the generally larger amount of compensation that is paid to the employees of corporate-oriented travel agencies. Comparing the results of the Davidoff study of personnel costs with the ASTA Profitability Study of personnel costs (and with earlier studies of personnel costs), there appears to be a difference in salary levels approaching 30 percent more compensation across the board for corporate-oriented travel agency employees as compared to leisure-oriented travel agency employees. The difference actually varies from job level to job level, of course. But the comparisons suggest that the variation is rather slight and that almost without exception the compensation levels are very close to 30 percent for all comparable jobs.

Another factor that affects the total compensation level is benefits. Leisure-oriented travel agencies, on the average, offer limited benefit programs (beyond a supply of free or reduced-rate airline tickets, hotel and car rental discounts, discounts on tours, and often generous FAMiliarization trip benefits). Corporate-oriented travel agencies, however, tend to offer far wider and more expensive benefits in order to attract the best and most capable staff members. Their benefit programs often include full medical coverage (sometimes even dental), several types of paid leave (often including maternity), and company-paid or partially company-paid retirement programs.

Still another factor affecting total personnel compensation levels in business-oriented travel agencies are the additional marketing, sales, and service oriented personnel. While it is rare for a leisure-oriented travel agency to employ a marketing staff, many corporate-oriented travel agencies employ a marketing staff which may consist of a marketing manager, one or several full-time salary plus bonus compensated salespersons, and often one or more full-time telemarketers. Full-time ticket delivery personnel are also found in many corporate-oriented travel agencies. Other service personnel often found in corporate-oriented travel agencies, but rarely found in leisure-oriented travel agencies, include hotel reservation experts, international travel specialists, incentive travel specialists, ticket processing staff, car rental specialists, and full-time accounting staff members.

When one considers productivity and what a single sales person can do if everything is set up for him/her, one must recognize that in a $2 million (or greater) volume agency, except for the marketing staff, the additional staff is working to pay for service personnel. This is a primary reason why corporate travel managers usually consider working with only very large travel agencies. Simply stated, after paying reservations personnel there is more money left over to pay for services one cannot get when working with an agency that is selling only $700,000. There is no way a small agency can offer these "people" services if it has no money to pay the required salaries. In terms of rebates, override sharing, profit sharing, and other monies being paid back to the business, these funds are usually not available in a small agency either. Therefore, the corporate travel manager does not receive any such funds back to his/her company when working with small travel agencies.

Rent and Utilities

Another factor that usually is considered strongly is rent/utilities. Now one is working with very different figures. The rent/utilities for the small travel agency constitutes 16.2 percent of total costs, figure 7–9. This goes down to 10.6 percent for the very large travel agency. The reason is that a lot of additional room is not needed to book a far greater amount of travel bookings. When one looks at those agencies booking $2 million or more (some book $20 million to $50 million and more annually), the average spent is only 10.6 percent. This is a very large difference in the cost of rent/utilities.

Automated Reservations

In this category of expense there is also a much larger percentage of expenditure by smaller travel agencies as compared to the larger agencies, figure 7–9. There is a large, fairly flat fee for automated reservations equipment. This means that as a percentage of total costs, it goes down substantially as volume increases. Larger travel agencies not only get the cost breaks on computer equipment, but they are also in a position to negotiate for lower per-unit equipment costs. In some cases they receive automation equipment at a very low cost. In a very few cases equipment is provided by air carrier vendors on a totally gratis basis.

Automated Accounting

The costs, as a percentage of total costs, for automated accounting is much higher for larger travel agencies, figure 7–9. Corporate travel managers want reports. They expect reports. They want and expect all types of data categorized in a number of different ways to meet each department's, executive's, or other end-user's needs. The expectations of the clients who work with small travel agencies, however, tend to be very much less. Clients do not get even the simplest cost savings report from small travel agencies doing under $700,000 annually because these agencies cannot afford to have automated savings report software or hardware. Any automated accounting small agencies may have will just do the ARC Report or it may do an end-of-month income statement and/or balance sheet. But it will not include corporate-travel client report features.

Advertising and Promotion

The small agency has to spend more, on a percentage basis, on marketing because it has fewer clients. The larger agency is spending the smallest amount, on a percentage basis, but they spend considerably more in terms of total dollar figures. Keep in mind that this does not include personnel costs for marketing staff. That is budgeted in the personnel costs category, not in the marketing costs figures.

Communications

There is a decrease in the percentage of cost allocated to communications for larger travel agencies. Again, this is because of the savings in terms of bulk buying and negotiating ability.

Office Supplies and Postage

The cost of office supplies and postage varies, but generally it will increase with larger travel agencies—primarily because there is some bulk buying, but with most items savings on per-unit costs are minimal.

Travel and Entertainment

This figure varies as well. Smaller travel agencies will often include FAM trips in the travel and entertainment budget figure. Larger agencies generally do not.

Other Expenses

The large travel agency has much more in terms of "other expenses" than does the small travel agency. That is because this is the category in which costs are allocated for many special services rendered to the clients. The large agency must provide those services in order to retain large corporate clients.

The comparison of expenses between large and small travel agencies is important to consider relative to budgets. In projecting expenses, one can conclude that the percentage of expenses in any particular category may vary considerably between large and small agencies. Therefore, if one is preparing the budget for a small agency, one should look at comparative national figures for small agencies. Of course, the same is true for large agencies. Yet many in the industry make the mistake of using all-agency national average comparison data as base data for determining whether they are doing well or badly in comparison.

COMMUNITY SIZE COMPARISONS

In comparing community size with employee salaries and benefits, one finds that there is little difference between the salaries and benefits of travel agency employees in large communities and smaller communities, figure 7–10. The salaries will be larger in larger communities, but to some extent this is offset by other employee costs.

YEARS IN BUSINESS COMPARISON

Employee costs (salaries and benefits) are greater for those travel agencies that have been in business longer than for those that have been in business for only a short amount of time, figure 7–10. One can hypothesize that this may be due to annual cost of living increases, raises, and promotions based on longevity rather than productivity. In addition, older agencies tend to have a larger range of benefits and more expensive benefits than do newer travel agencies.

Rent/utility figures for older travel agencies are lower than for newer agencies, figure 7–10. This may be due to long-term contracts negotiated when rates were lower and an ability to negotiate better with experience.

Reservation cost figures, i.e., computers, show a similar trend, figure 7–10. There is a slightly lower cost for older travel agencies and again, one can assume that negotiating experience and earlier (lower rate) contracts account for this difference.

All other expenses are similar. There is some variation, but very little.

TYPE OF BUSINESS AND SIZE OF BUSINESS—MAJOR DIFFERING FACTORS

When one compares expenses based on any factor other than the type of business that is done, one finds that there is very little difference. There is a substantial difference, however, in two factors or areas. One is the kind of business that the travel agency is doing, figure 7–11. There is a substantial difference if it is a leisure-oriented travel agency as compared to a corporate- or business-travel oriented travel agency.

COMPARATIVE EXPENSE PATTERNS

Expense	By community size		By years in business		By consortium membership	
	Over 1 million	1 million or less	Under 4 years	4 years or more	Member	Nonmember
Employee Salaries	41.9%	40.6%	38.4%	41.5%	41.1%	41.3%
Other employee costs	6.8	7.1	6.0	7.3	7.3	6.9
Rent/Utilities	13.2	11.1	15.0	11.3	11.5	12.4
Automated reserverations	6.1	7.3	8.8	6.5	6.6	7.0
Automated accounting	1.7	1.6	1.5	1.7	1.7	1.4
Advertising/Promotion	4.6	5.8	5.3	5.3	5.4	5.1
Communications	6.6	6.8	7.2	6.6	6.7	6.6
Office supplies/Postage	4.6	5.4	4.9	5.0	5.1	4.8
Travel/Entertainment	3.5	3.8	3.1	3.9	3.8	3.5
Other expenses/Depreciation, etc.	11.1	10.6	9.9	10.9	10.6	11.1

Figure 7–10 (Courtesy of ASTA)

COMPARATIVE BUSINESS-MIX EXPENDITURES		
Expense	**Business Mix**	
	Over 70% vacation travel	**Over 50% business travel**
Employee Salaries	39.4%	43.6%
Other employee costs	6.7	7.4
Rent/Utilities	13.3	11.6
Automated reserverations	7.6	6.0
Automated accounting	1.3	1.8
Advertising/Promotion	6.1	3.7
Communications	6.8	6.3
Office supplies/Postage	4.8	5.0
Travel/Entertainment	4.0	3.7
Other expenses/Depreciation, etc.	10.0	11.0

Figure 7–11 (Courtesy of ASTA)

The other factor is the size of the sales volume of the travel agency, figure 7–9. The larger the sales volume of the travel agency, the greater the difference between a smaller agency and a larger agency.

In the Davidoff study, which was completed at about the same time as the ASTA study, a comparison was made between salaries paid to employees of predominantly leisure- or vacation-oriented travel agencies and salaries paid to employees of corporate-oriented travel agencies. The statistics coming out of that report indicated 29.7 percent greater salaries and benefits paid to those people working in corporate- or business-travel oriented travel agencies as compared to those paid to people working in leisure- or vacation-travel oriented travel agencies. Those statistics carried through all the way from entry-level personnel clear up to management. This included every salary level and every job level. This nearly 30 percent difference is substantial for employees in terms of income.

When looking at salaries and benefits in terms of percentage of total costs and expenditures, about 46 percent of total costs is spent on salaries and benefits in leisure-travel oriented travel agencies and about 51 percent of total costs is spent on salaries and benefits in business-travel oriented travel agencies. Even here there is quite a bit of difference. Keep in mind, however, that the ASTA study did not include remuneration to owners and principals. Since owners and principals of many leisure-travel oriented travel agencies work in their travel agencies and account for a large percentage of the total agency staff (especially in smaller agencies), this 46 percent figure is probably substantially skewed.

This 46 percent versus 51 percent difference does not reflect the 29 percent average salary difference. Part of the reason is that there are fewer employees earning that additional salary when one considers the business-travel oriented travel agency. That statistic is hidden in these statistics, i.e., that there are fewer people per million dollars of travel handled in larger agencies than in smaller agencies.

Corporate-travel oriented agencies spend a smaller percentage of their income on utilities than do leisure-travel oriented agencies, figure 7–11. This is because they can be located in office buildings. In many cases, they have virtually no walk-in traffic. Some of the very large travel agencies are located in areas where they get low rent and have low utility costs. They do not have expensive lighted signs. They are usually closed on the weekends and therefore do not have to leave the heat and air-conditioning on. Perhaps most important, they have fewer people employed per million dollars of travel sales and, therefore, have lower square footage on which to pay utility costs per million dollars of sales.

Corporate-travel oriented travel agencies also pay a lower percentage for automated reservation equipment and usage than do leisure-oriented travel agencies, figure 7–11. Again this is because of volume and the ability to negotiate.

When it comes to automated accounting, however, business-travel oriented agencies pay more than do leisure-travel oriented agencies, figure 7–11. That is to be expected. Corporate travel managers expect a large number of reports—mostly financial—and they get them. Leisure-oriented travel agencies have no similar financial reporting demands.

The advertising and promotion cost statistics are interesting, figure 7–11. One might expect the business-travel oriented agencies to be spending considerably more on advertising and promotion than do leisure-travel oriented agencies. However, on a percentage basis, the reverse is true. There are several reasons. Business-travel oriented agencies usually depend primarily on sales and marketing people to bring in accounts. They spend little on advertising and promotion. The leisure-oriented travel agency, on the other hand, usually has no full-time marketing or sales employees. They find that advertising and promotion activities help to make up for the marketing/sales staff shortage. They probably do not spend more money on advertising and promotion than business-travel oriented agencies do. However, because their volume of sales as a group is so much smaller, the amount they do spend on advertising and promotion constitutes a larger percentage of their total expenditures.

Communications, office supplies, and postage are line items that reflect similar percentages of costs for both leisure-travel and business-travel oriented agencies, figure 7–11. This is probably because these costs reflect few economies of scale, and in the travel industry they are fairly uniform per income incremental, i.e., per $1,000 of income.

Probably because familiarization trips are often included in the Travel and Entertainment budget line, this expense accounts for a larger percentage of costs for leisure-travel oriented agencies than for business-travel oriented agencies, figure 7–11.

The business-travel oriented agency has a larger percentage of other expenses and depreciation than does the leisure-travel oriented agency, figure 7–11. This, too, is understandable since most business-travel oriented agencies have a wide range of both sales and service programs that are funded in order to remain competitive. Also, they tend to have a lot of equipment. Because the equipment they own tends to be both more sophisticated and more expensive than that owned by leisure-travel oriented agencies, depreciation accounts for a larger expense line item.

In terms of comparisons, these statistics provide indications of the pros and cons of various forms of agency size and specialization. They also provide a starting point for determining how well or how badly an individual travel agency is faring, when comparing its previous year's financial status with the national figures for agencies of a similar size and specialization. The statistics also provide a starting point for projecting line-item budgets for future years. It can be projected that as there is more specialization in the industry, there will also be more efforts on the part of the national associations—especially ASTA—to provide nationally based statistical cost (and income) comparisons so that individual member agencies can have a foundation base against which to make comparisons.

There are two major areas of concern. One is personnel cost. The other is *commission income per square foot,* figure 7–12. This is broken down in several categories. By region there is not a lot of difference. The West has more in terms of commission income per square foot, but on average all areas of the country are close to the same.

When it comes to both size of travel agency and volume of business of the travel agency, there are some major differences in *commission income per square foot.* For travel agencies doing $700,000 or less in volume of sales the commission income is $53 per square foot. For travel agencies selling $2

COMMISSION INCOME PER SQUARE FOOT OF OFFICE SPACE

By Region	Commission
East	$114
South	$134
Central	$117
West	$141

By Size (volume)	Commission
Under $700,000	$ 53
$700,000 to $999,000	$ 79
$1 million to $1.19 million	$110
$1.2 million to 1.99 million	$124
$2 million plus	$186

By Business Mix	Commission
Over 70% vacation/personal	$105
Over 50% commercial	$159

By Locale	Commission
Office building	$ 162
Storefront	$ 118
Mall	$ 117

Figure 7–12 (Courtesy of ASTA)

million and more the commission income per square foot is almost four times larger, figure 7–12. This is a major statistical difference.

A similar dramatic statistical difference is seen when comparing the type of business a travel agency does. Vacation/leisure-oriented travel agencies show a commission income per square foot of $105. Commercial/business-oriented travel agencies, on the other hand, earn an average of $159 in commission income per square foot. This is a dramatic difference.

The commission income per square foot statistics, therefore, reinforce the same results seen earlier. The major factors change on the basis of business mix and travel sales volume. Only the location of the agency reflects any other major statistical difference and this also reflects the type of business. In other words, business-travel oriented agencies are normally located in office buildings. This location, in turn, shows a greater earning level than suburban or mall locations. But this, of course, is not so much a reflection on the business location, but rather a reflection on the type of business being done at the location.

When looking at *commission income per advertising dollar spent,* the patterns seen above are reinforced, figure 7–13. Again, by region there is very little difference. However, by size and volume the difference is substantial. Large volume travel agencies are earning $27 in commission income for every $1 spent on advertising. But smaller volume travel agencies are earning only $19 in commission income for their $1 spent on advertising. Again, the difference is almost one-third more for the large volume travel agencies. By business mix a similar major statistical difference can be seen. Again, no other factor except location reflects a statistically significant difference. Location differences are probably more a reflection of the type of business being done in the location.

The *commission income per sales employee* statistical data reinforces information considered when studying employee productivity/profitability (in earlier chapters) as well as the conclusions drawn from the statistics seen earlier in this chapter, figure 7–14. By region the commission income per sales employee is again quite similar. When looked at by volume of sales, however, the differences are again substantial. The average commission sales level per employee in large volume agencies is almost four times greater than it is in small volume agencies. The average commission sales per employee in small volume agencies is $12,561. In large volume sales agencies, however, the average commission sales per employee is $46,000. Considering the average commission of approximately ten percent, one can see that the average agent in the large volume sales travel agency sold almost one-half million dollars of travel annually (about $460,000 based on these rough statistics).

The sales per employee statistics is perhaps the most important statistic seen thus far. As noted in earlier chapters, the reasons for the almost four times difference in booking income are clear. Simply, if a travel agency has a total sales level of only $700,000 and employs just two agents at a 10 percent rough average commission earnings level, the entire agency can only bring in $70,000 in commission income. This is $35,000 per employee. Obviously, without the travel agency increasing its volume of business, there is no way

COMMISSION INCOME PER ADVERTISING DOLLAR SPENT

By Region	Income
East	$27
South	$26
Central	$19
West	$24
By Size (volume)	**Income**
Under $700,000	$19
$700,000 to $999,000	$20
$1 million to $1.19 million	$19
$1.2 million to 1.99 million	$24
$2 million plus	$27
By Business Mix	**Income**
Over 70% vacation/personal	$20
Over 50% commercial	$34
By Locale	**Income**
Office building	$29
Storefront	$22
Mall	$21

Figure 7–13 (Courtesy of ASTA)

that either agent could increase his/her individual sales level, unless one increases it at the expense of the other. This hypothetical small volume agency data is skewed, since it is rare that a small volume agency, doing less

COMMISSION INCOME PER SALES EMPLOYEE

By Region	Commission
East	$27,249
South	$33,408
Central	$28,282
West	$27,913

By Size (volume)	Commission
Under $700,000	$12,561
$700,000 to $999,000	$18,577
$1 million to $1.19 million	$21,101
$1.2 million to 1.99 million	$26,472
$2 million plus	$46,226

By Business Mix	Commission
Over 70% vacation/personal	$22,044
Over 50% commercial	$35,447

By Locale	Commission
Office building	$32,835
Storefront	$28,860
Mall	$25,916

Figure 7–14 (Courtesy of ASTA)

than $1 million in annual sales volume, could get along with only two sales agents.

Reinforcing these statistics is the statistical difference between the business orientation of travel agencies, figure 7–14. Again, the difference between commercial- or business-travel oriented travel agencies and vacation/personal- or leisure-travel oriented travel agencies is substantial. This is not quite as much of a difference as that seen when looking at the volume of business.

A continuing similar pattern is seen when looking at the statistics for locale of the travel agency, figure 7–14. As noted when reviewing earlier study results, the best figures are for those agencies located in office buildings. Again, this is probably because this is where large volume, corporate-travel oriented agencies are predominantly located.

Next consider the statistics for the *dollar of profit per square foot of office space,* figure 7–15. Earlier the statistics for the cost per square foot of office space were considered. Here the profit per square foot is considered. As with cost, the differences are significant. In looking at the size and volume, the $700,000 volume of sales travel agencies show a dollar of profit per square foot of only $8. This compares with the $44 profit per square foot for the travel agency that is selling a volume of business of $2 million plus annually. The one-third difference statistic comes back when looking at the difference in profit per square foot based on the differences in business mix. The leisure-travel oriented agency average profit per square foot is $20, while the business-travel oriented agency average profit per square foot is $34.00. In terms of locale, there is not a lot of difference, but as usual, office building is leading.

Total profit is the most important factor for those concerned with the accounting and financial management of travel agencies. Owners and investors can be expected to be more concerned with the level of profits than with any other statistical factors. Therefore, when considering travel agency national statistics relating to costs, income, and sales, those statistics dealing with profits deserve heightened attention.

The first profit statistic considered will be the *dollars of profit per sales employee,* figure 7–16. By region there is little difference, although the South has the highest figure. By size of business, however, (as usual) the difference is considerable. The amount of profit earned per employee in the larger business is over five times that earned per employee in the smaller travel agency. Not quite, but almost twice the profit per employee is found in the commercial/business-travel oriented agency as compared to the vacation/personal- or leisure-travel oriented agency. Leading in terms of locale is office building, again reflecting the fact that this is where commercial- or business-travel oriented agencies are found.

DOLLAR PROFIT PER SQUARE FOOT OF OFFICE SPACE

By Region	Profit
East	$25
South	$35
Central	$20
West	$27

By Size (volume)	Profit
Under $700,000	$ 8
$700,000 to $999,000	$16
$1 million to $1.19 million	$16
$1.2 million to 1.99 million	$26
$2 million plus	$44

By Business Mix	Profit
Over 70% vacation/personal	$20
Over 50% commercial	$34

By Locale	Profit
Office building	$38
Storefront	$24
Mall	$24

Figure 7–15 (Courtesy of ASTA)

DOLLAR PROFIT PER SALES EMPLOYEE

By Region	Profit
East	$ 5,844
South	$ 8,424
Central	$ 4,907
West	$ 5,376

By Size (volume)	Profit
Under $700,000	$ 1,860
$700,000 to $999,000	$ 3,543
$1 million to $1.19 million	$ 3,176
$1.2 million to 1.99 million	$ 5,537
$2 million plus	$10,872

By Business Mix	Profit
Over 70% vacation/personal	$ 4,435
Over 50% commercial	$ 7,429

By Locale	Profit
Office building	$ 7,140
Storefront	$ 5,967
Mall	$ 5,475

Figure 7–16 (Courtesy of ASTA)

COMPARATIVE PROFIT FIGURES

The comparative profit picture chart, figure 7–17 needs to be explained in terms of how it will be analyzed. The chart shows a series of expenses coming down the left column. The analysis will consider what those expenses are for very profitable travel agencies (30 percent or more), high profit agencies, moderate profit agencies, and low profit agencies.

Starting with total personnel costs, one can see that they are right at 50 percent for very profitable travel agencies. For low profit agencies, the same costs are between 48 and 49 percent. There is not a lot of difference. This reinforces the concept of trying to keep personnel costs in the 50 percent (of total costs) range. For utilities, however, there is considerable difference. There is a slight difference between the most profitable and the least profitable travel agencies when it comes to automated reservation costs. In the accounting cost area, again there is very little difference in costs. In advertising and promotion, there is some, but no substantial difference in costs. The same applies to communications, office supplies and postage, and travel and entertainment.

What is seen, therefore, is that the cost figures as a percentage of costs for the most profitable travel agencies are almost identical to the percentage of cost figures for the least profitable agencies. One conclusion is that profitable travel agencies, no matter what their degree of profitability, tend to have similar percentages of costs. This suggests that if unprofitable agencies wish to attain profitability, they should seriously consider the percentages of costs of the profitable travel agencies. This is not to suggest, however, that just because an agency may be able to duplicate the spending patterns of profitable agencies it will become equally profitable or able to move from unprofitability to profitability. It is unlikely that this alone will be enough. However, in most cases, it would probably be a move in the right direction. By having these guidelines, agency management and their accountants have some targets to work toward. For many agencies they will no doubt be realistic targets, but for some they may be unrealistic in the short run. This is helpful. Until recently, the industry lacked valid national statistics on which to base such targets.

IMPORTANCE TO CUSTOMERS

The profitability status of a travel agency can readily be seen as important to agency management, but it is also important to travel agency clients—especially corporate clients. Therefore, the financial status—especially the profitability status—needs to be documented by accounting and financial management executives for corporate accounts. Almost all corporate account R.F.P.s

COMPARATIVE PROFIT PICTURE

Expense	Profit*			
	Very High (30% or more)	High (20 to 29%)	Moderate (9 to 19%)	Low (0 to 8%)
Employee Salaries	42.1%	39.6%	39.3%	42.6%
Other employee costs	6.9	7.7	7.5	6.4
Rent/Utilities	11.6	10.6	12.6	11.5
Automated reserverations	6.6	6.4	7.3	6.3
Automated accounting	1.7	1.7	1.7	1.5
Advertising/Promotion	4.9	5.4	5.6	4.9
Communications	6.7	7.0	6.7	6.4
Office supplies/Postage	4.8	5.4	5.4	4.8
Travel/Entertainment	3.8	4.3	3.8	3.9
Other expenses/Depreciation, etc.	11.1	12.0	9.9	11.7

*Profit includes remuneration to principals and owners.

Figure 7–17 (Courtesy of ASTA)

(Requests for Proposal) require this type of documentation. But it should be kept in mind that the documentation required normally only relates to meeting the minimal needs of the client company. Usually they will only ask for documents verifying the financial stability of the travel agency. These are profit and loss statements, balance sheets, and other end-of-year financial data. Almost all businesses, however, look with considerable favor on supplying more than minimal documentation. Those travel agencies which can document that they not only have a history of profitability and stability, but that their cost figures are at least as good as, if not better than the national figures often have an edge over other agencies when it comes to the review of their proposals by current and potential corporate accounts. Therefore, it would appear that profitability may beget profitability. It certainly helps to earn additional business.

IMPORTANCE TO EMPLOYEES

Few in the travel industry stop to consider how accounting and financial management positively impact agency employees and the ability to recruit top quality employees. Maslow's *Hierarchy of Needs* highlights how important security is to people as a whole. Travel agency employees and potential employees are no exception. Many travel agencies promise employees and potential employees far more than they can deliver and agencies that are in business for some time establish reputations. A travel agency must manage its resources in such a way that it attains profitability, hopefully doing better than the national averages. When it is doing better than most agencies and is in the high profitability range, and when that success is communicated to employees and potential employees by publicizing selected accounting and financial data, employees and potential employees can be comfortable with the security of knowing that the business will still be there in the future and that they have a steady job. They know that the business has the money to pay a competitive salary and to provide periodic increases when earned. This too becomes a reason to understand the national comparative statistics and to use them as a goal.

BUDGETING COMPARATIVE DATA

The comparative data statistics seen in this chapter are of importance to agency management, agency clients, and agency staff members (employees). But one aspect of comparative data that is of special and unique value to travel agency accountants and financial executives is the ability to have goals to work toward and/or exceed when preparing budgets for the travel agency. When considering any and all budget figures, agency accountants want and need to have a standard against which to measure. They need more than just how the agency did in this category of expenditure last year. Last year's figure is a good starting point. But if last year's figure and the national figure can be compared, the travel agency accountant has much more to work with in identifying realistic, yet challenging budgeting goals.

SUMMARY

Several profitability indicators have been discussed. The chapter started with a review of return on equity and it pointed out both the short-term and the long-term importance of equity return to investors. It also noted the frequent difficulty of getting money out of travel agencies when the return on equity is not as high as investors would like it to be.

The return on assets was also discussed. This is one of the better measures of managerial performance.

The performance measures reviewed started with the single most important performance measure, i.e., the ratio of personnel costs to total costs. It was noted that a 50 percent of total costs ratio is a general average within the retail travel industry, but that agencies expecting profitability will often strive for a ratio of 45 percent or even lower. However, as personnel costs are lowered, the ability to provide customer service also tends to lessen. Therefore, agency management must attempt to maintain a low employee cost as a percentage of total costs while at the same time providing excellent service—a challenge for anyone.

Long-range decision ratios started with a recognition of the difficulty of obtaining too much business from one single account. Generally in the industry, if 60 percent or more of a travel agency's business comes from a single account, most executives feel that there is considerable potential for danger. Some are concerned when a single account constitutes 50 percent, 40 percent, 30 percent, or even as low as 10 percent of an agency's business.

Long-term debt to total equity ratios are also important. An example of an approximately one to two ratio was provided and it was pointed out that generally agencies would prefer to have a better ratio than one that is this bad.

Comparative studies provide the opportunity to establish and determine additional ratios. The comparative studies presented are based on both the ASTA 1988 study and the Davidoff 1988 study. They start with an analysis of employee costs, but also review all other major costs, commission income relationships, profit ratios, and comparative profits. Several conclusions are suggested from these analyses, but one of the major factors pointed out is the conclusion that large travel agencies and corporate-travel oriented agencies tend to be more profitable than smaller travel agencies and those specializing in leisure travel.

❑ DISCUSSION QUESTIONS

1. Why are most businesses in business? Explain how this relates to profitability/performance measures in the retail travel industry.
2. What is equity and how is return on equity calculated?
3. What are assets and how is return on assets calculated?
4. What is the single most important performance measure and why?
5. How is the long-term debt to total equity ratio calculated?
6. When preparing a budget for a large travel agency, why should one not utilize comparative national figures for percentage of cost baseline comparisons?
7. What type and size of business constitutes the most profitable group of travel agencies?
8. Is the commission income per square foot of office space greater for travel agencies with under $700,000 of sales or for travel agencies with annual sales of $2 million and over? What are some potential reasons for this?
9. What are some reasons for the almost four times difference in booking income between the booking level of an average agent in a small volume sales travel agency and that of an average agent in a large volume sales travel agency?
10. Why is it that owners and investors can be expected to be more concerned with the level of profits than with any other statistical factors?

❑ ROLE-PLAYING EXERCISE

Two students may participate in this role-playing exercise either as an out-of-class, or an in-class, fun way to review the importance of national statistics as a foundation base against which to compare individual agency financial achievements and against which to set financial goals. One student plays a new travel agency bookkeeper working in a large corporate-travel oriented travel agency. The other plays an experienced travel agency bookkeeper working for the same large travel agency. Please read the script and then pick up the conversation in your own words.

New Travel Agency Bookkeeper: I appreciate your sharing all the data with me indicating the national statistics regarding expenditures and profits. It was interesting seeing how our travel agency compares with the national statistics. However, I really don't understand the practical value of this information. What good will it do us?

Experienced Travel Agency Bookkeeper: This gives our travel agency a point of reference in making comparisons and in setting financial goals. Last year we made a profit, but it was only a small profit. As you know, last year we paid out 50 percent of our operating income (net revenues) for salaries and benefits, 14 percent in rent and utilities, 9 percent in automated reservations payments, and 11 percent for communications. All of these figures were higher than they should be compared to national statistics for urban travel agencies with a $4 million annual gross sales level. Now let me explain what kind of figures we should strive for in each of these areas and what we, as the agency's financial staff, can do to help management achieve greater profitability. Let's start with personnel costs. For our size of agency we should be paying no more than. . .

CONTINUE ON YOUR OWN

❑ *CHAPTER SEVEN EXERCISE*

INSTRUCTIONS: Determine the equity position for Nina Bleedso twelve and a half months after she purchased AAAdventure Travel from Jane Harbison. Utilize the information provided below to determine the amount of equity she will have.

FACTS TO CONSIDER

1. AAAdventure Travel had a gross sales level of $3,600,000 in the year immediately before its sale.
2. AAAdventure Travel sold for 6.7 percent of its average gross sales for its previous year of business.
3. Nina paid 26 percent of the total purchase price as her down payment for the travel agency.
4. Nina made interest payments in the first year of owning the travel agency. These payments amounted to 12 percent on the balance due for the agency. This is simple interest, not compound interest.

5. On the first year anniversary of ownership of AAAdventure Travel, Nina paid 1/20th of the balance of the principal due for the purchase of the travel agency.
6. During the first year that Nina owned AAAdventure Travel, gross sales were increased to $3,850,000.
7. The profit earned by AAAdventure Travel on the $3,850,000 gross sales during Nina's first year of ownership was 2.5 percent after paying taxes on the profits.
8. The principal payment made at the end of Nina's first twelve months of owning AAAdventure Travel was paid from profits earned after corporate taxes were paid.

NOTE: Calculate your answer and show how you reached the equity figure you calculated.

THE ARC REPORT

OBJECTIVES

Upon completion of this chapter, the student will be able to:

- ❑ Explain the procedures for preparing the weekly ARC Report
- ❑ Complete a simple Sales Report Settlement Authorization Form
- ❑ Prepare the required adding machine tapes that accompany a simple Sales Report Settlement Authorization form
- ❑ Identify all key calendar dates inherent in the completion and processing of an ARC Report

INTRODUCTION

The report that is referred to most often in the travel agency industry is called the ARC (Airline Reporting Corporation) Report. Though commonly referred to as the ARC Report throughout the industry, that is not the technical name. The correct name is the *Sales Report Settlement.* The *Sales Report Settlement Authorization Form* is the basic document constituting the ARC Report.

BACKGROUND

Before considering the Sales Report Settlement and the Sales Report Settlement Authorization Form, background on the ARC Report will be beneficial. The ARC Report is a form that is utilized to report all sales of airline tickets and anything else that goes through the standard airline reporting system. Most of that is airline tickets. Historically, it was only airline tickets.

The airlines first joined together shortly after World War II and formed the Air Traffic Conference. One of their goals was to eliminate the need for every travel agency to reach some type of accounting settlement with every airline on every ticket sold on a regular basis. This was the industry norm prior to World War II and when there were steamship agencies selling tickets. But that system had created a great many problems, duplicating efforts that could be handled by a single organization.

Therefore, when a waiver of the antitrust laws was extended by the United States government (through the Air Traffic Conference) to air carriers and to a limited extent to travel agencies, one of the systems established was a system whereby the Air Traffic Conference-appointed travel agencies would make weekly reports to several central banks throughout the United States. Agencies sent in reports of all sales made throughout the week for all member airlines of the Air Traffic Conference. Originally, it was limited to only member airlines. Although this included most domestic air carriers, it did not include them all.

The service that was rendered was a benefit both to travel agencies and to the air carriers. It meant that the airlines were able to farm out a tremendous amount of their accounting processing work to the central banks. For the travel agent, it meant that instead of sending in a separate report and money to thirty, forty, or fifty airlines on a weekly basis, they could send in one report on all airline sales and simplify the process.

The system works quite well. But keep in mind that the system hindered competition to some extent and it was allowed only because of the waiver of antitrust regulations. When the antitrust waiver was taken away through the deregulation act, there was some discussion that the air carriers would no longer be able to continue having a centralized reporting system. However, the airlines agreed to continue with the system under ARC pending a potential court ruling that the area settlement plan (utilization by air carriers of the central bank clearance system) would be a violation of antitrust law. That has not been firmly established yet. The trade press has carried articles reflecting both pro and con positions. However, until a court case establishes precedent, there is no certainty that the area settlement program will be found to be a violation of antitrust law. Thus far the major actions have resulted in out-of-court settlements. There are still those in the industry who have taken the position that the central processing system utilized through area banks is a violation of antitrust laws. However, the air carriers and the travel agencies continue to utilize the system until such time as it is found to be a violation. If that occurs, then the system can be expected to change.

HOW THE SYSTEM WORKS

Therefore, it is important to understand the system as it works today. As airlines have expanded their activity and especially as air carriers sponsoring the computer reservation systems have expanded on-line capabilities (e.g., making reservations for non-air vendors; issuing tickets or vouchers for those non-air vendors on airline ticket stock run through the computer systems), other vendors (non-air) have become participants in the weekly ARC settlement program. For example, when travel agents sell cruises through the computer reservation system and issue a ticket that looks like an airline ticket but recognizes a transportation purchase for a cruise or the sale of a cruise, that product goes through the central bank system as well. The same thing is true with tours, and that is a little bit easier to understand since tour orders are utilized. Although in most cases these are handwritten, they still are processed through the weekly ARC Report. The same applies to some hotel packages. In other words, we now have many non-air vendors participating in what was originally an airline-sponsored and an airline-only accounting system.

The way this system works is that one starts with a report that is due every seven days. It is due at or before midnight of Tuesday every week, unless there is a Monday holiday which is listed in the ARC Handbook. The due date is then moved to Wednesday midnight.

ARC does make some exceptions to the once-a-week Tuesday reporting rule, but the exceptions tend to be more difficult to meet than the standard rule. For example, ARC has allowed some very large travel agencies and travel agency chains to submit an ARC Report on a daily basis, if they so desire. They have to seek permission to do so. There are a few travel agencies that have done so and now submit a daily rather than weekly ARC Report. But by far, the majority (well in excess of 99 percent) stick with the standard regulations and do not ask for a waiver.

THE TWO ARC REPORTS

The ARC Report is really two reports. One is prepared each week by Tuesday midnight reporting all sales of airline tickets and other related products. The other is a report that is received back into the travel agency several weeks later. It is issued by the Airline Reporting Corporation. Basically it is a computer generated report that identifies the tickets processed by ARC and provides a verification of what ARC has done with the travel agency's money and the agency's payment for tickets that were issued. However, when industry executives talk about the ARC Report, they are normally referring to the one that is prepared on Tuesday and sent to ARC by Tuesday midnight. That one is the focus of this chapter.

ARC REPORT OUTCOMES

The ARC Report has several outcomes. One is the division of sales into categories. The travel agency must not only report all sales, but it also must report how much was paid for by credit card and how much was paid for by what the airlines refer to as "cash." In this case, it is more than just cash (paper money and coins). It is cash, checks, travelers checks, and any tickets that are considered accounts receivables by the travel agency. This latter category needs further explanation. Sometimes the travel agency will issue airline tickets and bill the client, usually business clients, with payment expected later (usually within fifteen or thirty days). The airline treats monies due to the travel agency for the sale of tickets as actual cash in hand. They require the travel agency to report such transactions as cash sales, because from the airline point of view, the airline will receive its money from the travel agency. They are not concerned with whether the travel agency has received payment or not, since this is a matter between the travel agency and the agency's corporate client. The airline will receive its payment through an authorized cash withdrawal from the travel agency's bank account.

CASH VS. CREDIT SALES

All non-credit card forms of payment are grouped into the one category of "cash" for the purposes of the ARC Report. Therefore, the two major things that must be reported are the amount of credit card sales and the amount of cash sales.

ARC HANDBOOK GUIDELINES

The guidelines for preparing the ARC Report appear in each issue of the *ARC Handbook.* The *ARC Handbook* is sent to all participating member travel agencies on a quarterly basis. If the agency is an appointed travel agency (authorized by the Airline Reporting Corporation to sell airline tickets on behalf of ARC member air carriers), a handbook subscription is included in the annual membership fee paid to the Airline Reporting Corporation. One copy is sent to each appointed agency. There is an entire section on how to prepare the ARC Report and the processes that are involved. It is fairly clear. The accountant, or other agency employee responsible for preparing the weekly ARC Report, should go back to the ARC Report chapter in the handbook and review those pages prior to preparing the report for the first time. A glance at the ARC Report chapter in each new issue of the handbook is wise, since occasionally, but rarely, some aspect of the report or the report preparation process changes and when it does, the change is discussed in detail in the next new issue.

THE ARC REPORT PROCESSING SCHEDULE

The ARC Report processing schedule is very specific regarding when each aspect of the report is due and regarding the time windows covered by the report. The report week starts at 12:01 Monday morning and concludes the following Sunday at midnight. Looking at a calendar for the month of July and part of August, figure 8–1, the first full week in July is the week of 2 July through 8 July. Therefore, if the agency is reporting the whole first week of July, it reports all sales from Monday the second (starting at 12:01A.M.), through Sunday the eighth (ending at midnight). This report of all sales made during the first full week of July is due to be mailed to the Airline Reporting Corporation's designated area bank by midnight on Tuesday the tenth. In other words, the accountant or other finance executive of the travel agency has all day Monday and all day Tuesday to prepare the report. If the travel agency is like most travel agencies, it will be closed on Sunday and there will be no activity that day. Therefore, the ARC Report could theoretically be prepared on Sunday, as well. A number of travel agency accountants, especially those who contract their services to several agencies, arrange to go in on Sundays to prepare the weekly ARC Report. Since no other staff

JULY

SUN	MON	TUE	WED	THU	FRI	SAT
1	2	3	4	5	6	7
8	9	10	11	12	13	14
15	16	17	18	19	20	21
22	23	24	25	26	27	28
29	30	31				

AUGUST

SUN	MON	TUE	WED	THU	FRI	SAT
			1	2	3	4

Figure 8–1

members are in the agency, there are no interruptions or other disturbing activities. There are many agency executives, however, who feel that there could be substantial benefits to the agency and its clients by waiting until the last minute to process the report. They, therefore, do not allow it to be completed until the last minute on Tuesdays.

After the central bank receives the ARC Report from the travel agency (and ARC Reports from all other travel agencies in its designated region), the central bank undertakes the initial processing of the report. On Wednesday the eleventh and Thursday the twelfth the central bank will review all ARC Reports to make certain that they have received one from each agency. If a report is missing, the bank will notify the Airline Reporting Corporation, which in turn contacts the travel agency by phone. If necessary, an inspector will be sent to the agency office, normally either the same day or the next day, to find out what the problem is. ARC is very concerned about the timeliness of reporting and watches it carefully.

The travel agency will have its account automatically debited (the signature on the ARC Report form authorizes this withdrawal) for no more than the amount authorized by the travel agency on the ARC Report form. This will take place approximately nine to ten days after the report completion date. For the first week of July report, which is sent in on the tenth, the authorized amount of money would be deducted from the travel agency's account normally on the second Thursday following the Tuesday that it is sent in. For the first week of July report, which is sent in on 10 July, therefore, the authorized amount would be deducted from the travel agency's account on Thursday the nineteenth. Occasionally, the actual deduction will not occur until Friday, rather than Thursday. Much depends upon the time the electronic transfer takes place on Thursday. Since most banks process deposits and withdrawals the next day if they come after 3:00P.M., any transfer request coming in from the central bank after 3:00P.M. Thursday will not normally show up in the travel agency's account until the next day, Friday.

Keep in mind that the travel agency basically deducts its (average) 10 percent commission. But all the rest of the money from the sale of the airline tickets and other vendor products that are sold and reflected on the ARC Report belongs to the airlines or the vendor involved. That money (approximately 90 percent) will be deducted by the Airline Reporting Corporation from the travel agency's account.

This is why the Airline Reporting Corporation requires a travel agency to set up two separate accounts at the time the agency first receives its airline appointments. One account is for depositing all money received from clients in payment for airline tickets and other travel purchases that go through the central bank clearance system. It is from this account that ARC Report money is drawn. The other account is an operating account to which the 10 percent commission is to be transferred after the authorized deduction has been completed.

If the travel agency operates by having only one account and all money is put into it and all expenses are drawn from it, problems could arise. If this single account is used to pay ARC and to pay for current operating expenses, the travel agency might very well find itself using ARC's money to pay for operating expenses. This has happened many times in the industry.

What it means, for example, is that when ARC comes to the travel agency's bank on 19 July to withdraw the money due for sales of the second through the eighth, the money will not be there and the bank will refuse payment. Consequently there will either be a fine, or the travel agency will be penalized through a system of applying fine "points" that may result in the loss of its ticket stock. The agency could well have a problem with ARC, possibly lose its airline appointments, and possibly be put into a position of not being able to stock, sell, or process airline tickets. That is one of the problems of trying to operate out of a single account.

A second problem of working from a single account is that occasionally the central bank makes mistakes. They have, from time to time, put through a draw for considerably more money than the amount that was authorized. Since the travel agency's bank does not have a copy of the ARC Report, the bank does not know how much the travel agency authorized for withdrawal by the central bank. The travel agency's bank can only process the request it has received from the central bank. Since the travel agency authorized the agency's bank to honor all draws from the central bank, the agency's bank transfers the amount detailed on the electronic transfer it receives from the central bank. If the travel agency is operating with only one account and is using that account to pay both ARC and its own operating expenses, when a mistake is made by the central bank, the agency may very well find its account drawn down so low that it may suddenly be in a position of having insufficient funds to pay operating expenses. In essence, all of its money went to ARC because of a central bank error.

Therefore, the obvious recommendation is to have two accounts. After 19 July, when the money is deducted from the travel agency's account to pay for tickets issued between the second and the eighth, the travel agency can transfer its approximately 10 percent commission (the balance in its ARC account from those sales) to its operating account. This could be done on Friday the twentieth, after the ARC Report draw has been completed. In fact, since ARC makes an authorized withdrawal each Thursday, many travel agencies make it a habit to transfer the balance in the weekly sales income from the week of the authorized withdrawal each Friday. If the calculations are correct, there will always be enough money in the ARC account to pay ARC, yet there will not be considerable additional funds that could possibly disappear because of a central bank processing error.

It was noted earlier that there is another report—the computer report that the travel agency gets back explaining what ARC did with the money for the tickets. It is run on a ticket numerical-sequence basis. That report normally takes another week to prepare and will generally come back to the travel agency one week from the following Monday or Tuesday after the money was withdrawn from the agency's bank account. In the case of our travel agency generated ARC Report for the first week of July, the report back from ARC should arrive in the travel agency on either Monday, 30 July or Tuesday, 31 July.

Therefore, the entire process takes approximately one month and during that month there are several key dates to be aware of. To review: the report itself covers one full week of sales. In this case, it is from 12:01A.M., Monday, 2 July through midnight, Sunday, 8 July.. All sales made during that period of time are reported by midnight the following Tuesday (the tenth) on the travel agency prepared ARC Report. On the report there is an authorized amount that the central bank may withdraw from the travel agency's account. That amount is normally withdrawn a week from the following Thursday (approximately nine days from when the report was submitted), in this case, on the nineteenth. Then ARC prepares a report indicating what they did and the processing they utilized. That report is received back into the travel agency normally a week from the following Monday or Tuesday, in this case on Monday, 30 July or Tuesday, 31 July. Therefore, as one can see, for tickets sold during the first week of July, in relationship to ARC handling, one goes back and forth between the agency, the agency's bank, and ARC throughout the month of July.

ARC REPORT FLOAT

This ARC Report processing time means that the travel agency can take advantage of the financial *float* involved. The concept of float has not been addressed yet, but it will be reviewed in detail in a later chapter. Float is a term that is utilized to mean the use of money that belongs to someone else while it is in your possession. Working with the July calendar and the processing dates just reviewed, one starts by tracing where the money is throughout the ARC Report processing time.

In this fictitious example, a client comes into the travel agency and buys an airline ticket that costs $100, paying for it in cash. After deducting the 10 percent domestic tax of $10.00, the balance left for payment to the air carrier and the agency's commission is $90.00. If the agency commission is 10 percent ($9.00), the balance due to the air carrier is $81.00. However, the travel agency is not expected to give the $81.00 to the air carrier for quite some time. That sum came into the travel agency on 2 July. However, it will not be withdrawn from the travel agency's account by the air carrier until the nineteenth. Therefore, the travel agency has seventeen days to use this $81.00 that belongs to the air carrier; and the airlines allow that. There is nothing illegal about it. Many travel agencies will put all such monies into an interest-earning account. In fact, the American Society of Travel Agents has established a money market fund that pays interest on a daily basis. By putting the money owed to air carriers into that fund or a similar investment prior to the time the withdrawal is made by the air carriers, the travel agency earns interest on the $81.00 (and all other similar monies the travel agency has put into the fund) for that period of seventeen days. (The amount of time varies, of course, depending upon when and how the ticket was actually paid for.) The agency can accrue a substantial amount of income earned from interest over a period of time, especially when the interest rates are high. Yet a large number of travel agencies have not utilized this source of income. So float earning potential is one of the beneficial ramifications of the Area Settlement Plan process which has been initiated by the ARC Report.

Another very important ramification, alluded to before, is the fact that all of the money is sitting in an account held by the travel agency during this period of time (between the collection of the money from the client and the withdrawal of funds from the account by the central bank for ARC). It is very easy for a travel agency that is losing money to be tempted to pay operating costs from it. Many travel agencies over a period of time have done that. But sooner or later the money is requested through a withdrawal by the central bank for ARC and its air carrier members. Then a problem is created because the money is not there.

PROCESSING OF THE ARC REPORT

Now that there is an understanding of the time/date calendar for the ARC Report, the processing of the ARC Report should be considered. There are several steps involved. The first is that in most travel agencies all tickets and all invoice/receipts (or similar documents) will be gathered together by the agency accountant, financial executive, or other person responsible for preparing the report (referred to as the agency accountant, from here on). These documents then need to be numerically stacked. The first determination that needs to be made is whether or not all airline tickets and other accountable documents are on hand, i.e., in the stack to be processed. For each numerical series of tickets or other accountable documents, it is necessary to make and keep available a note of the number of the last such ticket or other accountable document that was issued and reported. Whether the last transaction involving a particular series took place a week ago or a month ago, it is important to keep a record of the number of the last ticket or accountable document issued and reported. The central bank does keep that record and does check to make certain that all reports pick up each series of tickets and documents numerically sequential to the last previous ticket or document reported to the bank. If someone wants to steal a ticket and is knowledgeable about travel agency procedures and accounting, he/she will often steal the first ticket issued after the close of the last ARC Report. This is because of two things. First, this theft may not be noticed, perhaps, until the next ARC Report is done. Therefore, the thief has the maximum amount of time to get away. Second, in some travel agencies, the person preparing the ARC Report neither keeps records of nor refers to the last report for the last number in each series reported. The report preparer simply starts with the first ticket or document in the stack collected for the week for which the report is being prepared. If there is no problem preparing the report starting with the first ticket in the stack, the preparer feels that there is no problem. So if the ticket numbered after the last ticket accounted for on the last report is stolen, the agency accountant never knows it until a debit notice is received approximately twelve to eighteen months later. There are some additional ways of checking built into the system, but if the agency report preparer is skipping the last-report/last-number check, the person is probably skipping the work involved in conducting any other optional but time-consuming system checks available to agency accountants. Again, therefore, the best place to start is to keep a record of last week's last ticket numbers in each series.

There may be several ticket and other document series. One series will be the computer-generated tickets. This is the source of a majority of the tickets generated in most travel agencies. However, there will be other ticket stock series as well which will be reported for most travel agencies. For example, MCOs (Miscellaneous Charge Orders) cannot be issued by the computer. They must be handwritten. They have their own numerical series. Tour orders are the same way: they cannot be issued by the computer, they have to be handwritten, and they have their own series numbers. The agency may also have handwritten normal airline ticket stock. These used to come in a different series of ticket numbers for one-coupon, two-coupon, three-coupon, and four-coupon handwritten ticket stock. Today, they are only being issued in four-coupon ticket booklets. Some travel agencies still have a supply of other coupon numbered stock and generally the air carriers allow their use until the stock is used up. Most travel agencies avoid using handwritten ticket stock, unless they have to. When the computers go down, or for some other reason, handwritten stock is occasionally used. Therefore the travel agency will usually have several ticket series to work with when preparing the ARC Report. The agency accountant starts by numerically stacking each series, looking at the last number from last week (or the last week in which there was a last number for each series), and identifying whether or not there is a ticket missing.

It is very important that missing tickets be identified and hopefully located, whether they be the first tickets that should have been issued for the current week's report or if they are missing from anywhere else in the series. The fine for lost and unreported tickets is quite substantial. The fine for lost tickets which are reported is also quite high. Prior to deregulation, if a travel agency had a lost ticket, the repercussions were even more substantial. In many cases, an ATC (the predecessor to ARC) inspector would visit the travel agency; and in a few cases, when this happened several times within a year, the travel agency could have its entire ticket stock lifted (taken away), either for a short time or permanently, and no longer be able to issue airline tickets. In other words, the air carriers consider ticket stock loss to be a serious problem.

In addition to having a violation of an ARC regulation, there is always the possibility that the lost ticket is actually a stolen ticket. If it is stolen, the regulations to protect a travel agency require that the missing ticket be reported to ARC as a stolen ticket (not a lost ticket) immediately. Therefore, most well-run travel agencies will make a daily check of all tickets issued to make sure that somebody in the agency (usually the agency accountant, the owner, or the manager) knows the status of every ticket on a daily basis. A daily ticket report is prepared. Even if that is not done, it certainly becomes part of the ARC Report, because one must show a numerical sequencing of the tickets with all tickets accounted for at the time the ARC Report is completed.

VOID TICKETS

Void tickets should also be included in the numerical sequencing. Prior to deregulation, the loss or the nonaccountability of a void ticket was much more severe than it is now. At that time, all voided tickets had to be included in the ticket batch that was sent to the central bank (this process is discussed later in the chapter). Under current rules, voided tickets no longer have to be sent to the central bank, but they still need to be accounted for. The incident of a new employee throwing away a ticket on which a mistake was made and then having to search the trash for the thrown-away ticket is an experience many an agency has had to go through at least once in its history.

INVOICE/RECEIPT ACCOUNTING

After making certain that all tickets are accounted for, most travel agencies will also require that the agency accountant prepare a numerical series of invoice/receipts (or similar billing documents). The invoice-receipt (I/R) total should balance with the ticket total. In other words, there should be an invoice for every ticket issued and there should be a ticket or some other document for every invoice issued. The dollar amount of tickets issued should also be the same as the dollar amount of the invoice/receipts for those tickets. There will, of course, be invoice/receipts for services or charges not relating to tickets. These should be excluded from consideration when balancing the total dollar amount of the ticket invoice/receipts with the total dollar value of the tickets issued during the week.

TICKET TYPE BREAKOUT

The next step is to break tickets out according to type of ticket. After clients get their tickets, there are two types of coupons that stay with the travel agency for every ticket and for most accountable documents. The traveler has the ticket with all the flight coupons and the passenger receipt. The travel agency has the auditor's coupon and the agent's coupon. These are located at the very top of the ticket booklet and are usually never seen by the customer/traveler. The first coupon in the ticket booklet is the auditor's coupon and the next one sequentially is the agent's coupon. Since the computer prints directly on the auditor's coupon (or for handwritten stock, the agent prints directly on the auditor's coupon), this coupon is the original and is normally the most easily read of all the ticket book coupons.

There are two exceptions to the auditor coupon being the top (original) coupon. One is when an optional form of computer-generated ticket stock is used. This optional ticket stock has a credit card charge form on top. This optional stock is used by many agencies to avoid handwriting credit card charge forms. The other is the ticket exchange form. The coupon arrangement on these forms is slightly different because of the nature of exchanges.

The next step in the process is to divide all tickets into agent coupons and auditor coupons. The agent coupons must be kept in the travel agency in a numerical series for at least five years. Most travel agencies do this each week by binding that week's series of agent coupons and a copy of the corresponding ARC Report with a rubber band. They store them sequentially by week in a box appropriately marked. On the outside of the storage box the number series of the enclosed tickets is listed together with the starting date and the ending date of the machine-issued ticket stock coupons kept in the box.

After determining that there is an agent coupon for every ticket issued and that the coupons are in numerical order, and after taking an adding machine tape total of the value of the agency coupons, one can simply rubber band that stack of ticket coupons and put it aside for awhile. There is nothing more that needs to be done with that stack until the ARC Report is completed and a copy of the report is wrapped around the agent coupons prior to their being filed.

The working stack, used by the travel agency accountant to prepare the ARC Report, is the auditor coupons. Therefore, the next step is to go through all of the auditor coupons making certain that they are in numerical order and that the agency has an auditor coupon for every ticket issued.

The auditor coupons are divided according to tickets that were paid for by credit card and those that were paid for in any other way (labeled cash). There are several factors relating to the cash tickets that one should consider. The cash amount will include all tickets paid for by cash, all tickets paid for by check, and all tickets not paid for at all. (Normally one will write 'agent check' in the "Form of Payment" block for unpaid tickets, because it means that the travel agency is owed the money by a client—usually a corporate client.) Keep in mind the meaning of the term "cash." For example, travelers checks or other tickets that are used in exchange for the ticket being issued—any of these other forms of payment (except credit card) are lumped together and called "cash" on the ARC Report. Therefore, all of the auditor coupons for tickets issued with these forms of payment will be stacked in one stack.

All of the auditor coupons from tickets paid for by credit card will be in the other stack. The reason for this is that the airline ultimately receives 100 percent of the monies when issued tickets are paid for by credit card. The travel agency does not get any of it. It is the airline that processes this and it is the airline, not the travel agency, that is paid by the credit card company. Therefore, the airline treats the commission part of credit card payments as an account payable to the travel agency. Their position is that all commissions earned on credit card sales constitute money that the air carriers owe to the travel agency. This is because the credit card company does not pay the travel agency. They pay the airline on which the ticket was validated. For all other tickets, paid for in any other way, the payment arrangement is different. The travel agency deducts its commission before sending the ARC Report to the central bank authorizing the withdrawal of the airline's 90 percent of payment. (This includes tax payment, since the airline pays the government an 10 percent tax on domestic tickets and a $6 departure tax on international tickets.)

ADDING MACHINE TAPES

Once the agency accountant has divided all of the auditor coupons according to credit card payment and all other kinds of payment, it is necessary to run an adding machine tape on each stack of auditor coupons so that the total amount of each stack will be shown on the appropriate tape, figure 8–2. If a mistake is made, a rerun is required. ARC does not allow any tapes to be processed which have any errors or corrections on them at all. They must be totally correct. The result will be one adding machine tape which reflects every auditor coupon paid for by credit card and another adding machine tape which reflects every auditor coupon paid for in some manner other than by

CASH SALES TAPE	CREDIT SALES TAPE
217.00+	174.00+
302.00+	190.00+
307.00+	304.00+
305.00+	128.00+
357.00+	174.00+
1,488.00 S	970.00 S
181.00+	346.00+
8.00+	252.00+
412.00+	275.00+
1,616.00+	206.00+
100.00+	233.00+
3,805.00 S	2,282.00 S
412.00+	598.00–
269.00+	50.00–
136.00+	
4,622.00 S	1,634.00 T
272.00–	
4,350.00 S	
18.30+	
7.37–	
4,360.93 T	
ABC TRAVEL	ABC TRAVEL
00 12345–6	00 12345–6
123 MAIN ST	123 MAIN ST
HOMETOWN, USA	HOMETOWN, USA
AUTH# 880104	AUTH# 880104
01/31/88	01/31/88

Figure 8–2 (Reset from and courtesy of *ARC Handbook*)

credit card. At the top of each tape will be a label. One will be "Cash Sales" while the other will be "Credit Card Sales," figure 8–2. At the bottom of each tape, one must enter the date of the ARC Report (ending date of the report week). Above the date (still at the bottom of the tape), show the agency's name, ARC number, address and the report authorization number. All of this information that is entered at the top and at the bottom of the adding machine tapes should be typed. Hand printing of the information, however, is an acceptable (but not preferred) alternative.

Tape Originals and Photocopies

It is a good idea to double-check figures in the report, because it is possible to make a mistake. Another option is to photocopy each of the tapes. The photocopies (or rerun tapes) are usually wrapped around the agent coupons prior to placing them into storage. They are banded together. The original cash sales tape should be rubber banded around the stack of auditor coupons representing tickets that have been paid for in some manner other than by credit card. The original credit card tape should be rubber banded around the stack of auditor coupons representing tickets paid for by credit card. Keep in mind that the agent coupons should be kept in numerical order prior to being banded and placed in storage, and that the stacks of auditor coupons should be kept in numerical order prior to their being banded and prepared for sending to the area bank.

THE ARC REPORT FORM AND COMPLETED FORM DISBURSEMENT

Once the adding machine tapes have been completed, the copies made and banded with the agent coupons, these stacks placed in storage, and one original tape banded around each of the two stacks of auditor coupons, the hardest part of the ARC Report has been completed. There is still one job left, however: completing the ARC Report itself. Look at the *Sales Report Settlement Authorization* form, figure 8–3.

This form, commonly referred to as the ARC Report, comes in three copies. It is a nonaccountable form that may be ordered along with supplies of ticket stock. There is no charge for the form. Since the order can sometimes take several weeks to process, most travel agencies order a good supply of forms at the same time they order ticket stock. Since this is a nonaccountable form, if an agency runs out of forms before getting in a new order, a blank form may be borrowed from another travel agency in order to complete the report and send it to the area bank on time. Also, if an error is made in

SALES REPORT SETTLEMENT AUTHORIZATION

The Airlines Reporting Corporation is authorized to draw a check against agency specified bank account to be presented no earlier than the tenth day following the ending date of this report period, such amount not to exceed the amount stated on this authorization.

REPORT PREPARATION DATE

AREA BANK COPY

AGENCY TELEPHONE NUMBER (OF PERSON PREPARING REPORT)

AREA CODE TELEPHONE NUMBER

( ) -

FILL ALL BOXES – USING 0'S WHERE NECESSARY

Report Period Ending — MONTH DAY YEAR

Authorized Signature ____________________

Name of Agency ____________________

Authorized Amount — DOLLARS CENTS

Authorization Number

Enter Tape Totals From Batches Being Submitted:

CREDIT CARD — DOLLARS CENTS

CASH — DOLLARS CENTS

Check if No Sales for This Period ☐

Figure 8–3 (Courtesy of *ARC Handbook*)

completing the form, it can be torn up and thrown away and a new form completed. This may seem like a luxury-in-abandon compared to the way other ARC documents (airline tickets and other accountable documents) must be watched and cared for.

The original copy of the ARC Report goes to the area settlement bank. It is usually rubber banded around the two stacks of auditor coupons before being placed into an envelope for mailing. The second (carbon) and (if one wants to retain it) third copies of the report stay with the travel agency. They are usually rubber banded around the stack of agent coupons (along with the copies of the adding machine tapes) prior to their being placed in storage.

The original of the Sales Report Settlement Authorization Form is identified by the words, "Area Bank Copy," located in a block at the top toward the right-hand side. This is the top copy and is the one that is typed or printed. It is this copy that goes with the original adding machine tapes and the two stacks of auditor coupons to the area bank each Tuesday by midnight.

COMPLETION OF THE ARC REPORT FORM

The process of completing the Sales Report Settlement Authorization Form starts with running it through the travel agency's validator. This imprints the agency's ARC plate identification information in the top right-hand corner of the form. This information includes the name of the agency, the city and state in which the agency is located, and the agency's ARC number.

Since the validator has a dater on it, the date on which the report was prepared also appears on the form. This is shown in the section titled "Report

Preparation Date." Make certain that the date on the validator is set to the day after the ARC Report week is over. Sometimes the validator date is not moved forward from the last working day and, if the report is prepared on a Monday morning, for example, the date appearing on the form may be the previous Friday's. However, if any sales were made on Saturday (still considered part of the report week) and reported in the ARC Report, the area bank will receive a report that includes sales made after the date on the report form. Therefore a quick check to make sure the date on the validator is correct can prevent having ARC return the report because it was dated improperly. The date should reflect either Monday or Tuesday. If the report is prepared on Sunday when the travel agency is closed, it will not hurt to move the validator date to Monday's date prior to running the ARC Report form through it. After all, there will be no more ticket sales prior to that date since the next business day will be Monday.

After running the blank Sales Report Settlement Authorization Form through the validator, the next thing to do is complete the "Credit Card" and "Cash" sections at the bottom left corner of the form. Because the adding machine tapes on both of these ticket coupon stacks have already been run, completing these sections is a simple job of copying figures. The same totals that appeared on each of the adding machine tapes are transferred to the appropriate blocks on the form. The total from the adding machine tape for credit card sales is entered into the blocks under "Credit Card" and the total from the adding machine tape for cash sales is entered into the blocks under "Cash." Because it is very important to get each number into the correct box, it is suggested that one complete the "Cents" blocks first and then enter the dollar amount, working from right to left rather than the normal way of entering data from left to right. After completing the transfer of figures, always check to make sure the numbers are correct and that they have been entered into the correct blocks.

The "Report Period Ending" section is the next part of the report to be completed. In this case, numbers are used for each date element. The two-block "Month" section is completed by showing the numerical month of the year. If it is for a month between January and August, the first digit will be zero and the second digit will be the number of the month (from one to nine). The next two-block series is for the day of the month. If the Sunday (last day of the report period) is one of the first nine days of the month, again the first digit in the two-block "Day" series will be a zero. Finally, the two-digit "Year" section of the date is completed. This will always be the last two numbers in the current year. For example, if the report is completed in 1993, the two figures in the "Year" blocks will be 9 and 3, figure 8–4. Again, it is important to remember that this block calls for the date of the report period ending. This will not be the same date as the report preparation date, unless the

SALES REPORT SETTLEMENT AUTHORIZATION

Agency Name
City/State
ARC # 00000

Initials

The Airlines Reporting Corporation is authorized to draw a check against agency specified bank account to be presented no earlier than the tenth day following the ending date of this report period, such amount not to exceed the amount stated on this authorization.

July 08, 1993
REPORT PREPARATION DATE

AGENCY TELEPHONE NUMBER
(OF PERSON PREPARING REPORT)
AREA CODE TELEPHONE NUMBER
(111) 222-3333

AREA BANK COPY

FILL ALL BOXES – USING 0'S WHERE NECESSARY

	MONTH	DAY	YEAR
Report Period Ending	0 7	0 8	9 3

	DOLLARS	CENTS
Authorized Amount	1 2 6 2 0	1 9

Authorization Number: 9 3 0 8 0 7

Authorized Signature ________________

Name of Agency Fictitious Travel

Enter Tape Totals From Batches Being Submitted:

CREDIT CARD DOLLARS	CREDIT CARD CENTS	CASH DOLLARS	CASH CENTS
4 3 7 8 9	2 1	1 6 2 2 0	7 9

Check if No Sales for This Period ☐

Figure 8–4 (Courtesy of *ARC Handbook*)

report is prepared on the Sunday before the report is due to be mailed to the area settlement bank on Tuesday. This "Report Period Ending" date always will be a Sunday date because all report periods end on Sunday at midnight. For the first week of July sales studied in the calendar example earlier, figure 8–1, the report week ended on Sunday the eighth. Therefore, for the report prepared for that sales week, the "Report Period Ending" date would be 07 for the month (July), 08 for the day (the eighth), and the year would be the last two digits of the year in which the report is completed, figure 8–4.

The next section, working down the right-hand side of the Sales Report Settlement Authorization Form, is the "Authorized Amount." This is considered by most to be the most difficult part of filling out the ARC Report. The airlines allow the travel agency to deduct the amount of money that the airlines owe the travel agency for credit card sales. The way this is done is to deduct 8 percent of the credit card sales and 8 percent of the cash sales from the total reported in cash sales in order to come up with the maximum figure authorized for the central bank to draw from the travel agency's account for the sales week being reported. Therefore, the authorized amount will be the same as the total of both credit card and cash sales reported less 8 percent of that total. After calculating the authorized amount figure, enter that figure into the appropriate blocks on the "Authorized Amount" line of the Sales Report Settlement Authorization Form, figure 8–4. Again, when entering this amount, it is recommended to complete the two-block "Cents" section first and then enter in the dollar amount working backward, i.e., from right to left. Again, when the figure has been entered, check all calculations to make certain they are correct and check the calculated figure to make sure it was entered correctly.

This is a simplified approach toward calculating the authorized amount. The exact formula to use for multiplying the percentages is in the current ARC handbook and that formula should be followed. The ARC formula changes from time to time. Therefore it should be reviewed each quarter when a new edition of the *Handbook* is received. It takes into account both the tax considerations and the fact that commissions vary, depending upon the air carrier on which the ticket is validated and whether the ticket is for domestic or international air transportation. The travel agency cannot take commission on tax collected as a part of the ticket sale just as the air carrier is unable to retain the tax collected. It must send that tax to the United States government. So the multiplication formula is more complicated than that shown above, but this is the process that is used. Therefore, one should follow the steps in the current issue of the *ARC Handbook,* figure 8–5, in order to calculate the exact authorized amount. Many will save time by using this simplified calculation approach since it is faster and since authorizing a maximum allowable draw that is only slightly above the exact amount due to the carriers will not hurt the travel agency. The central bank should only draw from the account what is due to them.

Obviously, if the credit card sales are substantially better than the cash sales, the travel agency may find itself in the enviable position of having the air carriers owe them money (rather than vice versa) when the ARC Report is processed. An increasing number of very large business-travel oriented agencies insist that their clients work on a corporate travel credit card billing system, thus finding themselves in the position of having the air carriers owe them money at the end of virtually every report week. When this occurs, the authorized amount is zero.

The last series of blocks, located near the bottom on the right side of the Sales Report Settlement Authorization Form, is labeled "Authorization Number." The authorization number should always be different than any number previously used. It is an arbitrary number decided upon by the travel agency. Its purpose is to reduce the possibility of someone other than an authorized agency employee completing a Sales Report Settlement Authorization Form and sending it to the area bank with incorrect information. Obviously, someone trying to hurt a travel agency financially could theoretically prepare a report showing an amount of sales considerably larger than actual sales and authorizing a draw that would be high enough to harm the agency financially. The likelihood of this happening is small, but some degree of protection is afforded through the vehicle of having an authorization number. Most travel agencies do not consider the authorization number to be an important part of the report, but they recognize that it must be completed in order to have a complete report. This avoids getting the report back because it is considered incomplete —necessitating the preparation and submission of a replacement report.

SECTION 12.0

SALES REPORTS

GENERAL INFORMATION

Sales reports are to be submitted each week for the value of all ARC Standard Tickets, Miscellaneous Charges Orders, PTA's, or Tour Orders issued on behalf of all ARC carrier participants.

Each report will include all sales made between the start of business each Monday and the close of business each Sunday. The report shall be mailed or delivered no later than midnight each Tuesday (or Wednesday if Monday or Tuesday is a holiday under the ARC Agent Reporting Agreement). See also holiday information in Section 12.10 of this Handbook.

Should you discover that a sale was inadvertently omitted from its proper sales report, you should include it with your next report.

In the event a carrier fails to meet ARC financial standards a refund restriction may be imposed which requires all documents of such a carrier to be submitted for refund, in a separate batch. There would then be three batches to the weekly sales report (cash, credit card and carrier XYZ refunds). This procedure is not to be used unless notified by ARC to do so. Refer to Section 11.0 of this Handbook for further information.

The agent is responsible for all accountable forms including completely voided ticket sets. Totally voided ticket sets should not be reported to the area bank. A well organized and effective plan safeguarding and accounting for all voided tickets must be maintained. Suggested procedures to follow are:

Establish an internal record of voided tickets for audit purposes. This record shall consist of no less than:

A listing of voided tickets showing the ticket number and the date such ticket was voided; or

a file of Agent Coupons of voided tickets in form and serial number order; or

a record of voided tickets that may be an integral part of a larger inventory control system.

Continue to invalidate accountable tickets manually at the time of voiding by writing the word "VOID" across the face of all coupons.

Voided tickets refer to completely voided ticket sets, not individual surface or voided coupons within a valid ticket set. Voided coupons within a valid ticket set are to be handled in accordance with the instructions in Section 5.2, page 1.

Voided tickets should be completely destroyed by means of shredding, mulching, etc. since the agent is ultimately responsible for the use of any ticket supposedly voided/destroyed.

REPORTING PROCEDURES

PREPARATION OF SALES REPORT

The weekly report will consist of the following three components:

Sales Report Settlement Authorization

Credit Transactions with Adding Machine Tape/ Printout (credit batch)

Cash Transactions with Adding Machine Tape/ Printout (cash batch)

Each of the above components of the report is explained below:

Sales Report Settlement Authorization

This document will be submitted on the top of the agent's report. Instructions for completion of this form are found later in this section.

Credit Card Transactions (with Adding Machine Tape/Printout)

When the form of payment is one of the following, place the transaction into the credit card sales batch:

Manual or automated credit card charge form

Direct Form of Payment credit plan

Government Transportation Request (Section 5.4)

Fly Now Pay Later credit plan

Transaction Definitions

Credit Sale Transaction

Represents a purchase of a ticket where a credit card was accepted as payment for the sale. A credit sale will consist of one credit card charge form and at least one primary auditor's coupon. EXCEPTION: A credit sale for family travel may contain up to ten new auditor's coupons per charge form. The credit sale transaction is listed as a (+) amount, as indicated on the auditor's coupon, on the credit card sales tape/printout.

Exchange Transaction with an Additional Credit Collection

Represents the reissuance of an old transportation document for a new ticket of greater value. The additional collection amount is paid using a credit card. This

Page 1

Figure 8–5 (Courtesy of *ARC Handbook*)

SECTION 12.0

Transaction Definitions (Cont'd)

transaction consists of a manual ARC credit charge form for the amount of the additional collection, one ticket exchange notice, one or more new auditor's coupon(s) and one or more support documents. This transaction is listed as a (+) amount, as indicated on the ticket exchange notice, on the credit card sales tape/printout.

Credit Card Refund Transaction

Represents the refund of unused flight/value coupons where a credit card was used as the form of payment on the original sale. The credit refund transaction consists of one credit card refund notice and one or more unused flight/value coupon(s). This transaction is listed as a (–) amount, as indicated on the CCRN, on the credit card sales tape/printout.

Exchange Transaction with a Credit Card Refund

Represents the reissuance of an old ticket for a new ticket of lesser value. The old ticket indicates a credit card form of payment. This transaction consists of one credit card refund notice, one ticket exchange notice, one or more auditor's coupon(s) and one or more unused flight/value coupon(s). This transaction is listed as a (–) amount, as indicated on the CCRN, on the credit card sales tape/printout.

Suggested Procedures

Organize the credit card sales transactions into numeric sequence by form number.

Ensure that the credit card charge form or the credit card refund notice is stapled to the front of the auditor's coupon, ticket exchange notice or the unused flight/value coupon(s).

Only one passenger itinerary (ticket, MCO or PTA) is permitted per credit card charge form or credit card refund notice.

Run a carbon or thermal adding machine tape off of the total sale or refund amounts of the auditor's coupon, ticket exchange notice or credit card refund notice.

Subtotal at least every fifty items, or if less than fifty items, between the credit sales and the credit refunds. Rubber band at the subtotals.

Total out the tape/printout and transfer the credit card sales tape total to the Sales Report Settlement Authorization Form. Documents must be batched together in the same order as they appear on the tape/printout.

Verify the accuracy of the credit card sales tape by checking amounts indicated against the agent's coupons. Hand corrections to rectify incorrect entries or deletions do not insure an accurate total. If your tape or printout contains an error, it should be rerun with proper figures.

Cash Transactions (with Adding Machine Tape/Printout)

When the form of payment is one of the following, place the transactions into the cash sales batch:

Cash or travelers check

Personal or company check

Transaction Definitions

Cash Sale Transaction

Represents the purchase of a ticket where cash or check was used as payment for the sale. The cash sale consists of one primary auditor's coupon and may contain one or more conjunction auditor's coupon(s). This transaction is shown as a (+) amount, as indicated on the primary auditor's coupon, on the cash sales tape/printout.

Exchange Transaction with an Additional Cash Collection

Represents the reissuance of an old ticket of greater value. The additional collection amount is paid using cash or check. This transaction consists of one ticket exchange notice, one or more auditor's coupon(s) and one or more flight/value coupon(s). This transaction is listed as a (+) amount, as indicated on the ticket exchange notice, on the cash sales tape/printout.

Cash Refund Transaction

Represents the refund of unused flight/value coupons where cash or check was used as the form of payment on the original sale. This transaction consists of one cash refund notice and at least one or more flight/value coupon(s). This transaction is listed as a (–) amount, as indicated on the cash refund notice, on the cash sales tape/printout.

Exchange Transaction with a Cash Refund

Represents the reissuance of an old ticket for a new ticket of lesser value. The old ticket indicates cash as the form of payment. This transaction consists of one ticket exchange notice, one or more auditor's coupon(s) and one or more exchanged flight/value coupon(s). This transaction is listed as a (–) amount, as indicated on the ticket exchange notice, on the cash sales tape/printout.

Even Exchange Transaction

Represents the reissuance of an old ticket for a new ticket of equal value. This transaction consists of one ticket exchange notice, one or more auditor's coupon(s) and one or more exchanged flight/value coupon(s) and is listed as ZERO on the cash sales tape/printout.

Page 2

Figure 8–5 (Continued)

Industry Agents' Handbook

SECTION 12.0

Transaction Definitions (Cont'd)

Carrier Adjustments

Represents a single document transaction forwarded to the agent in order to correct a sales figure involving prior reporting period.

Debit Memo: Is listed as a (+) amount on the cash sales tape/printout.

Recall Commission Statement: Is listed as a (+) amount on the cash sales tape/printout.

Credit Memo: Is listed as a (–) amount on the cash sales tape/printout.

Agent Automated Deductions

Permits the immediate reimbursement to an agent for an amount not to exceed $25.00. If the amount is between $0.00 and $10.00, this transaction will consist of only the Agent Automated Deduction. If the amount due is between $10.01 and $25.00, this transaction will consist of an Agent Automated Deduction and a copy of the agent's coupon on which the error occurred. This transaction will be listed as a (–) amount on the cash sales tape/printout.

Suggested Procedures

Organize the cash sales auditor's coupons into numeric sequence by form number.

Assemble the cash refund notices ensuring that the refund notice is securely fastened to the unused flight/value coupons

Assemble any adjustments such as Debit Memos, Recall Commission Statements, Credit Memos or Agent Automated Deductions.

Include all Even Exchange Transactions regardless of the form of payment and any free tickets.

Run a carbon or thermal adding machine tape off of the total sale, total refund, adjustments and/or Agent Automated Deductions.

Subtotal at least every fifty items or if less than fifty items, between the cash sales; cash refunds and adjustments. Rubber band at the subtotals. It is recommended that you subtotal after the cash refunds and before any adjustments. This subtotal should equal the cash sales processed.

Total out the cash tape and transfer the cash sale tape total to the Sales Report Settlement Authorization Form. Documents must be batched together in the same order as they appear on the tape/printout.

Verify the accuracy of the cash sales tape by checking amounts indicated against the agent's coupons. Hand corrections to rectify incorrect entries or deletions do not insure an accurate total. If your tape or printout contains an error, it should be re-run with proper figures.

The following sequence is suggested for the cash sales tape/printout:

Auditor's coupons (+), Including Ticket Exchange Notices (+ or –)

Cash Refund Notices (–)

Subtotal (Recommended for balancing)

Debit Memos (+)

Recall Commission Statements (+)

Credit Memos (–)

Agent's Automated Deductions (–)

IMPORTANT: Once a ticket has been reported as a cash sale, it may not be converted to a credit card sale (or vice versa).

Variable Remittance Options

Agents participating in one of the Variable Remittance options should refer to Section 13 of this Handbook for special instructions.

Figure 8–5 (Continued)

Industry Agents' Handbook

SECTION 12.0

ILLUSTRATIONS OF ADDING MACHINE TAPES AND COMPUTER PRINTOUTS

EXAMPLE OF CURRENT FORMAT FOR ALL AGENTS SUBMITTING STANDARD ADDING MACHINE TAPES

CASH
SALES
TAPE

217.00+
302.00+
307.00+
305.00+
357.00+
1,488.00 S
181.00+
8.00+
412.00+
1,616.00+
100.00+
3,805.00 S
412.00+
269.00+
136.00+
4,622.00 S
272.00–
4,350.00 S
18.30+
7.37–
4,360.93 T

ABC TRAVEL
00 12345-6
123 MAIN ST
HOMETOWN, USA
AUTH# 880104
01/31/88

CREDIT
SALES
TAPE

174.00+
190.00+
304.00+
128.00+
174.00+
970.00 S
346.00+
252.00+
275.00+
206.00+
233.00+
2,282.00 S
598.00–
50.00–
1,634.00 T

ABC TRAVEL
00 12345-6
123 MAIN ST
HOMETOWN, USA
AUTH# 880104
01/31/88

EXAMPLE OF CURRENT FORMAT FOR ALL AGENTS SUBMITTING COMPUTERIZED PRINTOUTS (CREDIT LISTING)

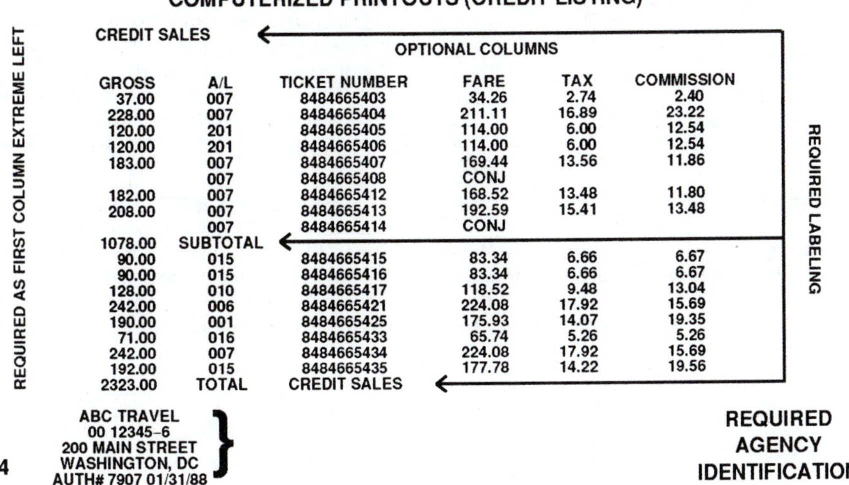

CREDIT SALES ← OPTIONAL COLUMNS

REQUIRED AS FIRST COLUMN EXTREME LEFT

GROSS	A/L	TICKET NUMBER	FARE	TAX	COMMISSION
37.00	007	8484665403	34.26	2.74	2.40
228.00	007	8484665404	211.11	16.89	23.22
120.00	201	8484665405	114.00	6.00	12.54
120.00	201	8484665406	114.00	6.00	12.54
183.00	007	8484665407	169.44	13.56	11.86
	007	8484665408	CONJ		
182.00	007	8484665412	168.52	13.48	11.80
208.00	007	8484665413	192.59	15.41	13.48
	007	8484665414	CONJ		
1078.00	SUBTOTAL ←				
90.00	015	8484665415	83.34	6.66	6.67
90.00	015	8484665416	83.34	6.66	6.67
128.00	010	8484665417	118.52	9.48	13.04
242.00	006	8484665421	224.08	17.92	15.69
190.00	001	8484665425	175.93	14.07	19.35
71.00	016	8484665433	65.74	5.26	5.26
242.00	007	8484665434	224.08	17.92	15.69
192.00	015	8484665435	177.78	14.22	19.56
2323.00	TOTAL	CREDIT SALES ←			

REQUIRED LABELING

ABC TRAVEL
00 12345-6
200 MAIN STREET
WASHINGTON, DC
AUTH# 7907 01/31/88 }

REQUIRED
AGENCY
IDENTIFICATION

Page 4

Figure 8–5 (Continued)

Industry Agents' Handbook

SECTION 12.0

CALCULATION OF AUTHORIZED AMOUNT

The authorized amount merely establishes a maximum amount for which the bank can present a check to your account. It in no way affects your net remittance or your commission.

The authorized amount is calculated by using one of the following formulas:

Use the total of the cash sales tape.

OR

Add the cash and credit card tape totals, multiply the results by .06 to arrive at 6% of total sales.* Subtract this amount from the *cash total*. The final result is the authorized amount. For example:

Add: Cash Sales Tape Total	$ 4,360.93
Credit Card Sales Tape Total	+ 1,634.00
Total Sales Tapes	5,994.93
Multiply × .06	× .06
6% of Sales Tapes Total	$ 359.70
Cash Sales Tape Total	$ 4,360.93
Subtract: 6% Sales Tapes Total	359.70
AUTHORIZED AMOUNT	$ 4,001.23

If excessive credit card sales, cash refunds or other factors cause a negative figure, use "0" as the Authorized Amount. For Example:

Add: Cash Sales Tape Total	$ 1,275.00
Credit Card Sales Tape Total	+24,200.00
Total Sales Tapes	25,475.00
Multiply × .06	× .06
6% of Sales Tapes Total	$ 1,528.50
Cash Sales Tape Total	$ 1,275.00
Subtract the 6% Total Sales Tape Figure	− 1,528.50
	− 253.50
AUTHORIZED AMOUNT	0.00

*The 6% figure is not intended to replace a commission level, but is a tested figure that in most instances provides a reasonable authorized amount. If this figure is not satisfactory for your agency it may be adjusted (e.g. 5%).

For Agents participating in one of the variable remittance options, please refer to Section 13.0 of this Handbook for calculation of the authorized amount.

ADDITIONAL INSTRUCTIONS FOR COMPUTERIZED PRINTOUT FORMAT SUMMARY (CASH & CREDIT)

Computer printouts will be accepted in lieu of adding machine tapes, provided the format of the printout conforms to the tape format; i.e. a column of cash and a column of credit sales, each showing proper headings and totals.

The first column of data (extreme left) of both the Cash and Credit Sales/Refund listings *must* be the *Gross* amount (i.e. fare plus applicable taxes).

All other columnar listings are *optional*.

If however, due to programming capability and/or related *economic* factors, you do not wish to format your printout as described in (A) above, you may alternately keep your Gross Amount Column where it is but:

The Gross Amount Column will be cut-out *neatly* from the print-out and submitted in lieu of an adding machine tape. Do *not* submit other columns of information.

The cut-out Gross Amount Column must conform in all respects to tape specifications outlined throughout this section (i.e. subtotals, agency identification, labeling, etc.).

If more than one Gross Amount Column must be cut-out for the Cash and/or Credit listings (i.e. several pages of sales listings), then these columns will be securely attached to each other (scotch tape on both sides) in consecutive listed order, creating one composite Cash tape, and one composite Credit tape.

As in the example, GROSS sales amounts or CCRN refund amounts (if applicable) *must* appear in the extreme *LEFT* hand column. All other columns are optional but labeling of totals and subtotals must appear as above. CREDIT sales must be so labeled. Identify printout with agency name, address and other information as above.

Figure 8–5 (Continued)

A simple way of calculating an authorization number that meets with the ARC requirement of never having a duplication in authorization numbers is to use a variation of the Report Period Ending date numbers. Go back to the 8 July 1993 Report Period Ending date, which was used as an example when discussing the "Report Period Ending" blocks earlier in this chapter, figure 8–3, and which was taken from the example used when looking at the ARC Report calendar toward the beginning of this chapter, figure 8–1. This Sunday was the last day of the sales week. To turn this same date into an authorization number, show the year in the first two blocks of the authorization number block series. This will mean that the authorization number starts with 93. Next show the day, 08. Finally, show the month, 07. Therefore, the authorization number for the Sales Report Settlement Authorization Form completed for the report period ending on 8 July 1993 is 930807, figure 8–4. Because the date will never be repeated, neither will the authorization number ever be repeated. This very simple way to create an authorization number is used by many travel agencies.

Simply because many in the industry utilize this easy system for determining an authorization number, it defeats the purposes for which it was intended. If agency management is concerned about the slightest possibility of having a forged report submitted (and all agency owners should be) this commonly-used approach at creating an authorization number should not be used. Therefore, a better approach is to develop another technique to use in creating authorization numbers. Use a system that is known by the person who prepares the ARC Report—a system known only by the preparer and no one else, except possibly a member of top management.

COMPLETING OTHER ARC REPORT SECTIONS

Unless there were no sales made by the travel agency during the sales report period, there are only three more sections of the Sales Report Settlement Authorization Form that need to be completed. If there were no sales made by the travel agency during the report week, the block at the very bottom right-hand corner should be clearly marked with an X. If that is the case, the "Credit Card" and "Cash" blocks will show zeros in all blocks. The "Authorized Amount" will also show zeros in all blocks. All other sections of the form will be completed in the same way as discussed above. However, if there were any sales during the sales week for which the ARC Report is being prepared, the block at the bottom right-hand corner of the form is left blank. Obviously, most of the time there will be sales and the block at the bottom right-hand corner of the form will be left blank.

Each of the remaining three sections that need to be completed is easy to complete. Two require little discussion. These are the "Name of Agency" and the "Agency Telephone Number" blocks. Type in or clearly print the name of the travel agency, as well as its phone number, making sure that the area code is listed.

SIGNING CONSIDERATIONS

The final step in completing the Sales Report Settlement Authorization Form is signing the form on the "Authorized Signature" line. The signature should be that of a person authorized with the Airline Reporting Corporation to prepare the report. This is usually the qualifier, one of the officers of the travel agency, or one of the owners of the agency. In many agencies the person preparing the ARC Report is expected to sign the report and, as noted above, this is frequently the travel agency's accountant or bookkeeper.

Whoever signs the ARC Report is taking the responsibility of authorizing a draw from the travel agency's bank account for the amount of money indicated on the report. They are signing the following statement: "The Airlines Reporting Corporation is authorized to draw a check against agency specified bank account to be presented no earlier than the tenth day following the ending date of this report period, such amount not to exceed the amount stated on this authorization."

Signing this statement has some ramifications. There are cases where absentee owners of travel agencies have sued report preparers, stating that the preparer did not have authority from the owner to authorize withdrawal of funds because that person's name did not appear on the bank account signature card. There are cases where persons suing a travel agency also named to the suit the person who prepared and signed the ARC Report for the agency, suggesting that authorizing payments for the travel agency constitutes responsibility for the actions of the travel agency. Perhaps most unfortunate was the case of an agency manager who signed ARC Reports for over a year, but who never had any ownership in the agency. She was held responsible for back taxes owed by the agency to the government. This agency manager never saw any of the agency's bank accounts. The working owner kept these to himself. One day the owner left the country with all the agency money and the funds owed to the Airline Reporting Corporation. The Internal Revenue Service got involved in the matter because back taxes were owed. In spite of the fact that the agency manager was able to prove to the Internal Revenue Service that she had no ownership position and did not have access to any of the financial records of bank accounts, the Internal Revenue Service held her responsible for the back taxes. She ultimately paid them, plus accrued interest. The contention of the I.R.S., according to the manager, was that she took on the responsibility for the taxes when she took on the responsibility for authorizing agency payments to the airlines by signing the weekly ARC Report. Therefore, if one signs the report, one should understand the ramifications that go with that signing. Many owners feel that they are paying a qualifier a manager's salary to take on this responsibility. However, the person signing the report needs to understand the potential risk involved even though that risk in most cases is quite small.

ENVELOPE PREPARATION AND DISTRIBUTION

The completion of the Sales Report Settlement Authorization Form is the last part of preparing the ARC Report. After it has been completed, the original is banded to both stacks of ARC copies of the ticket coupons, which themselves have been banded with the original adding machine tapes encircling each stack. The entire banded batch of material (i.e., the original authorization form, both of the original adding machine tapes, and both stacks of ARC copies of the ticket coupons) is placed in an envelope and the envelope is sealed. (Most agencies must use a large manilla envelope with a clasp gummed seal.) The envelope is addressed and then mailed to the appropriate area bank. It is not sent to the Airline Reporting Corporation. The *ARC Handbook* provides the address of each area bank and its geographic territory. Travel agency report preparers simply identify the bank serving the territory in which the agency is located and send the report to that area bank.

Because of the penalties involved if the report does not arrive on time to the area bank, agencies are urged to document the fact that the report is mailed by the deadline, i.e., by midnight Tuesday. Although the error may lie with the post office in losing the report or, more often, in a delay in the delivery of the report, the travel agency is held responsible unless the agency can prove that the report was mailed on time. Therefore, some type of receipt needs to be obtained when the ARC Report is mailed. It does not have to be signed for at the area bank. Sending the report registered mail, return receipt requested is an expensive way to send weekly reports. All that is needed is to ask for a certificate of mailing. The post office will document the date of mailing and the address to which the envelope was addressed and will charge only the cost of a regular stamp. This is the process, therefore, that is suggested. However, the certificate of mailing should be retained for at least two weeks. Many travel agencies will band the certificate of mailing right on top of the weekly filed agent coupons and copies of the adding machine tapes for the weekly report.

SUMMARY

The ARC Report is considered by many to be the most important report prepared in a travel agency. All appointed travel agencies are required to complete the ARC Report, which is a synopsis of airline and related sales for each week. The report week ends on Sunday at midnight and is due to be mailed to the agency's central bank by midnight on the following Tuesday. The ARC Report not only provides information to air carriers, it also provides a financial status report to agency management. Although, in many cases, this report does not include all sales made during the week, agency management can get a good rough idea as to what the agency's weekly sales were from the ARC Report.

The process of completing the ARC Report usually starts by separating all tickets into those paid for by cash or check and those paid for by credit card. Next, an adding machine tape is run for each of the two forms of payment. The results are transferred to the Sales Report Settlement Authorization Form and then the other blocks on the form are completed. The form is validated and signed before sending the report to the area bank.

The ARC Report is the foundation report that is utilized for many other financial management analyses as well as a number of other agency reports. Much of the data discussed in this chapter will be referred to in future chapters. It will be shown how this data contributes to the development of additional reports and how it is used for other aspects of accounting and financial management.

❑ DISCUSSION QUESTIONS

1. When the ARC Report is completed each week and put in the mail, where is it sent?
2. What type of report is sent back to the travel agency by the Airline Reporting Corporation and what information does this report give to the agency's accountant?
3. What forms of payment are included in the category of "cash"?
4. Why does the Airline Reporting Corporation require travel agencies to have two separate bank accounts?
5. What is meant by "ARC Report float," and how might a travel agency take advantage of this?
6. Why do most who prepare ARC reports keep a record of the last ticket issued in each series at the end of each week's report?
7. What information appears on the adding machine tapes that accompany the weekly ARC Report?

8. How is the authorized amount calculated for the Sales Report Settlement Authorization Form?
9. How do many travel agencies devise an authorization number for the Sales Report Settlement Authorization Form?
10. What considerations should one keep in mind when signing the Sales Report Settlement Authorization Form?

❑ *ROLE-PLAYING EXERCISE*

Two students may participate in this role-playing exercise either as an out-of-class or in-class fun way to review the ARC Report preparation procedures. One student plays the agency's bookkeeper. The other plays the travel agency's senior agent. Please read the script and then pick up the conversation in your own words.

Bookkeeper: I appreciate you offering to complete the ARC Report for me while I am on vacation. You have read through the *ARC Handbook* and reviewed our procedures manual to understand how the report is prepared, haven't you?

Senior Agenct: No, I will glance at them if I run into any problems. It seems pretty straightforward. All I do is stack the auditor and agent coupons by form of payment and then fill out all of the blocks on the ARC Report form. Isn't that pretty much how it works?

Bookkeeper: It's more complicated than that. Let me go through all the steps of preparing the report with you. The first thing to do is. . .

CONTINUE ON YOUR OWN

❑ *CHAPTER EIGHT EXERCISE*

INSTRUCTIONS: You are working for ABC Travel, a new travel agency. You are completing their ARC Report for the week that ended last Sunday. The agency is located at 229 State Street, Phoenix, Arizona; and the phone number is (505) 995–2832. The ARC number for the agency is 72 654 3. Only ten tickets were sold last week, the second week this agency has had its airline appointments. Complete the blank Sales Report Settlement Authorization

Form on the next page, figure 8–6, filling in all appropriate blocks. Also complete the blank adding machine tapes on the following page, figure 8–7, hand-printing the header and bottom-of-tape data at the top of each tape and hand-printing the figures for the amounts of the tickets and totals. The tickets sold last week are as follows:

TICKET NUMBER	FORM OF PAYMENT	TOTAL TICKET PRICE
0018402970274	Cash	$270.00
0348402970275	American Express Card	$140.00
0068402970276	Agency Check	$210.00
0018402970277	UATP Card	$420.00
0018402970278	Check	$260.00
0018402970279	Check	$316.00

SALES REPORT SETTLEMENT AUTHORIZATION

The Airlines Reporting Corporation is authorized to draw a check against agency specified bank account to be presented no earlier than the tenth day following the ending date of this report period, such amount not to exceed the amount stated on this authorization.

REPORT PREPARATION DATE

AGENCY TELEPHONE NUMBER
(OF PERSON PREPARING REPORT)
AREA CODE TELEPHONE NUMBER
(　　)　　–

AREA BANK COPY

Authorized Signature ______________

Name of Agency ______________

FILL ALL BOXES – USING 0'S WHERE NECESSARY

Report Period Ending　MONTH　DAY　YEAR

Authorized Amount　DOLLARS　CENTS

Authorization Number

Enter Tape Totals From Batches Being Submitted:

CREDIT CARD　DOLLARS　CENTS

CASH　DOLLARS　CENTS

Check if No Sales for This Period ☐

Figure 8–6

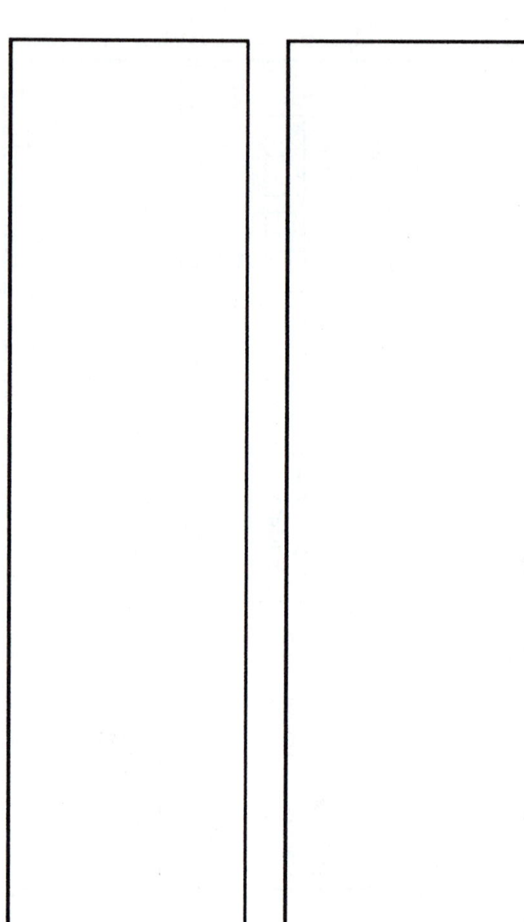

Figure 8–7

9

LEDGERS AND JOURNALS

OBJECTIVES

Upon completion of this chapter, the student will be able to:

- ❑ Identify the major ledgers and journals utilized in a travel agency and the purpose for each
- ❑ Prepare a simple ticket delivery routing based upon a ticket delivery log
- ❑ Explain how data is entered on a miscellaneous receipt log
- ❑ Identify the reason(s) why a miscellaneous receipt log might be considered more of a disbursements log at the end of some months

INTRODUCTION

Ledgers are books that list documents and the sales of similar types that are not kept in other source data, such as journals, figure 9–1. The ledgers that list documents are normally used for accountable documents, the major one relating to airline tickets. Other accountable documents, such as miscellaneous charge orders, tour orders, and prepaid ticket advices are normally kept in ledger format as well. The purpose of *accountable document ledgers* is to provide a financial cross-check and to guard against theft or loss. In some cases, accountable document ledgers are kept in a single book with sections of the book devoted to each type of accountable document. In other cases, there is a separate ledger for each type of accountable document.

SALES PRODUCT LEDGERS

Sales product ledgers, on the other hand, are usually breakdowns of vendor journals and they provide similar (but not as detailed) data for vendors. Usually these are kept only on sales for suppliers who pay override commissions and are used solely for the purpose of tracking override commissions. In other cases, they may be utilized for in-house productivity tracks, such as

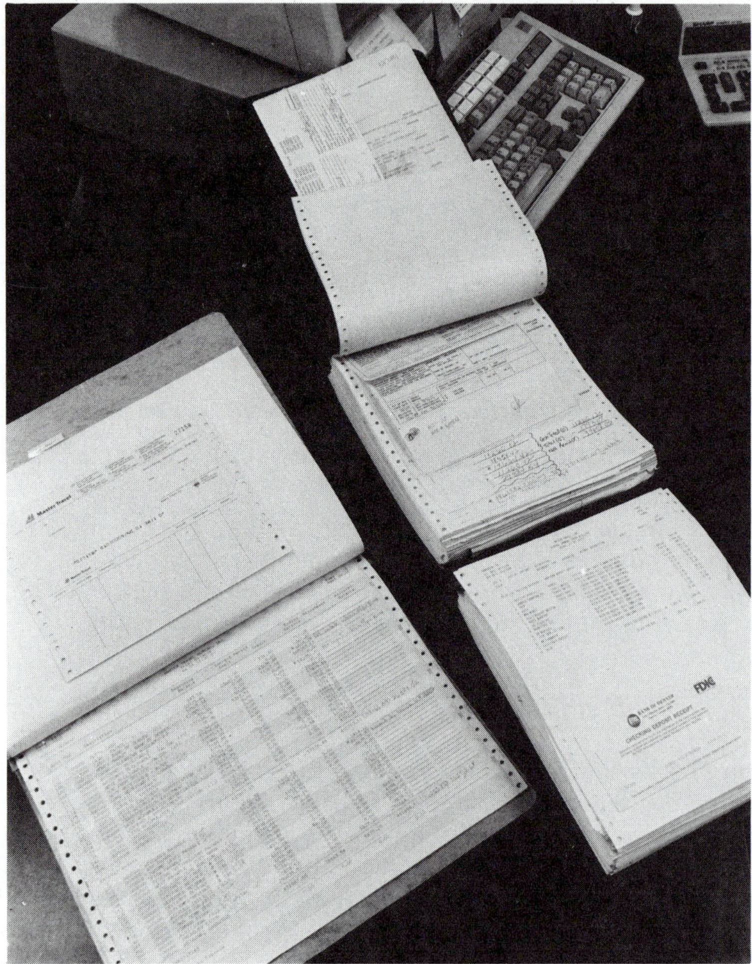

Figure 9–1 Journals and Logs (Courtesy Master Travel, Denver, CO)

F.I.T. (Foreign Independent Tour) bookings and bookings of tours that are developed and run by the agency itself. Still other ledgers are for special charges, such as service charges levied by the travel agency.

CRS TICKET LEDGER

Perhaps the most important of all ledgers is the *machine ticket ledger*, figure 9–2. Often this is kept on or near the ticket printer, a convenient location for

TICKET LEDGER FOR ____DAY ____MONTH ____YEAR				
Ticket No.	Client Name	I/R No.	Agent	Disposition

Figure 9–2

recording tickets generated from the printer. In many agencies this procedure is required whenever a ticket is generated. Normally the agent who generates a ticket is required to enter the ticket number, client name, invoice/receipt number, and/or other data for each ticket generated. The accountant or bookkeeper is expected to balance the machine ticket stock at the end of each day against the numbers of the tickets generated, making certain that every ticket is accounted for on the machine ticket log. In this way, a possible loss of a ticket is identified right away and the potential for internal ticket theft is considerably reduced.

HANDWRITTEN STOCK LEDGER

A similar ledger is kept for handwritten ticket stock, normally by type of ticket. In many agencies the accountant is expected to physically review all tickets in the reserve supply on either a daily or a weekly basis and to review the ticket ledgers of all tickets issued on a daily basis. This initial review is usually a very rapid one consisting of only identifying that there is an entry for the ticket across from each ticket number. At the time that the ARC Report is prepared, a check mark is made in the ledger indicating that the auditor coupon for each ticket has been sent to the central bank with the report. Voids are also checked off at the same time. An entry for which a check mark has not been made is considered a flag to the accountant/bookkeeper, indicating that there is a need to identify the status of that particular ticket. Again, this process assists in reducing loss and the potential for internal theft.

MISCELLANEOUS RECEIPTS LOG

A special type of ledger is the *Miscellaneous Receipts Log*. This form is used to record funds received in the agency from sources other than clients. Perhaps the entries most often found in the Miscellaneous Receipts Log relate to commissions. Both override commissions and retroactive commissions are listed in the Miscellaneous Receipts Log (MRL). However, in addition to override commissions and retroactive commissions, this is the place where refunds (either refunds from suppliers or operating expense refunds or reimbursements) are listed. It also records transfers of funds, either from sources outside of the agency (usually new capitalization) or when funds from other agency accounts are transferred into the agency's operating account.

A sample of a blank Miscellaneous Receipts Log appears in figure 9–3. When entries are made on the Miscellaneous Receipts Log, they are normally entered by starting with an entry in the column on the left and working one's way to entries further and further right until the line is completed. The first item entered is in the "RCPT Date" column. This is the date when monies are actually received in the agency. Next is the "Deposit Date" column. This is the date on which the bank deposit is made. The next entry is the "Received From" entry. Here one enters the name of the person or company from which the funds were received. It is normally also the company or individual who issued the payment (Payor). The "Amount" column comes next. This is the amount of monies that have been received.

The "Value" column, completed next, is for the gross amount of the sale. The gross times the percentage of sale should give the commission amount.

MISCELLANEOUS RECEIPTS LOG RECORD						
RECORD NUMBER ________ MONTH ________						
RCPT DATE	DEPOSIT DATE	RECEIVED FROM	AMOUNT	VALUE	COMMISSION	ACCT NO.

Figure 9–3

Keep in mind that if the transaction being listed in the log is a refund, the value of the booking will be a negative value and therefore will have a parenthesis before and after the figure. Because refunds are reflected on the Miscellaneous Receipts Log, travel agencies sometimes do show a negative balance at the end of the month. Therefore, the Miscellaneous Receipts Log is more of a disbursements log than it is a receipts log for those months. However, the goal of most agencies is to reduce the number of refunds and always have the Miscellaneous Receipts Log show a positive figure at the end of each month.

The next column to be completed is "Commission." This is for the dollar and cent value of the commission received or refunded.

The last column is the "Acct No." (Account Number) column. In this column one enters the appropriate chart-of-accounts number for the transaction being recorded. This will be a chart-of-accounts line number.

Some of the funds received will not have any affect on commissions or commission income. Therefore, these funds will be recorded in the column which is titled "Amount." But no entry will be made in the "Commissions" block. Examples include reimbursement of an expense by a vendor or an overpayment reimbursement.

THE TICKET DELIVERY LOG

Another special type of ledger is the *ticket delivery log*, figure 9–4. The ticket delivery log acts as another check form to identify the status of issued airline tickets. In corporate or business oriented travel agencies many (in some cases all) tickets are delivered to the client by an employee of the travel agency. Because responsibility for the ticket is transferred from the agency to the client at the time that the ticket is actually handed over to the client, most travel agencies require the client's employee who physically receives the tickets to sign for them on a ticket delivery log. This way, if the client complains at a later time that the ticket has not yet been received, a quick check of the ticket delivery log will determine whether or not the ticket has been delivered to someone at the client work place.

It is not uncommon for the tickets to be delivered to a client's receptionist, who signs for the ticket, and for the traveler or the traveler's secretary to phone complaining that the ticket has not yet been received. By checking the ticket delivery log and advising the traveler or the traveler's secretary of the name of the person who received the ticket, the matter can usually be resolved rapidly.

Efficiency of ticket delivery can be accomplished by using the addresses on the ticket delivery log to determine the fastest routing for the delivery person. After matching addresses on the log to locations on a map, one can rapidly schedule delivery with a minimum of backtracking.

In leisure-travel oriented agencies, it is frequently common for a client to pick up a ticket at the agency. In this case, a *ticket receipt log* is frequently kept at the agency. When the ticket is received by the client, the ticket receipt log is signed. This too shows that responsibility for the ticket has transferred from the agency to the client. Again, it is not too uncommon for a housewife to pick up her family's tickets early in the day and her husband to stop in for the tickets on the way home from work. When a ticket receipt log is kept, one can rapidly turn to the log after determining that the tickets are no longer in the agency, and advise the husband that his wife has already

TICKET DELIVERY LOG FOR ____DAY ____MONTH ____YEAR PAGE NUMBER ___ of ___			
Ticket No.	Company Name	Delivery Address	Rcvd By (Signature)

Figure 9–4

picked up the tickets. This can save considerable concern on the part of both agent and client, eliminating a considerable search for tickets that have already been turned over to the client.

VENDOR JOURNALS

Override commissions are providing an increasingly greater important source of income for travel agencies. This is especially true for high-volume travel agencies. Because override commissions are based upon increased volume of sales or the ability of an agency to move sales from one vendor to another, it behooves agency management to keep accurate vendor use records. Most travel agency executives wish to make certain that clients are happy and not push specific vendors on clients who would otherwise be unhappy with those vendors. It has become common in the industry for agencies to select *preferred vendors* and to offer the products of these vendors first. By keeping detailed journals of each ticket, hotel booking, tour sale, cruise sale, or other product sold according to vendor, it is easy at the end of each month, each quarter, and each year for the agency's accountant to identify the dollar volume of bookings with each vendor and the percentage of total bookings within the type of sale (cruises, tours) for each vendor. After identifying that an override level has been met that will provide a previously negotiated and agreed upon override commission or flat payment, the agency is then in a position to bill the vendor for the appropriate override commission/payment. Those agencies not keeping vendor journals are in the position of depending upon the vendor to keep these records and provide the override commission/payment. The *vendor journals* kept in the travel agency provide a cross-check against the record keeping maintained by the individual vendors. Agency management can then be secure in the knowledge that they are receiving all override monies earned.

SUMMARY

Although some travel agency owners, managers, and accountants do not keep detailed ledgers and journals because of the considerable time and work involved in keeping them, many have found that the ledgers and journals provide specific benefits in addition to providing the customary financial cross-checks which verify accounting and guard against theft or loss.

The most common ledger is one that records accountable documents, such as airline tickets. By periodically checking the reserve of each accountable document against the ledger of used and issued accountable documents, the agency's accountant is able to identify the status of each document for which the agency is held accountable. In addition, when staff members are aware of this process, the potential for internal theft of accountable documents is considerably reduced.

Sales product ledgers and vendor journals are kept in order to provide a cross-check to determine receipt of all earned override commissions and to provide an in-house productivity track. The CRS ticket ledger is the most commonly found ledger. This provides detailed information on each ticket generated through the computer reservation system. Supplementing the CRS ticket ledger are ledgers for each form of handwritten ticket stock. The

Miscellaneous Receipts Log is a special type of ledger which provides detailed information on both miscellaneous income and refunds.

By maintaining ledgers and journals travel agency executives are able to ensure greater security of documents, track the status of documents, and make sure that a cross-check on monies due to the agency is maintained. There is a trade-off that is generally recognized. This is that the more accurate and detailed the record keeping, the greater the amount of work in recording transactions. While good accounting practices call for very detailed reporting of transactions in journals and ledgers, some agency executives feel that the amount of additional work is not worth the potential additional income and the security that may come from ledger/journal maintenance. Each agency finds its own most suitable balance.

❑ *DISCUSSION QUESTIONS*

1. What are ledgers?
2. What is the major ledger?
3. What is the purpose of accountable document ledgers?
4. On what type of suppliers are sales product ledgers normally kept and why?
5. Against what does the accountant or bookkeeper balance machine ticket stock in order to make certain that every ticket is accounted for?
6. What type of item becomes a flag to the accountant/bookkeeper, indicating that there may be a need to identify the status of a particular ticket and how does the recognition of this flag come about?
7. What type of information is recorded on the Miscellaneous Receipts Log?
8. Why might a Miscellaneous Receipts Log be considered more of a disbursements log at the end of some months?
9. How might a ticket delivery log resolve the concern of a business client who might believe that tickets had not been delivered on time?
10. In what way might vendor journals provide a cross-check against vendor-kept records in ensuring that all override commissions which are due are claimed?

❑ *ROLE-PLAYING EXERCISE*

Two students may participate in this role-playing exercise either as an out-of-class or in-class fun way to review how a travel agency's ticket receipt log can assist in overcoming uncomfortable situations. Suppose a client thinks a ticket has either been lost by the travel agency or that the ticket may not have ever been issued. One student plays the agency's client who has just come by to pick up his/her tickets. The other plays an agent working in the agency. Please read the script and then pick up the conversation in your own words.

Client: I have come to pick up my tickets for our vacation trip to Spain.

Agent (after searching): I'm sorry, but I am unable to find your tickets. Is it possible that someone else in your family may have already picked them up?

Client: No, we discussed it this morning and I said I would pick them up on the way home after work. We are scheduled to leave tomorrow morning and you are closing in just about ten minutes. If you have lost the ticket. . .

Agent (calmly interrupting): Don't worry. Just let me check our log. Whatever it takes to make things right we will take care of it. (Agent reviews the ticket receipt log). . .

CONTINUE ON YOUR OWN

❑ *CHAPTER NINE EXERCISE*

INSTRUCTIONS: Utilizing the listing of checks received that should be recorded on the Miscellaneous Receipts Log Record, complete the recording of the transactions on the Miscellaneous Receipts Log Record provided on page 148, figure 9–5. Calculate the total value of the five transactions and show that value at the bottom of the page in the appropriate column. Note: leave the "Acct No." block blank since the determination of the appropriate account number for several of the items listed will vary from agency to agency depending upon how agency management decides it wants to account for the receipt.

TRANSACTION NUMBER ONE

An override commission check in the amount of $2,147.50 was received on the eleventh of last month from Fly By Night Airways.

TRANSACTION NUMBER TWO

A reimbursement is received from the Put Em Up Hotel in Cody, Wyoming. It is for $246.10 and represents a refund to the agency for overpayment for a group that was booked into the hotel last week. The check came in yesterday.

TRANSACTION NUMBER THREE

Calamity Cruises sent the agency a check last Tuesday. It is for $54.09. This is a reimbursement for the flowers ordered to be put into the stateroom of the agency's clients, Mr. and Mrs. Giglesea. Attached to the note was a message indicating that the floral request was received after the ship had sailed, too late to provide the flowers.

TRANSACTION NUMBER FOUR

HackMe Car Rentals sent the agency a check for $3.00 as part of its new "Cash Bonus" program. For one month, it is issuing checks of $1.00 per booking to the clients' travel agency for every agency booking, paid at the end of each week and based on clients who actually pick up and return a rental car. The $3.00 check came in last Thursday and was deposited last Friday.

TRANSACTION NUMBER FIVE

A check for $19.18 from the agency's landlord, Strip Stripe Strip Malls Inc., was received the day before yesterday. This represents the agency's share of the balance of the money in the annual snow and leaf removal fund. According to the lease, one-tenth of one percent of each store 's annual lease fee is to be paid into the annual snow and leaf removal fund. Any balance in the fund is distributed back to mall stores at the end of the mall's fiscal year.

MISCELLANEOUS RECEIPTS LOG RECORD

RECORD NUMBER ________ MONTH ________

RCPT DATE	DEPOSIT DATE	RECEIVED FROM	AMOUNT	VALUE	COMMISSION	ACCT NO.

Figure 9–5

10

THE INCOME STATEMENT

OBJECTIVES

Upon completion of this chapter, the student will be able to:

- ❑ Explain the benefits to a travel agency of having detailed and accurate monthly and annual income statements
- ❑ Take line-item total expense and income figures for a one-month period for a travel agency and prepare a simple draft monthly income statement showing both end-of-month totals and year-to-date totals for both the month's income and the month's expenditures
- ❑ Explain the advantages and the disadvantages of considering familiarization trips to be marketing expenses
- ❑ Identify the three expense sections on the income statement and explain in general terms the line items included in each of the three expense sections

INTRODUCTION

The *income statement* is an instrument designed to tell executives of the company how much was earned and how much was spent each month. There are at least two terms used for this financial document. The term "income statement" is the most commonly used term among accountants. However, many small business owners and managers (and a large number of the executives in the travel agency industry) refer to it in a more descriptive way by calling it a "receipts and disbursements statement." In fact, this is exactly what the income statement does. It provides an inventory of all receipts (monies coming into the travel agency) and all disbursements (monies paid and therefore flowing out of the company) each month. The income statement, therefore, is an overview picture of the accounting or financial transactions that occurred during the month. In addition to monthly data, it also shows year-to-date figures for both receipts and disbursements. In this way it provides a basic overview picture of where the business stands on a year-to-date basis.

INCOME STATEMENT HEADER INFORMATION

To get a better understanding of how this works, review figure 10–1, a sample Income Statement. The form has the title "Income Statement" at the top. Normally after that comes the month for which the income statement is being prepared. Sometimes the income statement is prepared weekly—especially for a large business, and in that case the period will usually reflect the week of activity by indicating that it is the first, second, third, or fourth week of the month.

THE 'INCOME' PORTION OF THE INCOME STATEMENT

The income statement starts out by identifying the income received by the travel agency during the month. Basically the income will represent all of the money that came into the business during the month for which the statement is being prepared. This money is not total sales. This is commissions earned only. In other words, it is the money that is earned by the travel agency, not all sales (approximately 90 percent of total sales go to the supplier vendor—airline, tour company, etc.).

Air Commissions. In the case of the travel agency example shown, the business had an airline sales level of $21,828.58 in commissionable income. That is how much they earned in air commissions. In terms of actual sales, it was probably in the neighborhood of $218,286.00, since commissions on air average in the neighborhood of 10 percent. On a year-to-date basis up to the time of the preparation of this income statement, the commissions received on air sales is a little more than $145,000.00.

How does the accountant know that the commission earned during the past month for air sales is $21,828.58? Normally, the data for the income statement is taken directly from the ledgers in the agency. As each financial transaction is recorded on an invoice/receipt, the financial information from that invoice/receipt is transferred onto appropriate logs. If an invoice/receipt showed an air ticket sale, a tour sale, and perhaps airport transfers, the information from the invoice/receipt relating to the commissions earned for the air sale is transferred to the air ticket log. (In some agencies there will be one log for domestic air and another one for international air.) The invoice/receipt information about the tour sale commissions is transferred over to a log or journal recording all commissions earned from tour sales. The commissions taken for the airport transfer service are transferred to the agency journal documenting ground services commissions; or to the miscellaneous/general income log, if there are not enough ground services earnings in this

INCOME STATEMENT

FOR MONTH OF ___________, 19__

INCOME

ACCT. NO.	INCOME/EXPENSE FOR MONTH	ACCOUNT	INCOME/EXPENSE YEAR-TO-DATE
301	*21,828.58*	Air Commissions	*145,322.92*
302	*824.42*	Hotel Commissions	*5,056.32*
303	*1,235.47*	Car Rental Commissions	*8,892.75*
304	*296.70*	Cruise Commissions	*5,661.55*
305	*370.19*	Rail Commissions	*2,335.25*
306	*99.14*	Package Tour Commissions	*6,654.78*
307	*25.18*	Other: —*Service Charges*	*365.89*
308	*1,881.41*	Other: —*Own Tours*	*2,148.20*
	26,561.09	TOTAL INCOME	*176,437.66*
		EXPENSES	
		MARKETING EXPENSES	
401	*625.07*	Auto—Ticket Delivery	*2,493.75*
402	*310.19*	Auto—Other	*741.89*
403	*695.12*	Printing (Marketing)	*1,314.62*
404	*52.18*	Outside Sales Commissions	*461.23*
405	*324.60*	Advertising	*6,495.60*
406	*224.74*	Promotional Programs	*1,171.90*
407	*500.00*	Other: —*Educational Trips*	*774.45*
408	*54.38*	Other: —*Entertainment*	*264.40*
	2,786.28	TOTAL MARKETING EXPENSES	*13,717.84*
		PERSONNEL EXPENSES	
501	*7,106.61*	Inside Agent Salaries	*56,058.41*
502	*1,220.00*	Marketing Staff Salaries	*12,234.61*
503	*758.19*	Support Staff Salaries	*7,119.80*
504	*1,109.34*	Admin./Exec. Salaries	*16,333.41*
505	*860.44*	Taxes	*6,853.10*
506	*749.71*	Employee Benefits	*3,051.05*
507		Other:	
508		Other:	
	11,804.29	TOTAL PERSONNEL EXPENSES	*101,650.38*

Figure 10–1

INCOME STATEMENT

FOR MONTH OF ____________, 19__

EXPENSES

Acct. No.	Income/Expense For Month	Account	Income/Expense Year-To-Date
		ADMINISTRATIVE/OFFICE EXPENSES	
601		Accounting	*9,870.00*
602	*1,146.13*	Automation Costs	*10,318.88*
603	*105.15*	Dues	*1,243.42*
604	*10.00*	Educational Expenses	*637.73*
605	*38.00*	Fees	*319.08*
606	*603.42*	Insurance	*5,189.15*
607		Legal	*1,461.67*
608	*736.79*	Office Equip & Furn	*3,155.15*
609	*33.00*	Office Repairs & Maint	*136.56*
610	*356.09*	Office Supplies	*2,243.27*
611	*41.07*	Printing (Non Mktg)	*1,010.31*
612	*1,443.33*	Rent	*13,481.86*
613	*100.10*	Subscriptions	*783.45*
614	*1,421.18*	Telephone/Telex/Fax	*7,441.51*
615	*199.41*	Other: *—Postage & Express Mail*	*1,483.32*
616		Other:	
	6,233.67	TOTAL ADMIN/OFFICE EXP.	*58,775.36*
		SUMMARY	
	2,786.28	TOTAL MARKETING EXPENSES	*13,717.84*
	11,804.29	TOTAL PERSONNEL EXPENSES	*101,650.38*
	6,233.67	TOTAL ADMIN/OFFICE EXPENSES	*58,775.36*
	20,824.24	**TOTAL EXPENSES**	*174,143.58*
	5,736.85	**NET PROFIT (OR LOSS)**	*2,294.08*

Figure 10–1 (Continued)

agency to warrent having a separate category for ground services. Each month the totals of all logs and journals are balanced against such things as the ARC Report, bank deposits, accounts receivables, etc., to make sure that all figures are correct. Then the data totals are transferred to the appropriate columns on the income statement.

Some income statement forms break out air into domestic air and international air. This particular agency does not break out their air sales into domestic and international. They lump it all under one category, "Air Commission." Those agencies which sell little international air will often do this as they have not identified sufficient justification for breaking out all air sales into geographic type. On the other hand, some travel agencies break down the air sales into many categories, often by carrier for major carriers. This happens especially when they have (or hope to have) override commission agreements with one or more of the carriers. (These override commission agreements are bonuses for selling at or above negotiated quotas for an airline or for another vendor and are often tied to sales volume.)

Hotel Commissions. This agency also had hotel commissions. In the month covered by this income statement, the commissions received for hotel bookings was $824.42 and the year-to-date hotel commission income was a little over $5,000.00.

Car Rental Commissions. For many travel agencies, car rental commissions constitute either the second or third highest amount of income. Again, for this agency it is a major source of income both for the current month and on a year-to-date basis.

Cruise Commissions. Cruise commissions are shown next. In the example shown, as with tours, the commissions received for the month are less than normal, but in every category there will be some "off" months.

Rail Commissions. Rail commissions can be an important category for some travel agencies. With this particular agency, rail sales constitute a sufficient amount of income to be important.

Packaged Tour Commissions. The agency earned commission income on packaged tours. It would appear that this was a very light month for packaged tour commissions, however, since only slightly less than $100 was received as compared to well over $6,000 for the year to date.

Other Income. Other income category lines are provided. This agency has used one of them to reflect service charges. This particular travel agency levies only a small amount of service charges.

When a travel agency runs a number of its own tour groups as this one does, an "Other" column is assigned to "Other—Own Tours." Some agencies do not run any of their own tours while others run a large number of their own tours. When there is more than one tour being run by an agency, it is important to keep journal records separately on each tour being run. However, most travel agencies will show only one line entry on the income statement (as this one does) reflecting all commission income earned during the month for all of its own tours for which the agency received commissions. When agencies run many tours, especially several expensive tours, they will sometimes identify commission income (really profit rather than commission) from each tour on the income statement, assigning a separate line number to each tour rather than grouping all tours together.

This agency sold no F.I.T.s (Foreign Independent Tours). Some agencies, however, sell a large number of F.I.T.s, and for a few it is one of their top income generating sources. Because F.I.T.s (and their domestic equivalents, D.I.T.s) are priced differently than most other travel sales, it is good to have a separate line item on the income statement for them. Those agencies selling many F.I.T.s also typically sell a large number of D.I.T.s. In some cases they will lump both F.I.T.s and D.I.T.s into the same category (F.I.T.); in other cases they will separate them out, writing in a line item category for D.I.T.s. When this is done, one of the "Other" lines in the income portion of the income statement is used to show F.I.T.s or D.I.T.s.

At the bottom of the income column one adds all income lines for the month to determine the total income received for the month. In the case of the example in figure 10–1, it is $26,561.09. The total income year-to-date is also added up and calculated. In this case, it is $176,437.66. All of the income, therefore, is shown and summarized.

THE EXPENSE SECTIONS

Next, the agency's accountant, bookkeeper, or other financial executive determines the expenses incurred during the current month and on a year-to-date basis. Expenses are broken down into three categories: 1) Marketing Expenses, 2) Personnel Expenses, and 3) Administrative/Office Expenses.

Marketing Expenses

The disbursements/expenses section of the income statement starts with the Marketing Expenses. The major marketing cost which is not reflected here is the cost of marketing personnel. That cost accounts for more than 50 percent of the marketing costs of many travel agencies. It is shown in the "Personnel

Expenses" section of the income statement, since the actual line item expenses are for salaries, payroll and other employee related taxes, and benefits. Because of the common and accepted accounting practice of showing marketing personnel costs in the personnel expenses section and not in the marketing section, the real allocation of marketing expenses in travel (and many other) businesses is skewed and not truly representative of what the company(ies) actually spend(s) on marketing.

Automobile Expenses. Looking at the marketing (sales) expenses shown in figure 10–1, the first line item is for automobile ticket delivery expenses. In many cases automobile expenses cover the cost of ticket delivery. In some travel agencies, ticket delivery staff members are expected to use their own cars and are reimbursed on a mileage basis. In other cases the agency will buy, or more often lease, a car for the purpose of delivering tickets. A few agencies also have automobiles that the agency owns or leases for full-time salespeople as well. In some cases, full-time and/or part-time salespeople will be given either a flat monthly or mileage-based allowance or reimbursement. However it is calculated, what normally goes into the line item for automobile usually is an allocation to cover the cost of delivering tickets and/or the cost of transportation in conjunction with the sales effort.

Printing. Printing costs in some agencies can be substantial. Much of the printing costs are often for marketing materials. Many agencies break out the cost of printing, showing that which is for marketing in the "Marketing Expenses" section and other printing in the "Administrative/Office Expenses" section.

Outside Sales Commissions. The next line is for commissions paid to outside salespersons. This is normally commissions for outside sales representatives who work for the travel agency only on an outside sales basis—usually as independent contractors. Again, one must be careful in considering total marketing expenses. In this case, the salaries (called outside sales commissions here) are included in the marketing or the selling expenses category of disbursements or expenses; whereas full-time staff people who are partly or totally employed in the sales and marketing effort have their salaries and benefits shown in the "Personnel Expenses" section. Theoretically, if a part-time person is an excellent salesperson, then while that person is working on a part-time basis, his/her remuneration is shown as a marketing expense. However, when hired on a full-time basis, the compensation cost allocation moves to the Personnel Expenses category.

Advertising and Promotion. Some travel agencies, especially high volume leisure-travel oriented agencies, spend a considerable amount of money on advertising and promotional programs (efforts). Others spend almost nothing on advertising and promotion, preferring to spend marketing monies on other marketing strategies. The biggest problem here is sorting out what is advertising and what is a promotional program and then consistently allocating the expenses for each of these marketing strategies to the appropriate expense lines.

Other: —Educational Trips. Many agencies will call familiarization trips educational and allocate their costs to the marketing budget. Some in the industry do not consider familiarization trips to be a marketing expense. However, the reasoning behind placing it in this category of costs is that by having travel agents familiar with a destination, they are better able to sell that destination to clients. Therefore, the expense becomes a marketing expense. This reasoning is certainly justified when there is a direct relationship between the destination of the familiarization trip and the destination sold most of the time by the agent taking that trip. For example, if the agency divides the world into geographical specialization areas and the agency's Africa specialist takes a trip to the Union of South Africa, the allocation of the costs of that familiarization trip to marketing can be understood and most would consider that to be a reasonable allocation. However, when the travel agency's accountant takes a familiarization trip to the Union of South Africa and allocates the expenses to marketing, one might question the appropriateness.

"FAM" Trips. The reason given (by most who discuss it in the industry) for allocating FAM trips to "Marketing Expenses" is the fact that if it is a justifiable business marketing expense, it becomes a business expense. Therefore it is not considered to be personal compensation for the agency employee taking the trip. It does not become subject to individual income tax as a benefit or as employee compensation. However, many of these allocations add to the cost of marketing and, just as not considering marketing personnel a marketing cost skews the marketing budget and marketing expense figures to make them appear lower than they really should be, so also allocating FAM trip costs (that result in no additional sales for the agency) to the marketing budget skews the marketing figure to make it appear higher than it really should be.

Other: —Entertainment. The cost of client entertainment is a valid marketing expense for some travel agencies. Some agencies which specialize in business travel and actively solicit corporate accounts, often spend a considerable amount of money in taking potential clients to lunch or dinner, attending conventions, and having potential and current clients (corporate travel managers, company purchasing executives) up to a hospitality suite during conventions. They are continuously soliciting business in many ways. A number of travel industry executives are concerned with the semantics of calling this expense "entertainment," but that has become the common term in the industry for this expense. When an agency has this type of expense, it is usually entered on one of the "other" lines in the "Marketing Expenses" section.

Personnel Expenses

The next grouping of expenses is all those that are considered personnel costs. These come under the title "Personnel Expenses." If outside sales representatives are used, personnel expenses do not cover the costs of all personnel, however, since the compensation paid to outside sales people comes under "Marketing Expenses." Personnel expenses are especially important, nevertheless, because in the average travel agency they account for approximately half of the agency's total costs. They therefore need to be watched very carefully.

Sales Salaries. The first of the personnel costs to be considered is that of "Sales Salaries." As with some of the other category titles, the semantics are sometimes a problem. When one thinks of sales, one usually thinks of someone going out on the street and calling on clients or potential clients. However, the common use for this general expense allocation category is to record the salary costs of those in the travel agency who are commonly referred to as inside sales agents. It is used as well for the "outside" or "other" marketing staff. The inside sales agent is the person who sits at a desk or a counter in a travel agency and handles the travel needs of walk-in clients and of clients who call in travel trip requests. Outside sales agents are the people who go out on the street to make sales calls.

Marketing staff salaries, however, may include more than salaries for outside salespersons. They also include the salaries of telemarketers and customer service representatives.

Support Staff Salaries. The next line is "Support Staff Salaries." This is for those people in the company who are not actually selling tickets. They are not marketing people nor are they officers or administrators of the travel agency. In many cases there will be no salaries or amounts of money appearing in this column. This is especially true for small volume travel agencies. Some agencies choose to have people who are really administrative people listed on this line. The "Support Staff Salaries" line is designed to reflect the salaries of the following staff members: receptionist, full- or part-time secretaries, ticket delivery or a ticket delivery/ticket processing personnel, and full- or part-time accounting/bookkeeping personnel (there are several titles used for this position). There are others in some travel agencies whose titles result in their salaries being reflected in this category as well.

Administrative/Executive Salaries. The "Administrative/Executive Salaries" section, as the line suggests, covers all who are administrators or executives. In the small and many medium-sized travel agencies one often finds that no one works in a purely administrative/executive role. The typical owner/manager of a small travel agency will sell travel much of the time and then perform the administrative and executive duties whenever there is time. Often this means in the evening and on weekends. The income statement is designed with the idea in mind that the person who performs more than one role will allocate a break down of the salary in accordance with the time spent in each role. However, relatively few owner/managers of small agencies do this. The more common practice is for them to place their entire salary in the "Administrative/Executive Salary" category. When there are two or more partners/stockholders in a small volume agency, this practice can substantially skew the income statement making it appear to potential buyers that sales personnel were tremendously productive and that the agency is very much top-heavy with administrators and executives. However, the fact is that the people who show their salaries as administrators and executives have sometimes sold more travel than have the people whose salaries are shown in the "Inside Agent Salaries" category.

Taxes. The "Taxes" line is straightforward and self-explanatory. Occasionally one finds that a person new to bookkeeping will make a record on this line of tax commitment (those monies still owed to the government) rather than the payroll taxes actually paid (already paid). Or sometimes, they might show both paid taxes and tax commitments. These errors should not happen. This line is intended to reflect only actual payroll taxes already paid. It is not for payroll tax obligations that may have been incurred but not yet paid.

Employee Benefits. The last line (except for two "other" lines) in the "Personnel Expenses" section of the income statement is for "Employee Benefits." With the possible exception of FAM trip benefit expenses, all benefits paid to employees are reflected on this line. Even though insurance is listed as a separate line item under "Occupancy and Administrative Expenses," employee insurance premium payments are reflected on the "Employee Benefits" line. Employee life, accident, medical, and other personal insurance are normally considered to be company-paid or partially company-paid benefits.

Monthly and Year-To-Date Totals. As with the totals for "Marketing Expenses," the monthly totals for "Personnel Expenses" should be added up and reflected at the bottom of the left-hand (monthly) column. Likewise the total year-to-date "Personnel Expenses" should be added up and reflected at the bottom of the right-hand (year-to-date) column.

Administrative/Office Expense

The "Other" expenses title that is used to reflect all other agency costs on the income statement is titled "Administrative/Office Expenses." Actually there should be no "Other Expense" category on the income statement. Every expense should be allocated to some line on the income statement. One will note right away that there are more line items in the "Administrative/Office Expenses" section of the income statement than in either the "Marketing Expenses" or the "Personnel Expenses" sections.

Accounting. Accounting fees become a factor of consideration when the travel agency uses an outside accounting firm to prepare its monthly, quarterly, and annual accounting and financial reports. Most travel agencies will have bookkeeping tasks performed by someone within the agency, or the agency will use some type of automated accounting system. Some of these are also interface systems that transfer accounting data directly to the accounting software data base whenever a ticket is issued by the automated reservation system. Whether the agency is using internal staff or automated accounting interface systems, most travel agencies will have some costs reflected in this line item because most agencies will have their financial records at least checked by an outside accounting firm (sometimes a C.P.A.) once a year. This type of authentication of financial records is valuable when the owner(s) of the travel agency wish to sell and wish to document a history of a specific level of profitability over a period of years.

Educational Expenses. "Educational Expenses" are clear-cut expenses most of the time. These can be FAM trips, training programs, seminars, and workshops. Computer reservation training updates, especially for the agency's key or trainer-reservationist, usually need to be attended at least once a year. As can be seen by the sample income statement, many travel agencies spend very little on ongoing educational expenses.

Fees. The line item for "Fees" is sometimes confused with the "Dues" line. This expense category is normally reserved for federal, state, and local licensing and fee expenses, e.g., an annual business license. ARC and IATAN dues are sometimes included here, but most travel agencies carry these expenses in the "Dues" category.

Insurance. As noted above, the "Insurance" line-item in the "Administrative/ Office Expenses" section of the income statement does not reflect payments for individual employee insurance, since this is usually considered to be an employee benefit. Rather, the insurance line here is used to reflect payments for business insurance, such as fire, theft, key man, and so forth.

Legal. Many travel agencies have no legal expenses in most months—sometimes for several years. However, the line item is provided for agencies to reflect this expense when they need it.

Office Equipment vs. Office Supplies. "Office Equipment and Furnishings" and "Office Supplies" are two line-items in this section of the income statement that sometimes confuse the travel agent when deciding what expense to put in each category. The difference between office equipment and office supplies can be confusing. For a basic understanding of the differences, one should understand that those items that are considered permanent (e.g., desks, chairs) are normally accounted for in the "Office Equipment" category while those that are expendable (used up)—e.g., envelopes, pencils—are accounted for in "Office Supplies."

The Need to "Break Out" Office Supplies and Printing. Many in the industry are not comfortable with the grouping of office supplies and printing into the same category. Therefore, most agencies show these two expenses separately, rather than together as one expense. Even within the category of printing, some travel agencies keep breakdowns in the form of logs. They want to know how much is spent for specific types of printing. And, since for some agencies much of the printing costs are associated with tours and marketing, some break out the printing line into three categories: 1) General Printing, 2) Tour Printing (normally broken out still further by allocating these expenses on a tour-by-tour basis, either by tour number or by tour name), and 3) Marketing Printing (these expenses may also be broken out further by marketing project name or number, or by marketing strategy name or number). The Marketing Printing Expenses, of course, are marketing expenses. They are shown in the "Marketing Expenses" section of the income statement on line 403.

Office Repairs and Maintenance. For most travel agencies, the "Office Repairs and Maintenance" line represents small payment amounts. This covers normal wear-and-tear repair expenses as well as payments made for maintenance contracts.

Rent. Perhaps the most predictable line-item expense in the "Administrative/Office Expenses" section is the one devoted to rent. Unless there is a new contract or unless variables (such as utilities or common area maintenance fees) are included in monthly billings, the rent will remain the same from month to month.

Telephone, Telex, Fax. "Telephone, Telex, Fax" is a line item that also groups some costs that can be misleading when considering the terminology. Prior to deregulation of the telephone industry, business telephone systems were rented. Today the cost of the equipment itself is purchased, instead of rented, and it can be very expensive. Some agencies lump these monthly payments for telephone equipment (usually paying off a loan for the equipment) in the telephone/telex/fax costs. However, others consider telephone equipment costs to be an office equipment expense and reflect it on that line of the income statement. Still others will not show the expense on the income statement at all, but on the balance sheet as a loan obligation of the agency.

Ongoing telephone/telex/fax costs normally include monthly telephone line charges and monthly phone usage charges. In addition, there may be charges for fax equipment usage, teletype equipment usage, and telex charges. The telephone lines used for the travel agency's reservations computers are sometimes reflected in this section of agency costs. Some agencies, however, will show these costs as part of their "Automation Costs."

Postage. Many, especially small travel agencies, have little postage and pay all postage costs out of petty cash. Other travel agencies have a sufficient amount of postage expense to justify having postage as a separate cost line-item. They may even purchase and use a postage meter. This makes the tracking of postage costs easy. Some will buy stamps from petty cash and get receipts for items mailed from the post office, necessitating a breaking out of postage expenses from petty cash receipts at the end of the month if postage becomes a separate line item. Express mail can be handled either by contract with an express mail service (with an end-of-month bill for usage), or by using the United States Post Office express mail service and getting receipts at the post office every time the service is used. Those agencies with considerable express mail usually work with a monthly contract, the bill for which can work as a monthly log. Those with only occasional express mail needs will usually send the item through the postal service and get a receipt.

Additional Cost Items. The "Administrative/Office Expenses" section of the income statement provides two empty lines on which to write in additional cost item. As noted above, postage charges do not appear on the income statement. Therefore, many who use this form write in their postage costs here. Others use these lines for expenses that are unique to their travel agency.

Administrative/Office Expense Totals. As with the other expense subsections, the "Administrative/Office Expenses" monthly line costs should be added up and shown at the bottom in the left-hand column. The year-to-date figures should also be added to provide a total that is recorded in the right-hand column.

EXPENSE SUMMARY SECTION

At the bottom of the income statement one can summarize the total "Marketing Expenses," the total "Personnel Expenses," and the total "Administrative/Office Expenses." By combining all three expense categories, one can calculate total monthly expenses in the left column and total year-to-date expenses in the right column.

DETERMINING PROFIT OR LOSS

By subtracting total expenses from total income, it is possible to determine whether there was a profit or a loss for the month, and the amount of that profit or loss. On the sample income statement, figure 10–1, there was a monthly profit of well over $5,000; while the year-to-date figure shows a profit of about $2,300. This bottom line figure tells the travel agency's executives where the business stands both for the month just ending and for the year as a whole up to the end of last month.

OTHER INCOME STATEMENTS

Many income statements, ranging radically in size, style, and detail have been developed for travel agencies, but a large number of them were based on the early industry income statements.

SUMMARY

The income statement is a form that is utilized to provide basic data as to what the income is and what the expenditures are. There really are only two ways to create a profit and both are reflected on the income statement. One way is to sell more. That will be reflected when comparing the income section of the one's current income statement to the income section of the same month of the previous year. The other way is to spend less. This too will be reflected when comparing the current expense columns with those of the same month of the previous year.

Therefore, the income statement is and should be considered a crucial document. It is utilized in all major businesses. It is a basic starting point for looking at budgeting for the next fiscal year. One determines whether or not a profit was earned and what the level of profit was, and whether there was a loss and what the level of loss was. This document helps management to start taking some educated guesses as to what should be done differently to create profits or to build greater profits than existed before.

The income statement and the balance sheet are the two documents most businesses consider crucial for them to prepare at the end of each month and at the end of the business's fiscal year. The next chapter will address balance sheets and will show a close tie in with the income statement.

❑ DISCUSSION QUESTIONS

1. What information is in the "Header" section at the top of the income statement?
2. How does the agency accountant or bookkeeper know how much commission was earned during the past month for air sales?
3. What options do agencies use in reflecting sales of their own agency tour groups on the income statement?
4. What major marketing cost is not usually reflected in the sales section of the income statement, why does it not appear there, and where does it appear?
5. What are the pros and cons of considering familiarization trips as marketing expenses?
6. What problem(s) can arise out of showing the entire salary of both owners of a small travel agency as administrative salary?
7. What kinds of expenses are shown in the "office equipment and furnishings" category and what kind of expenses are shown in the "office supplies" category?
8. What are some of the line recording options open to travel agency accountants and bookkeepers for reflecting the cost of telephone equipment?
9. If agency management asks for the exact amount spent on telex messages last year, why might this question not be simply answered by glancing at the end-of-year income statement?
10. By examining the columns of figures on the income statement, how does the agency accountant or bookkeeper determine whether there was a profit or a loss for the month and the amount of that profit or loss?

❑ ROLE-PLAYING EXERCISE

Two students may participate in this role-playing exercise either as an out-of-class or in-class fun way to review the benefits of the income statement to a travel agency. One student plays the travel agency's bookkeeper. The other plays a senior agent who has just been offered stock in the travel agency and a position on the Board of Directors in exchange for signing a long-term employment contract. Please read the script and then pick up the conversation in your own words.

Senior Agent: This is the first company in which I have held any stock or a position on the Board of Directors. There are a number of financial documents I do not understand and I would appreciate it if you would give me a brief explanation of them.

Agency Bookkeeper: I will be happy to assist. Which document would you like to start with?

Senior Agent: The income statement. I understand that it shows the monies brought in and the monies spent during the past month, but I don't understand what purpose that serves or how it can be of any benefit to agency management or to our Board.

Agency Bookkeeper: The income statement is a very important document for the agency. Let me start my explanation by. . .

CONTINUE ON YOUR OWN

❑ CHAPTER TEN EXERCISE

INSTRUCTIONS: Utilizing the information from figure 10–1 and presuming that the data in the column on the left side reflects financial activity for the travel agency for the month before last month, complete the blank income statement (figure 10–2, the last pages of this exercise) incorporating the data and the figures from the information provided on the next page. These figures are for last month's financial activity in the travel agency. These totals come from logs, journals, and other sources kept in the agency.

LAST MONTH'S DATA TO BE USED IN PREPARING THE INCOME STATEMENT

1. Receipts and information from the ticket delivery person indicate a total expenditure on automobile expenses of $301.25.
2. Newspaper advertising bills total $125.10.
3. The cruise commission log indicates receipts of commissions totaling $331.20.
4. Check receipts for salaries show the following totals paid in salaries: 1) Agents — $8,412.22; 2) Marketing Staff — $1,219.18; and 3) All others — $1,427.39.
5. Compensation logs reflect payroll taxes paid in the amount of $780.21.
6. The rail commission log shows a receipt of commissions for the sale of Eurailpasses. This total was $56.00. Another rail entry indicates that Amtrak sales commissions were $201.95.
7. Agency contributions to agent FAM trips for this past month totaled $107.
8. The senior agent turned in automobile receipts reflecting expenditures during the time he/she covered for the ticket delivery person who was on vacation. These expenditures totaled $320.19.
9. Telephone usage charges for local calls and line charges totaled $1,025.18.
10. The cost for a booth taken at the Chamber of Commerce annual meeting was $94.50. A potential client met at the function was taken to dinner that evening and the cost for that dinner was $65.20, including tips.
11. The office supply house bill totaled $514.83.
12. Automation expenses totaled $1,092.21.
13. Airline commissions totaled $23,617.39.
14. Long-distance telephone charges totaled $63.51.
15. The company's share of payments for employee life and health insurance totaled $425.
16. The accountant's bill for the past quarter, which was paid last month, was $3,111.91.
17. The printer's bill for printing the newsletter and the Grand Bahamas tour brochure was $1,012.94.
18. Commissions paid to outside sales representatives totaled $94.30.
19. Rent costs totaled $1,443.33.
20. The car rental commissions log indicates commission receipts of $952.20.
21. The Chamber of Commerce membership fee was paid last month. The total paid was $94.
22. The postage meter total was $225.
23. The hotel commission log indicates a total receipt in hotel commissions of $715.12.
24. The *Travel Weekly* three-year subscription fee was $39.50.
25. The Federal Express monthly bill totaled $41.82.
26. The Errors and Omissions insurance premium payment totaled $413.43.
27. The package tour commission log reflected a commission income of $1,180.94.

INCOME STATEMENT FOR MONTH OF ____________, 19__ INCOME			
ACCT. No.	INCOME/EXPENSE FOR MONTH	ACCOUNT	INCOME/EXPENSE YEAR-TO-DATE
301		Air Commissions	
302		Hotel Commissions	
303		Car Rental Commissions	
304		Cruise Commissions	
305		Rail Commissions	
306		Package Tour Commissions	
307		Other:	
308		Other:	
		TOTAL INCOME	
		EXPENSES	
		MARKETING EXPENSES	
401		Auto—Ticket Delivery	
402		Auto—Other	
403		Printing (Marketing)	
404		Outside Sales Commissions	
405		Advertising	
406		Promotional Programs	
407		Other:	
408		Other:	
		TOTAL MARKETING EXPENSES	
		PERSONNEL EXPENSES	
501		Inside Agent Salaries	
502		Marketing Staff Salaries	
503		Support Staff Salaries	
504		Admin./Exec. Salaries	
505		Taxes	
506		Employee Benefits	
507		Other:	
508		Other:	
		TOTAL PERSONNEL EXPENSES	

Figure 10–2

INCOME STATEMENT

FOR MONTH OF ____________, 19__

EXPENSES

Acct. No.	Income/Expense For Month	Account	Income/Expense Year-To-Date
		ADMINISTRATIVE/OFFICE EXPENSES	
601		Accounting	
602		Automation Costs	
603		Dues	
604		Educational Expenses	
605		Fees	
606		Insurance	
607		Legal	
608		Office Equip & Furn	
609		Office Repairs & Maint	
610		Office Supplies	
611		Printing (Non Mktg)	
612		Rent	
613		Subscriptions	
614		Telephone/Telex/Fax	
615		Other:	
616		Other:	
		TOTAL ADMIN/OFFICE EXP.	
		SUMMARY	
		TOTAL MARKETING EXPENSES	
		TOTAL PERSONNEL EXPENSES	
		TOTAL ADMIN/OFFICE EXPENSES	
		TOTAL EXPENSES	
		NET PROFIT (OR LOSS)	

Figure 10–2 (Continued)

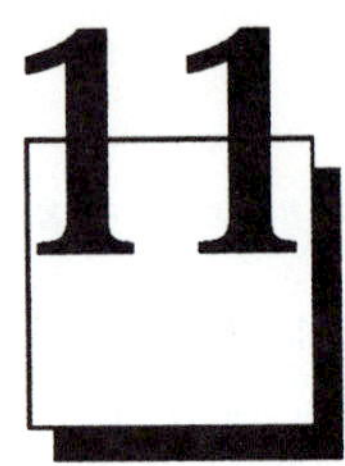

THE BALANCE SHEET

OBJECTIVES

Upon completion of this chapter, the student will be able to:

- ❑ Identify the titles of the categories of financial data needed to complete the travel agency balance sheet and several options for alternative titles and approaches
- ❑ Complete a simple balance sheet when the financial figures are provided in each required category of assets, liabilities, and capital
- ❑ List the reasons why some travel agencies list account numbers under the "Cash in Bank" section of "Current Assets"
- ❑ Explain the reasoning used by travel agency accountants to justify the elimination of a line on the balance sheet for "advanced deposits from customers"

INTRODUCTION

The balance sheet is normally the document that is considered and reviewed most by the owners of the business. They tend to be more concerned with this than with any other document. The balance sheet basically tells the reader where the business stands at any particular time. Usually the time that concerns people is the end of the fiscal year. The fiscal year, incidentally, does not have to coincide with or be the same as the calendar year, although in many cases it does. The fiscal year for many government entities, for example, starts on 1 July, while for other government entities it starts on 1 October.

THE BALANCE SHEET

The *balance sheet* shows how much money (or monetary equivalents) the company has and how much the company owes. In this regard, it is somewhat like the income statement, which shows income and expenditures. However, the balance sheet is not concerned with a flow of money, i.e., earnings and disbursements, but rather with the financial status of all aspects of the business at a point in time. It includes value or income from sources other than commission and fee earnings. For example, it will reflect the value of the building in which the travel agency is located, if the agency either owns or, more likely, is in the process of purchasing its own building.

Note figure 11–1. This shows a sample balance sheet from a standard industry accounting system. Like most balance sheets, it compares assets with liabilities and capital. Some prefer to compare assets with liabilities and equity. To some extent the difference is one of semantics, though many believe that equity is a more appropriate term when working with travel agencies.

ASSETS

Assets are cash, marketable securities (anything that can be exchanged quite rapidly), accounts receivables (this should be a net figure), and prepaid expenses and deposits. In some cases they are listed just this way. There are substitute titles for categories of assets and there are additional titles, as well. On the balance sheet in the example shown, figure 11–1, cash is broken down into "Cash in Bank" and "Petty Cash." This is a good breakdown because it reflects the reality of how cash is accounted for and how it is kept in, for, and by a travel agency. Some agencies will list account numbers under the "Cash in Bank" section, since the air carriers encourage agencies to maintain at least two current bank checking accounts (discussed in chapter 8).

Accounts Receivables

"Accounts Receivables" is listed next. These items appear in chart-of-accounts number 110. "Accounts Receivables" is the money that is owed to the business. This may or may not be good income. Some clients who have been billed will move or may simply disappear, resulting in some accounts receivables money having to be ultimately written off as *bad debt*. That usually happens either at the time that becomes a certainty or after repeated efforts to collect the money have failed. Sometimes part of a bad debt can be salvaged by selling the debt to a collection agency for a fraction of the amount of money owed.

Notes Receivable

Chart-of-accounts line-item 111 is "Notes Receivable." In most cases this will be the account where money owed to the travel agency (debts for loans or,

BALANCE SHEET

FOR: ___________ 19__

CURRENT ASSETS

Increase/ Decrease			Account	Balance	
			120 Cash in Bank—ARC Acct		
			121 Cash in Bank—Other Acct		
			122 Cash in Bank—Other Acct		
			123 Petty Cash		
			124 Other:		
			125 Other:		
			110 Accounts Receivable		
			111 Notes Receivable		
			112 Investment:		
			113 Investment:		
			114 Other:		
			199 TOTAL CURRENT ASSETS		
			OTHER ASSETS		
			200 Automation Equipment		
			201 Less Depreciation		
			202 Office Equipment		
			203 Less Depreciation		
			204 Automobile		
			205 Less Depreciation		
			206 Other:		
			207 Less Depreciation		
			299 TOTAL OTHER ASSETS		
			TOTAL ASSETS		

Figure 11–1

BALANCE SHEET

FOR: ____________ 19__

LIABILITIES AND CAPITAL

INCREASE/ DECREASE			ACCOUNT	BALANCE	
			LIABILITIES		
			910 Accounts Payable—ARC		
			911 Accounts Payable—Hotels		
			912 Accounts Payable—Car Rental		
			913 Accounts Payable—Cruises		
			914 Accounts Payable—Rail		
			915 Accounts Payable—Tours		
			916 Accounts Payable—Automation		
			917 Accounts Payable—Other:		
			920 Notes Payable		
			901 Federal Income Tax Withheld		
			902 State Income Tax Withheld		
			904 Local Income Tax Withheld		
			905 City Income Tax Withheld		
			903 FICA Tax Withheld		
			999 TOTAL LIABILITIES		
			CAPITAL		
			800 Invested Capital		
			801 Retained Earnings		
			810 Withdrawals		
			820 PROFIT OR LOSS (THIS YEAR)		
			830 NET CAPITAL		
			TOTAL LIABILITIES AND CAPITAL		

Figure 11–1 (Continued)

more often, for contracted services) are recorded. However, some agencies will also list prepaid expenses and deposits here as well. This category can be a very important one. Several travel agencies have had major problems when selling because several thousand dollars of cruise deposits had been sent to suppliers and they were either improperly accounted for or, in some cases, there were disagreements about the commissions involved. Were these monies construed to be the deposits themselves (in which case, it is generally agreed that they belong to the seller), or had the commissions already been paid (in which case the buyer gets the commissions)? Because of the problems that can occur in the event of a sale when "Notes Receivable" includes prepaid expenses and deposits, it is suggested that "Prepaid Expenses and Deposits" be a separate and distinct balance sheet line. Line number 114 provides a place on the balance sheet where this can be done.

Investments. "Investments" (chart-of-accounts number 112 and 113), come next on the balance sheet. Some agencies break this down into two categories: 1) Marketable Securities (those items that can be converted to cash quite rapidly, such as Certificates of Deposit), and 2) Other Investments (for example, the office building in which the travel agency is located, if the agency owns or is buying its own building).

The Current Assets Subtotal

The first subtotal is the one for current assets. All of the above lines are added up to provide the amount shown as "Total Current Assets."

Other Assets

"Other Assets" is the title of the second half of the "Assets" section of the balance sheet. Some will use the term "Long-Term Assets" to compare it with "Current Assets" and indeed the "Other Assets" section in figure 11–1 does reflect long-term assets. Some balance sheets go further and break down "Other Assets" or "Long-Term Assets" into the two subcategories of "Tangible Assets" and "Intangible Assets." This type of breakdown can be beneficial in the event of a sale when a buyer may be looking for a substantial amount of "Tangible Assets" that can ultimately be converted to cash.

Automation Equipment. Automation equipment can be a major asset for a travel agency. If it is old and outdated, however, it can be worthless or almost worthless. Including accurate, true valuations rather than inflated values is important.

Office Equipment. Office equipment is shown on line 202 and the allowance for the depreciation of office equipment is shown on line 203. By subtracting the allowance for depreciation from the office equipment cost one determines the balance sheet total for office equipment.

Automobiles. One of the "Other Assets" listed is "Automobiles," chart-of-accounts line-item number 204. This is followed by line 205, which is an allowance for depreciation. If the agency owned a car, the cost of the car would appear on line 204 and the depreciation would appear on line 205. Line 205 would be considered a negative figure.

Depreciation. Many accountants will put brackets around all negative figures, so that the depreciation allowances (for automobiles and for office equipment) would be seen as negative figures (sometimes referred to by accountants as "contra assets").

Tangible vs. Intangible Assets. As noted earlier, another way of treating "Other Assets" is to call them "Long-Term Assets." These can then be broken down into "Tangible Assets" and "Intangible Assets." When this is done, the accountant will usually show a total for each type of asset. There will be a "Total Tangible Assets" figure and a "Total Intangible Assets" figure to be added together in order to get the "Total Assets" figure for the company. Whether one works with the term "Other Assets" or "Long-Term Assets" (breaking down long-term into tangible and intangible) the "Total Assets" figure should be the same. The system used by the accountant depends upon how comfortable the accountant and the agency's management/owners are with the semantics involved and with the category breakdowns provided.

Leasehold Improvements and Goodwill. Some of the other terms that are used, but which do not appear on the industry example provided, are "Leasehold Improvements" and "Goodwill."

The "Leasehold Improvements" figure reflects the value of any improvements made to the building or the property where the travel agency is located. Many will consider only permanent improvements, i.e., things that can not be moved to a new location. Painting the offices and adding electrical wiring for the automation equipment are two examples of leasehold improvements.

Of special importance is the term "Goodwill." This is the term used to describe the value of the customers who buy from the travel agency. In the event of a sale of the travel agency, goodwill becomes a major factor. Typically, when a buyer purchases a travel agency, much of what is being purchased is goodwill. For example, if a buyer purchases a travel agency that is grossing (selling) $1,500,000 of annual business and the buyer pays $120,000 for that agency, it is probable that the total value of materials, supplies, and equipment in the agency will not exceed $40,000. The other $80,000 represents the purchase of goodwill. Therefore, the value of current and especially of current, repeat clients is very important.

LIABILITIES AND CAPITAL/EQUITIES

The second half of the balance sheet is called either "Liabilities and Capital" or "Liabilities and Equities," again depending upon the semantics and category breakdowns management prefers.

Liabilities

The first of the two sections of this part of the balance sheet refers to liabilities. One approach is to just list all liabilities, grouping them by type. This is the approach that the industry example shown in figure 11–1 uses. Another approach is to break down liabilities into types and to label the broad category appropriately. For example, some accountants show "Current Liabilities" and "Long-Term Liabilities." Some of the "Current Liabilities" subsections may be: 1) Accounts Payable—ARC (usually those monies reflected in the ARC Report); 2) Accounts Payable—Other; 3) Accrued Taxes Payable (this is often broken down further by type of tax); 4) Notes Payable—Short Term; and 5) Advance Deposits from Customers (monies the customers have paid to the travel agency, but which belong to suppliers and have not yet been sent to suppliers). The only long-term liability usually showing on a travel agency's balance sheet is "Notes Payable" and this is for long-term notes payable since short-term notes payable are usually considered part of current liabilities.

Accounts Payable—ARC. In the example seen in figure 11–1, the first line in the "Liabilities" section is "Accounts Payable—ARC." As noted above, this is usually the total of all money owed but not yet paid to ARC. For a better understanding of how this figure is calculated, see chapter 8.

Accounts Payable—Other Carriers. Agencies owing money to a specific carrier will usually reflect this on another line reading "Account Payable" and then name the carrier on this line. This usually occurs when a travel agency acts either as a general sales agent for an individual airline (usually a foreign carrier) or if the travel agency is allowed to have a particular carrier's ticket stock because of the high volume of tickets issued on that carrier. Under such circumstances a settlement arrangement similar to the ARC area bank settlement plan is devised between the travel agency and the airline for payment to be made on an agreed upon periodic basis. Theoretically, a travel agency might have several lines of "Accounts Payable" to individual carriers, listing a different line for each carrier to which money is owed. In practice, however, there are seldom more than two individual carriers at a time with which an agency might work out individual settlement arrangements. When this occurs, normally the point system is used. For example, the line for the first carrier (carrier A) might read: 910.1, Carrier A. And the line for the second carrier might read: 910.2, Carrier B.

Accounts Payable—Car Rental. Line 912 is "Accounts Payable—Car Rental." Most car rental transactions for travel agencies create receivables rather than payables. This is because in most cases a reservation is made for the client and the client is provided with confirmation numbers and other reservation information. However, the client does not pay the travel agency for the rental car. All payment is made by the client directly to the car rental company. After the client has returned the car and paid the car rental company, a check is written by the car rental company to the travel agency for the agency's commission for booking the car rental. The check is mailed to the travel agency at that time. Almost all car rentals handled by travel agencies are booked in this fashion.

However, there are circumstances where an accounts payable to the car rental company can be created. This normally happens under two circumstances. One is when a client wants a special car that requires an up-front deposit or up-front full payment for the rental. In this case the agency collects the money from the client and sends it (less the agency's commission) to the car rental company via a check drawn on the travel agency. There can be (and often is) a period of time between the receipt of the client's payment and the sending of the agency's check. It is during this period of time that an accounts payable situation may occur.

The other circumstance in which an accounts payable for car rental may take place is when the client/driver is under the age that the car rental company allows for initiating airport rental arrangements. With some car rental companies there is a minimum-age requirement for renting a car at the airport or, in some cases, at an in-town location. Where this restriction applies, the age limit is often twenty-five. Some companies will waive these restrictions and rent to a person who has a valid license and is between the ages of twenty-one and twenty-five, if all payment is made in advance to the travel agency and often if other restrictions are met. When this is the case, the client is usually provided with a voucher and the payment is sent (less commission) by the agency to the car rental vendor. Again, during the time between the receipt of the client's check and the mailing of the vendor's check, the travel agency has created a car rental account payable.

Accounts Payable—Cruises. Chart-of-accounts line 913 is "Accounts Payable —Cruises." For many travel agencies substantial accounts payable can accrue in this category since it is here that deposits for all cruises are shown. For agencies booking cruise groups, it is not unusual to group payments to the cruise line once the initial deposits have been made, and to send these additional payments to the line only once every two weeks or once a month. The amounts that accumulate between the payment distribution dates are accounts payable to the cruise companies.

Accounts Payable—Rail. Chart-of-accounts line 914, "Accounts Payable —Rail" is treated in the same way as the "Accounts Payable—ARC" line. It reflects the current account of money owed to all domestic and international railroads for rail tickets and other rail purchases made through the travel agency.

Accounts Payable—Insurance. Some agencies will have an "Accounts Payable—Insurance" line. This will appear only if insurance payments are processed by the travel agency and then sent to the insurance company. This is usually for baggage, trip cancellation, and accident/death insurance taken out by clients prior to undertaking their trip(s). Many travel agencies give the insurance forms to the clients, instruct them as to how to fill out the forms, and then advise them to send the completed forms together with their checks directly to the insurance company (often in pre-addressed and provided envelopes). Under such circumstances the travel agency receives commissions from the insurance company. But the agency does not hold premium payments from clients since all money paying for the insurance is sent by the client directly to the insurance company. With this type of arrangement, the agency will not need an "Accounts Payable—Insurance" line.

In some travel agencies, however, the practice is to have clients return the completed insurance application form(s) to a designated person in the agency and make the payment to the agency. The agency groups these payments, and once or twice a month the agency will write a check to the insurance company (after having deducted commissions). It is under these circumstances that an agency might accrue an account payable debt to the insurance company. This could be listed on line 917, "Accounts Payable —Insurance."

Special Accounts Payable Lines. Although the account lines in figure 11–1 do not show them, special accounts payable lines can be and are reflected in travel agency balance sheets depending upon the sales orientation and specializations of the individual agency.

For example, many travel agencies have an "Accounts Payable—Tour Operator" line. For those agencies which run their own tours, accounts payable to a wide range of ground operators may be reflected on the balance sheet. Such ground operator provided services as meet and assist, airport to hotel (and back) transfers, and sightseeing are examples of the types of purchases for which a special accounts payable may be incurred.

Notes Payable. Notes that are payable can be treated in several ways. As noted earlier, some prefer to break these down to short-term notes payable and long-term notes payable. When this is done, usually those that will be paid off within twelve months are considered short-term and those that will be paid off in twelve months or longer are considered long-term. Another option is to list each of the notes payable, identifying what it is for or to whom it is owed. Because of space limitations on the balance sheet, this is sometimes coded so that, for example, there might be a line for "Notes Payable—A," "Notes Payable—B," and so forth.

The third alternative, and one used by many agencies, is to group all notes payable together for balance sheet reporting purposes and, as in figure 11–1, simply have one line that reads "Notes Payable." This option is usually adopted by small-volume travel agencies that have no or very few notes payable.

Notes payable usually reflect loans to the business for any number of reasons. Sometimes these are loans from owners who wish to show additional monies (beyond initial capitalization amounts) as loans rather than additional capitalization. In other cases, notes payable can represent loans from vendors or banks, typically for the purchase of equipment. For example, if the agency wishes to purchase one or more small or personal computers for the business, typically it will do so by taking out a bank loan or by buying the computer on a lease-purchase arrangement, effectively having the supplier carry the loan. In both cases, the amount of money owed will be reflected as a "Notes Payable."

Advance Deposits from Customers. A line that is not shown in figure 11–1, but that appears on some travel agency balance sheets is "Advance Deposits from Customers." Some agencies eliminate the need for this line by reasoning that any advance deposit received from a customer is for a vendor-provided service. They will have an accounts payable line for the vendor involved and therefore will eliminate the need for an "Advance Deposits from Customers" line. However, other agencies group all advance deposits into this category and try to or do eliminate the "Accounts Payable—Vendor" lines. The third alternative, and one that is also followed by many agencies, is to have a combination of "Accounts Payable—Vendor" lines and an "Advance Deposits from Customers" line. Having at least one "Advance Deposits from

Customers" line is almost essential if an agency is running its own tours. Practically speaking, there is no other way to reflect monies paid to the agency as deposits for tours that the agency itself is running.

Taxes. The final subsection of the "Liabilities" section of the balance sheet deals with taxes that are owed by the travel agency. The easiest way to treat taxes is to have a single line titled "Accrued Taxes Payable" and to group all taxes that are owed into this one single category. However, many accountants and agency executives want to know on the balance sheet exactly what taxes are owed and how much of each tax is owed. Therefore, the more common practice is to list taxes in the manner shown in figure 11–1.

Federal Income Tax Withheld. Line 901 reflects the "Federal Income Tax Withheld." This is the money withheld from employee paychecks to pay their federal income tax. The amount withheld is determined by each employee's completed Internal Revenue Service "W-4" form. This form identifies the number of dependents the employee is claiming and whether or not the employee will be filing a joint (married) or single tax return. Based upon the number of dependents and how the employee will be filing his/her return, a chart furnished by the Internal Revenue Service (it can also be obtained from the agency's CPA or auditor) shows how much money should be deducted from each employee's paycheck to pay for federal income tax.

Because this tax is accrued and normally paid on a quarterly basis, it is shown as a liability on the balance sheet. Some travel agencies, especially smaller sales volume agencies and newer agencies struggling to get off the ground, do not separate these monies into a separate bank account for tax payments and are sometimes hard pressed when it comes time to make the quarterly federal income tax payments. Therefore, it is suggested that these monies be set aside each pay day in an account earmarked for the payment of taxes.

State Income Tax Withheld. The second tax normally reflected on the balance sheet is "State Income Tax Withheld." Except that the amounts involved are far less, this is handled in exactly the same way as "Federal Income Tax Withholdings." Again, each pay period these monies should go into a separate bank account earmarked for the payment of taxes.

Local Income Tax Withheld. The next tax shown on the balance sheet is one that appears only for a limited number of travel agencies. This is "Local Income Tax Withheld." It is on this line that county taxes are reflected. City Income taxes withheld may appear here as well. Alternatively they may be assigned a balance sheet line of their own, as in Figure 11–1. Many communities, especially smaller ones, do not levy a local county or city income tax. Therefore, these tax lines appear only on the balance sheets of those travel agencies located in communities where these taxes are levied.

FICA Tax Withheld. The last tax line is for "FICA Tax Withheld." This is for social security payments. This is a percentage-based tax similar in collection application to income taxes. The local social security office, the agency's CPA, or the agency's auditor can provide the charts, formulas, and directions for calculating the tax and remitting it.

'Capital' or 'Equity'

The last section of the balance sheet is titled either "Capital" or "Equity" depending upon how management wants to view it. Whatever it is called, the line items are the same.

Invested Capital. The first line (number 800 on the standard industry chart-of-accounts) is "Invested Capital." This is the money that was invested in the travel agency by those who started the business. It includes not only initial monies invested, but also any subsequent investment in the agency. If any monies have been paid back to investors from the funds they put in to start the travel agency, the amount of these funds may either be shown as "Capital Withdrawals" or, as is more often the case, the "Invested Capital" amount will be reduced on the balance sheet by the amount of money paid back to investors.

Retained Earnings. "Retained Earnings" is the next line. This is line 801 on the chart-of-accounts. "Retained Earnings" is profit made by the company, but not paid out to investors or stockholders. These profits have been put back into the company.

Withdrawals. It should be noted that the balance sheet shows a line (number 810) for "Withdrawals." This is for payments during the period which were made from "Capital." The amounts are shown as negative figures on the balance sheet (i.e., they are in parentheses). The total of "Invested Capital" plus "Retained Earnings" less any "Withdrawals" is the "Total Equity" of the travel agency. This is an important figure to keep in mind when calculating the "Return on Equity," which is discussed in chapter 7.

Profit or Loss. The next to last line in the balance sheet shows the profit or loss accrued by the travel agency both for the month just ending (in the left column) and for the year-to-date. This line, number 820 on the standard industry chart-of-accounts, is titled "Profit or (Loss) (This Year)." (The word "Loss" is purposely put in parentheses here since the figures, if they represent a loss, are shown in parentheses.)

Net Capital. The final line in the "Capital" section is a summary line, giving the totals for the section. This is "Net Capital." To calculate it, add "Invested Earnings," "Retained Earnings," and "Profit" and subtract "Withdrawals." If instead of a profit, the agency shows a loss, then the figure should be shown in parentheses.

Total Liabilities and Capital

The last line on the balance sheet is "Total Liabilities and Capital." This amount is calculated by adding "Total Liabilities" and "Net Capital."

BALANCING THE BALANCE SHEET

One way to check whether or not the balance sheet has been calculated accurately is to determine whether or not the balance sheet "balances." This is where this accounting document gets its name. The balance sheet, if it has been prepared properly, will always balance. To determine if it is in balance, make sure that the total for "Total Assets" is the same as the total for "Total Liabilities and Capital."

The "year-to-date" figures on the balance sheet should also balance. In other words, the year-to-date figure shown for "Total Assets" should be exactly the same as the year-to-date figure shown for "Total Liabilities and Capital."

BALANCE SHEET TIMING AND VERIFICATION

The balance sheet is prepared monthly and it presents a picture of the financial position of the travel agency at any point in time. The balance sheet for the twelfth month of the year is also the end-of-year balance sheet. It not only presents a picture of the financial position of the company at the end of the fiscal year, but it also provides an overview of how the company fared throughout the year. Because the balance sheet is considered by most financial executives to be the most important end-of-year financial document, many agencies arrange to have it (and, in many cases, the end-of-year income statement) audited by an outside accounting company—usually verified by a cover letter from a CPA (Certified Public Accountant).

OTHER BALANCE SHEETS

Throughout this chapter references have been made to alternative ways to reflect data on the balance sheet. As with income statements, there are several "versions" of balance sheets utilized in the travel agency industry. Figure 11–2 is an example of another balance sheet used by travel agencies.

BALANCE SHEET FOR 1989												
	JAN	FEB	MAR	APR	MAY	JUN	JUL	AUG	SEP	OCT	NOV	DEC
ASSETS												
CURRENT ASSETS												
Cash in Bank												
Accts Rcvbl												
Notes Receivable												
TOTAL CURRENT ASSETS												
LONG TERM ASSETS												
Furnishings												
Rent Deposit												
Depreciation												
TOTAL LONG TERM ASSETS												
TOTAL ASSETS												
LIABILITIES												
ACCOUNTS PAYABLE												
REVOLVING CREDIT LINE												
LONG TERM LIABILITIES												
Deferred Officer Sal.												
TOTAL LIABILITIES												
STOCKHOLDER EQUITY STOCK												
Common Stock												
Addtl Paid in Capital												
TOTAL STOCK												
RETAINED EARNINGS												
PROFIT/LOSS — PERIOD												
TTL STOCKHOLDERS EQUITY												
TTL LIABILITIES AND EQUITY												

Figure 11–2 (Courtesy of The Travel Society, Denver, CO)

SUMMARY

For owners of travel agencies, the balance sheet is the document most often scrutinized. It summarizes the financial status of the business and clearly identifies if a profit has been earned or if a loss has been incurred and the extent of that profit or loss. The balance sheet is broken down into the two broad categories of assets on the one hand and liabilities and capital on the other hand. The total of the assets should equal the total of the liabilities and capital. Assets are further broken down into the two broad categories of current assets and other assets; while liabilities and capital are broken down into the two broad categories of liabilities and capital.

In the section relating to capital, one identifies the amount of profit or loss. Frequently management decisions are based on the amount of profit or loss. Most investors are clearly most concerned by the amount of profit or loss. Because this is their major concern, they frequently make major management strategy decisions based upon the profit or loss position of the business.

The end-of-year balance sheet and the end-of-year income statement form the foundation for the travel agency's budget development. Once these two documents have been completed and verified for accuracy, the agency's accountant or other financial executive is ready to prepare the budget for the next fiscal year.

❑ DISCUSSION QUESTIONS

1. Why do owners tend to be more concerned with the balance sheet than with any other financial document?
2. In what ways are the balance sheet and the income statement similar and in what ways do they differ from one another?
3. What are assets?
4. What is another term used for "Other Assets" and why might this other term be more appropriate?
5. What are the two categories into which "Other Assets" can be divided?
6. What are the titles of some of the "Current Liabilities" subsections?
7. Why might a figure for "Accounts Payable—Insurance" never appear on the balance sheet?
8. Why is it that the "Accounts Payable—Car Rental" section seldom reflects any activity?
9. Under what circumstances might the "Local Tax Withheld" line not appear on a travel agency's balance sheet?
10. How is "Net Capital" calculated?

❑ ROLE-PLAYING EXERCISE

Two students may participate in this role-playing exercise either as an out-of-class or in-class fun way to review how a balance sheet works and its benefits to stockholders, officers, and board members of a travel agency. One student plays the travel agency's bookkeeper. The other plays the senior agent who has just been offered stock in the travel agency and a position on the Board of Directors in exchange for signing a long-term employment contract. Please read the script and then pick up the conversation in your own words.

Senior Agent: I appreciate you explaining the income statement to me. Probably even more confusing to me, however, is the balance sheet.

Agency Bookkeeper: Let me explain how the balance sheet works, why it is important, and what information is placed in each part. I'll also explain some options for you and why we have elected to utilize a standard industry balance sheet. Our Chairman of the Board decided several years ago that we will use this form. To begin, let me point out that. . .

CONTINUE ON YOUR OWN

❑ CHAPTER ELEVEN EXERCISE

INSTRUCTIONS: Complete the blank balance sheet (Figure 11–4 on the last two pages of this exercise) incorporating the data and the figures from the information provided below. These figures represent the financial status of the travel agency for the end of last month, which was the first month of the travel agency's fiscal year. An additional copy of the blank sheet (Figure 11–3) has been provided to use as a worksheet.

DATA FROM THE END OF LAST MONTH TO BE USED IN PREPARING THE BALANCE SHEET

1. In reviewing the money owed to the air carriers and not yet deducted by the central bank from the agency's account, it is found that the agency owes the air carriers $4,721.19.
2. Withheld taxes are as follows: $76.47 for Federal Income Tax; $22.14 for State Income Tax; and $26.02 for FICA Tax.
3. Amtrak owes the travel agency $206.12 in back commission payments and the car rental companies owe the agency $218.38 in commissions.
4. The total amount of cash in all of the travel agency's bank accounts is $1,582.31.
5. The accounts receivables total $3,219.16.
6. The financial books reflect a profit for this month of $629.41.

BALANCE SHEET FOR: ____________ 19__ CURRENT ASSETS					
INCREASE/ DECREASE			ACCOUNT	BALANCE	
			120 Cash in Bank—ARC Acct		
			121 Cash in Bank—Other Acct		
			122 Cash in Bank—Other Acct		
			123 Petty Cash		
			124 Other:		
			125 Other:		
			110 Accounts Receivable		
			111 Notes Receivable		
			112 Investment:		
			113 Investment:		
			114 Other		
			199 TOTAL CURRENT ASSETS		
			OTHER ASSETS		
			200 Automation Equipment		
			201 Less Depreciation		
			202 Office Equipment		
			203 Less Depreciation		
			204 Automobile		
			205 Less Depreciation		
			206 Other:		
			207 Less Depreciation		
			299 TOTAL OTHER ASSETS		
			TOTAL ASSETS		

Figure 11–3

BALANCE SHEET

FOR: ____________ 19__

LIABILITIES AND CAPITAL

Increase/ Decrease			Account	Balance	
			LIABILITIES		
			910 Accounts Payable—ARC		
			911 Accounts Payable—Hotels		
			912 Accounts Payable—Car Rental		
			913 Accounts Payable—Cruises		
			914 Accounts Payable—Rail		
			915 Accounts Payable—Tours		
			916 Accounts Payable—Automation		
			917 Accounts Payable—Other:		
			920 Notes Payable		
			901 Federal Income Tax Withheld		
			902 State Income Tax Withheld		
			904 Local Income Tax Withheld		
			905 City Income Tax Withheld		
			903 FICA Tax Withheld		
			999 TOTAL LIABILITIES		
			CAPITAL		
			800 Invested Capital		
			801 Retained Earnings		
			810 Withdrawals		
			820 PROFIT OR LOSS (THIS YEAR)		
			830 NET CAPITAL		
			TOTAL LIABILITIES AND CAPITAL		

Figure 11–3 (Continued)

BALANCE SHEET

FOR: ____________ 19__

CURRENT ASSETS

Increase/ Decrease			Account	Balance	
			Cash in Bank—ARC Acct		
			Cash in Bank—Other Acct		
			Cash in Bank—Other Acct		
			Petty Cash		
			Other:		
			Other:		
			Accounts Receivable		
			Notes Receivable		
			Investment:		
			Investment:		
			Other		
			TOTAL CURRENT ASSETS		
			OTHER ASSETS		
			Automation Equipment		
			Less Depreciation		
			Office Equipment		
			Less Depreciation		
			Automobile		
			Less Depreciation		
			Other:		
			Less Depreciation		
			TOTAL OTHER ASSETS		
			TOTAL ASSETS		

Figure 11–4

BALANCE SHEET

FOR: ____________ 19__

LIABILITIES AND CAPITAL

Increase/ Decrease			Account	Balance	
			LIABILITIES		
			Accounts Payable—ARC		
			Accounts Payable—Hotels		
			Accounts Payable—Car Rental		
			Accounts Payable—Cruises		
			Accounts Payable—Rail		
			Accounts Payable—Tours		
			Accounts Payable—Automation		
			Accounts Payable—Other:		
			Notes Payable		
			Federal Income Tax Withheld		
			State Income Tax Withheld		
			Local Income Tax Withheld		
			City Income Tax Withheld		
			FICA Tax Withheld		
			TOTAL LIABILITIES		
			CAPITAL		
			Invested Capital		
			Retained Earnings		
			Withdrawals		
			PROFIT OR LOSS (THIS YEAR)		
			NET CAPITAL		
			TOTAL LIABILITIES AND CAPITAL		

Figure 11–4 (Continued)

BUDGETING PRELIMINARIES

OBJECTIVES

Upon completion of this chapter, the student will be able to:

- ❑ Identify the raw data needed to prepare the annual budget
- ❑ Prepare a simple weekly status report when all required basic weekly financial information is provided
- ❑ Explain what is included on a source analysis report and why the report is important
- ❑ Explain why a comparison of weekly employee compensation with weekly travel agency income is important, and detail the steps that need to be taken to calculate the percentage of weekly employee salaries compared to weekly income

INTRODUCTION

The material discussed in this chapter relates to what is necessary prior to getting into budgeting. Much of the material relates to reports and data. There are six sources. The first is raw data. Timely reports make up the other five sources: daily reports, weekly reports, monthly reports, quarterly reports, and annual reports. Each will be analyzed.

RAW DATA

The first area of concern is raw data. Probably the most important raw data is *tickets.* Not all needed information comes from tickets, but a lot of the data constituting financial reports comes from tickets. Another raw data source that is very important is the invoice/receipt. The invoice/receipt is considered a foundation document. This is a document that is completed any time a financial transaction takes place. It is a single piece of paper that serves a dual purpose. It serves as a receipt and as an invoice when payment has not yet been received.

Deposit Slips

Another source of raw data often referred to during the budgeting process is *deposit slips.* Deposit slips can be important to an agency, but in a lot of travel agencies, deposit slips are not processed in ways as beneficial as they might be. Nevertheless, deposit slips can provide information that often can be retained in no other way. They provide the agency with essential tracking data. Much of the tracking data needed is found on the back of deposit slips for each item listed.

Complete Deposit Slip Information. On a deposit slip one reflects deposits of both checks and cash. The easiest way to write out a deposit check is simply to list the amount of each check and the total amount of cash being deposited. Many people do it this way. However, if this is what is done, much of the information that would be helpful in financial management will be lost to the agency. It is necessary to retain some data that may be available only before the check is cashed. Once the check has been deposited, there may be no other way to obtain the needed data. First, write down the total amount of money that is deposited for each trip. Let us say that we have received $150 from Mrs. Jones, who is taking a trip. We need to show that amount of money. We also need to show who it is for. In this case it would be for Mrs. K. Jones. In addition to that, we need to track what it was for. Mrs. Jones may come back and say that she has paid us. If our records are not complete, we may have no record of having received Mrs. Jones' payment. We only have a payment on our deposit slip for Mrs. Jones for $150, but she has purchased perhaps nine or ten tickets, all of which were for $150. We do not know if the particular ticket payment in question is the one that is represented by the $150 that we find listed on our deposit slip. This becomes an especially difficult problem for the person who travels every day, or even once or twice a week (a frequent traveler, in other words). So another item needed on the deposit slip is the invoice/receipt number or the I/R number. Since a separate invoice/receipt is filled out for each trip or for each transaction, there is now a way on the deposit slip to be able to go back and show an invoice/receipt number. This will indicate that the money received is the same as the amount of money that the agency is showing for Mrs. Jones for this particular trip. This allows the agent to track back if Mrs. Jones comes in and wants to know information about her payments and when her payments were made. Of course one needs to know that it was paid by check. Therefore, it helps to enter the check number of Mrs. Jones' check on the deposit slip. For example, it might be written as check number 1234. This is her check number. Again this is a rapid reference for the agency so that if agency management has any need to check this at any future time, there is a way of going back to get the data.

Cash Payments and Deposit Slips. But what happens if it is a cash payment? What many people do is to lump all cash payments together and enter this total amount as cash received on the deposit slip. It can be done this way, but a lumping approach does not give the travel agency any tracking data. If this is a cash payment, the agency accountant needs to know all the same things that appear on the deposit slip for a check payment, i.e., the client's name, the amount of money, the invoice number, and the form of payment (in this case, cash). Instead of check number, the word "cash" is substituted. Now one has a way on the deposit slip to be able to track back exactly what was involved in this particular transaction. This is one bit of raw data and if one keeps the raw data correctly, it will assist in being able to develop the annual budget.

Ticket Logs as Raw Data

It has been pointed out that raw data consists of tickets, invoice receipts, and deposit slips. There is additional raw data as well. Another raw data source is ticket logs. A *ticket log* is a list of every ticket that comes off the computer. It gives the travel agency a way of tracking tickets. When one looks at the potential for theft or loss in a travel agency, one starts to understand the need to track and log all accountable documents. All tickets are accountable documents. The ticket log provides a way of being able to track what happened to that ticket. It may not tell an agency staffer where a ticket is if it is lost, but it can tell the staffer if that ticket was generated. Most ticket logs can identify whether or not a ticket was voided. An agency is responsible for accounting for every ticket that comes through. If there is a ticket that is lost, there is a substantial fine. The bigger problem is the fact that if there is a ticket that has not been accounted for, that ticket might have been stolen. That becomes a greater problem than a loss. The ticket log can give a manager this information. Many ticket logs will provide additional information. In most cases, it will tell the agency staffer who the traveler on the issued ticket is. If the traveler comes in and says, "I didn't get my ticket," the agent who is assisting the client may not know whether the ticket has been generated or not. All the agent has to do is go to the ticket log to find out if the ticket has been generated and when. In large travel agencies that ability is sometimes very important because the people generating the tickets are different than those who made the reservations. In smaller agencies one does not run into that too often.

Ledgers and Reports as Raw Data

Ledgers and *reports* constitute still another raw data source. These are really not raw data, but are often treated as raw data by accountants and others who work with travel agency financial management. As pointed out, however, raw data is only one of the elements needed to start with when developing a budget.

DAILY FINANCIAL REPORTS

Daily financial reports are also important. *Daily reports* help to ensure some degree of security. When an airline ticket is generated, or a client pays for a cruise, a financial transaction occurs. What happens to the paperwork?

Systems and Security

Generally speaking, the agency runs into problems unless there is a system. In many small travel agencies there may be no system. The agent may be rushed and leave a client's check for payment on his/her desk. A receipt is written and left on top of the desk. If there is no system, things can get lost. The best approach is to have a place within the travel agency where, after every transaction has been completed, all documents relating to that transaction (as they pertain to financial paperwork) are placed. The Airline Reporting Corporation suggests that place to be the agency's safe. But some safes are too small to be able to handle all the paperwork, and some owners and managers are not too happy about having their employees go into the safe after every transaction. They want the safe to be reserved for access to the owner and/or manager. However, whether financial transaction documents are kept in the safe or somewhere else, it is important that they be kept under lock and key. This is important because of the potential for loss and theft.

Security and Theft. There have been a number of cases where documents have been stolen, where checks and money have been stolen, by people who call themselves clients when they come into a travel agency. In Los Angeles in 1989, for example, two people came into a travel agency on a Saturday afternoon. One distracted the owner, who happened to be the only person in the agency at the time. The other person went to the back of the agency, requesting beforehand if he could use the agency's restroom. He took several tickets and some cash. They had apparently identified where the tickets and cash were kept before coming into the agency; or, perhaps, they were familiar with the way agencies work and guessed rightly that the tickets and cash were kept in an accessible back room enroute to the agency's restroom.

Locked Money and Tickets

Returning to the incident related above, had the tickets and cash been kept in this room in a locked container (file cabinet, locked desk drawer), it is unlikely that the thief could have had the time needed to break the lock and steal the tickets and cash. If, however, all the material is kept in a locked facility (preferably a cabinet or a safe in a back room) and that facility is kept locked, the likelihood of loss or theft will be considerably reduced. Each agent could perhaps have a key during office hours to open the storage container when needed and lock it when finished. Theft still is a possibility, but it is a diminished possibility.

Cash Drawers

What many people prefer is to use a separate cash drawer, similar to a cash register drawer, as the designated place for financial documents.

Financial Document Drawer Convenience

The accountant or other person who prepares the daily report and/or the weekly ARC Report needs to have daily access to all completed paperwork for processing and the preparation of required reports. Therefore the location of the financial document drawer needs to be convenient for the accountant or manager, and easily accessible without disturbing any clients who may be in the agency at the time the report is being prepared.

Daily Financial Transaction Data

When one starts considering the preparation of daily reports, financial transaction documents are turned to. These are the daily financial reports and documents that are completed whenever a financial transaction occurs. Some document is completed reflecting the transaction whether or not the client has actually paid for the trip prior to leaving the agency. These daily financial reports and documents form the foundation for the preparation of the agency's Daily Report.

The Bank Deposit as a Daily Report. Looking at the daily reports, the first daily report should be a bank deposit. Many people don't think of a bank deposit as being a report. However, it really is a report of everything that was put into the bank that particular day. It is a document that helps the accountant balance all the financial activity of the day. That is why one needs to have the breakdown of information on the back of the bank deposit which was discussed earlier.

The Airline Reporting Corporation discourages travel agencies from keeping any cash on hand, i.e., in the agency overnight. One can have petty cash, of course, but keeping payments from clients in the agency overnight is discouraged. It is strongly recommended in ARC documentation that bank deposits be made every day. In most companies in the travel agency industry there is a concerted effort to get all cash received from payments into the bank at the end of each day. Therefore, around three or four o'clock in the afternoon (or pretty close to closing time), somebody is designated to take all of these financial transaction documents from the designated document drawer, sort through it, balance it with a deposit slip, and then deposit all the cash and checks in the bank. Therefore, if there is a break-in at the agency overnight, the thief will not be able to get the previous day's checks and cash. Some feel it may not be as important to deposit checks every day as it is to deposit the cash, but both are important. So, one starts the daily report with a bank deposit.

Daily Sales Balance. The next part of the daily report is a *daily sales balance.* At least that is what one attempts. To be able to reach the daily sales balance, one needs to undertake several financial balances. One is to balance the ticket log and the tickets issued to the invoice/receipts. Since it has been pointed out before that one has an invoice/receipt for every financial transaction, the agency bookkeeper must look on the ticket log to make sure that every ticket is accounted for in terms of having an accompanying invoice/receipt. Obviously, there will be no invoice/receipt for many of the voids. One may have a voided invoice/receipt to accompany a voided ticket, but some tickets, especially handwritten tickets, will be voided before an invoice/receipt is prepared. For every valid ticket that is going to be leaving (or has already left) the travel agency, one should have some type of an accountable document to back it up. For every ticket the agency needs to have some type of record showing either that payment has been received or that the client has been billed. This will be an invoice, a receipt, or an invoice/receipt. One of the first steps in preparing a daily sales balance, therefore, is to match up all of the invoice/receipts with every ticket that came off of the ticket log. If there is a ticket that came off of the ticket log that is neither matched nor a void, the accountant needs to find out why and what the problem is. Some travel agencies actually run a full Airline Reporting Corporation (ARC) Report every day. Most do not actually send it in every day (some do), but they go far beyond just matching up tickets and invoice/receipts. The majority of agencies, however, feel that it is enough to match the invoice/receipts with the actual tickets issued.

Financial Matching. As noted, one also needs to show that there is some type of payment or request for payment for every transaction. This requires another matching-up process. For every valid ticket that has been issued, the accountant needs to find out whether or not the agency received a check, a credit card form, cash, or a bill for payment for that ticket One should have one of these four documents for every ticket (except voided tickets) that has been issued. Again, one should have either a cash payment for it, a check to pay for it, a credit card slip showing payment, or a bill. There are, however, a few more unusual forms of payment that could be used which have not yet been discussed. These include MCOs (Miscellaneous Charge Orders), traveler's checks, or other (exchange) tickets. All three are acceptable forms of payment for airline tickets. The point is, some type of payment or expected payment is needed for each valid ticket issued. One must be able to balance every airline ticket issued with some form of payment or with the invoice portion of an invoice/receipt.

Balancing Non-Air Sales. The discussion thus far has related to airline tickets only. However, airline tickets account for only between 80 and 90 percent of all average travel agency sales. Travelers do purchase travel other than airline tickets. If a client purchases a cruise, the airline reservation computer may not be used to book the cruise. When the agency sends payment directly to the cruise line, a matchup of the deposit or the full payment can be reflected either in the computer (and one can request a hard copy of the invoice or receipt from the computer reservation system), or if the booking is on a manual system, an invoice/receipt will be issued. In other words, one must be able to match the payment with some type of invoice or a receipt, whether computer-generated or handwritten, in order to create a balancing of the records.

Employee Time Log. Another part of the daily financial report that many, though not all, travel agencies have is an *employee time log.* Employee cost in a travel agency averages between a low of 45 percent and a high of 55 percent of all costs. Therefore a rough average of employee cost is 50 percent of expenses. Since this is such a high percentage of all agency costs, many agencies include data from employee time logs in their daily sales reports. A 50 percent average is an easy figure to be able to work with. Because employee expenses are by far the major single costs involved, most agencies feel that it is important to have a daily record of the employee hours. They want to know how many employees worked how many hours and what it cost the agency. It is not just because of the major expense of employees that agency management wants these figures. It is also because of the ramifications involved. For example, the tax ramifications are important. The Internal Revenue Service likes to have accurate records and there have been some major problems in travel agencies when it comes to keeping accurate employee time and work records.

WEEKLY FINANCIAL REPORT

The major areas to be considered on a daily basis when preparing the daily sales report have been identified. Now let us review what is included in the weekly financial reports.

The Weekly ARC Report

For most travel agencies, the most important weekly report by far is the ARC Report. The details of how to develop the Airline Reporting Corporation weekly report are discussed in chapter 8. The ARC Report basically gives the airline information as to how much money is due to the airline for sales that occurred that week for the travel agency. The ARC Report was designed by airline employees, not by or for travel agencies. It is a report that is designed to give information to air carriers and not to travel agencies. Nevertheless, the information that is contained in the ARC Report can be of great value to a travel agency. Basically the ARC Report is a very simple, straightforward report.

What is and is not Included on the ARC Report. The ARC Report supposedly shows the total amount of airline sales. That really is a misnomer today. It used to reflect just airline sales, but with computerization and the ability to provide assistance for non-air vendor sales, we now are finding that the ARC Report includes cruise sales, rail sales, and in some cases hotel sales, tours, and other products. So to say that it just reports air sales today is no longer accurate. Nevertheless, everything that was issued during the week on an airline ticket (either hand-issued or computer-generated) is accounted for on the weekly ARC Report with the exception of those documents that were issued on individual airline stock. For most travel agencies this is a mute point, since few have any airline tickets issued on non-ARC stock. But there are some agencies that do such a large volume of business with individual carriers that they have negotiated with those carriers to have their ticket stock provided to the agency. The travel agency then issues tickets on the individual carrier's ticket stock. When this is done, a separate settlement arrangement is made and it does not go through the Airline Reporting Corporation. But for all standard ticket stock, which includes both computer-generated ticket stock and hand-issued tickets ordered through the auspices of the Airline Reporting Corporation, the ARC Report provides a weekly settlement or accounting.

Data Provided on the ARC Report. The ARC Report does a couple of things. First, it provides information to the airlines and to the travel agency regarding the total amount of sales. It also breaks down that total amount of sales into that which is paid for by cash and that paid for by credit card. Again, this is a little bit misleading, because that which is reported as being paid for by cash can actually be at least three different forms of payment. Tickets that are paid for by cash are shown in this category, but in addition, tickets that are paid for by check are also included. Also, tickets which have not yet been paid for at all are shown as being paid for by cash. As far as the airlines are concerned, the travel agency owes money for all tickets that are issued whether the travel agency has collected for those tickets or not. They therefore include accounts receivables for the travel agency (tickets companies have ordered, but not yet paid for) in the "cash" category.

ARC Report Financial Information. There are several ways in which this information can be of value to the travel agency. One is that it shows the travel agency the total volume of sales that are submitted and processed through the Airline Reporting Corporation. For most travel agencies this is at least 80 percent of all sales. For many travel agencies it will be a much higher percentage than that. By looking at the ARC Report, agency managers should have a good idea as to whether they made money that week, if they broke even, or if they lost money. This is especially true if the manager, owner, or other person analyzing the data knows what the agency's expenses are. Only if the commissions received exceed expenses does the agency make money. If one has a good idea of what the expenses are on a weekly basis, and if one understands what the ARC Report figures are, one can have a good idea as to whether the agency made money, broke even, or lost money for the week. Other factors need to be added in, but one can get a good feel for profit or loss from the ARC Report. In their book, the Davidoffs suggest that there are basically only two ways of being able to make money. These are to either reduce costs or to increase sales. Since the ARC Report gives such a good sense of weekly profit or loss when compared to expenses, agency management can use it to signal immediate cost cutting measures if at any time a pattern of excessive expenditures over income is seen. Therefore, the ARC Report tends to be the most important single report.

The Source Analysis Report

Another weekly report that many agencies expect to have because it is beneficial in terms of doing an annual budget is a *client source analysis report.* Basically what it does is give the amount and percentage of sales for the preceding week broken down by source of client. The source analysis is designed to determine where the agency got its clients. One needs to identify what dollar amount was received and what the percentage of sales was from all the clients who purchased travel during the previous week. This is determined for each source of clients and it is necessary to know both factors.

Repeat Clients

For an established travel agency the major source of clients for the preceding week will normally be repeat clients. If one is doing a good job and the agency is satisfying the clients, repeat clients will definitely be the largest source of weekly clients. One agency owner once said that if he could keep every client he ever had, he would be a rich man. Unfortunately, sometimes something happens whereby a client is lost. The agency makes mistakes, the client moves to another city, or any one of a number of other factors occurs that accounts for clients not coming back. Nevertheless, repeat clients should be the major source category.

Other Sources and Report Benefits. Other sources of clients might be: 1) walk-in clients, 2) those who come in response to advertising, and 3) those brought in by outside sales representatives. In addition, there are any number of other sources. The client source analysis shows the agency where its marketing strengths are and where additional work might be needed. It also provides a way to measure the return on investment of monies spent for marketing. It is important to have return on investment figures before undertaking budgeting, since ROI figures may dictate or help to dictate where marketing monies are to be allocated.

Source Analysis Completion Process. To develop the client analysis report, agents must ask clients how they found out about the agency. A form is completed by agents to determine how clients learned about the agency, why they used the agency in the first place, and why they keep returning to it.

The Weekly Petty Cash Report

Still another weekly report is a *petty cash report.* Petty cash is a fund from which to pay ongoing small and emergency expenses. Most travel agencies have a petty cash fund. The weekly petty cash report is important to have because when one does the annual budget, one needs to budget for petty cash. If it is left out, the agency may wind up with no petty cash or, more likely, the budget will be thrown off because checks to cover daily small miscellaneous costs will still be written. Most agencies also find that unless they balance out their petty cash fund on a regular basis (usually once a week) one of two things can happen. One is that they may run out of petty cash monies altogether; the other is that they may spend petty cash money on expenses for which the petty cash fund was not intended. Therefore, many agencies implement a weekly petty cash fund report and balancing process. This means that one starts the week with the highest amount of petty cash that the agency would designate and one finishes the week with very little left in the fund.

The Cash Balance Report

Next, is a *cash balance report.* Most owners are very concerned with their cash balances. The cash balance form normally starts with the agency name. It has room for dates. One lists all of the check numbers for disbursements. There is room to record the deposits and what they were for. The system works like a check book. There is a balance column to show the current cash status of the travel agency. This report clearly shows the amount of the disbursements, the amount of the deposits, and the balance. When applied to each of the agency's accounts on a weekly basis, the report shows the total amount of money that is left at the end of each week in each of the agency's accounts.

The Airline Reporting Corporation suggests that travel agencies have at least two accounts. One account should be maintained just to pay for the ARC Report. One or more other accounts are used as operating accounts. Many agencies have several additional accounts.

Travel agency accountants prepare a weekly cash balance report to show management the status of each account. They do not mix two or more accounts on the same report. There is a separate report for each account. By just glancing at the balance at the bottom, agency management immediately knows how much money it has. Most owners want the weekly report to not only show the balance in each account, but to show an end-of-the-week balance for all accounts.

Expense Forecasting

Determining weekly expense levels is important in constructing the annual budget so that the level of expenditure and the level of income for each week (cash flow) can be projected. By analyzing expense data over a period of time one can identify trends.

The cash balance report is most beneficial in this regard. It allows management to look at levels of income and expenditures each week over a period of time and to be able to plan in terms of budgeting. It does not always work this way. Just because the first week of May every year for the last five years has been a very profitable week for an agency does not necessarily mean that next year the first week of May will also be very profitable. However, trends do seem to repeat themselves. Therefore, one considers trends and patterns when undertaking financial planning.

It may be possible to forecast which weeks in the year traditionally (perhaps over a five-year period) show the agency has a lot of income coming in and which weeks of the year traditionally (again, over a five-year period) show the agency has little income coming in. Every travel agency experiences the uncomfortable fact that incomes and expenditures do not equal out. There are periods of the year when the agency has a great deal more money coming in than it has going out in expenditures. While this is an excellent situation and one that agencies strive for, the reverse is also true. There are periods of the year when the agency has a great deal more money being spent than it has coming in. Cash flow patterns can be identified, and peaks and valleys of income and expenditures can be planned for in the budget. If the agency is not prepared for low cash flow periods, it may have to draw money from sources from which principals (owners) would rather not have to draw (e.g., from additional capital income paid in by the owners). Most owners would prefer to avoid doing this, if possible. It may well be that had cash flow been analyzed and planned, the need for new inputs of capital into the company might have been avoided.

The Weekly Status Report

For many agency owners and managers the *weekly status report* is their most important report. It shows them where they stand financially at the end of the week. The cash balance report tells them what the balance is in each of the accounts. This is important. However, the weekly status report does more than that. It is a summary of the most important weekly financial activities.

Weekly Ticket Sales. Usually this report starts with the *total weekly ticket sales.* This is not just the total number of tickets sold, but it is the total amount of money received from selling tickets during the previous week. This information comes from the weekly ARC Report. The amount is reported in dollars. If the data is compared showing the amount of ticket sales this week of this year and the total amount of ticket sales during the same week last year, the agency knows where it is versus last year. Some agency accountants go further and compute an average of the amount of ticket sales for the week going back to the same week for the last five years. That is even better. It gives agency management some feel for how well it is doing.

Client Loss Problem Identification. Another way weekly financial comparisons benefit a company is their ability to help identify problems. Recently, an agency manager stated, "Our sales are about the same as they were last year. They are okay. We made a profit last year and we will this year too. However, the number of tickets issued is down by almost 15 percent." One conclusion is that the tickets being sold are based on higher average fares, possibly because of fares increasing. The real problem is not a problem in losing money, but a problem in losing clients. If only total sales were reviewed, agency management might mistakenly believe that it is doing well (at least staying the same) when, in fact, client loss is steady and can ultimately be considerable. In other words, the reason why the agency is profitable is not because of anything the agency has done. It is because the average ticket price has gone up. Therefore, the number of tickets issued is just as important a factor as the dollar amount of sales when identifying where the agency really stands compared with the past year or an average of the past five years.

Weekly Tickets Issued. Tickets-issued comparisons are important. This report considers the total number of tickets issued during the past week compared with the total number of tickets issued during the same week last year (or compared with the average total for the same period over each of the last five years). This also provides important information, especially when the information is compared to average ticket price. For example, if the number of tickets issued this week this year is down about 4 or 5 percent from the total number of tickets issued during the same week last year, it tells agency management that the agency may be losing clients. However, an individual week loss in number of tickets issued this year compared to the same week last year, may be because of a skew of some type. A single week comparison showing a small loss (4 or 5 percent) should not be a matter of great concern. However, if there is a pattern and there are several weeks (or worse, several months) in a row where there is a 4 or 5 percent decrease in total number of tickets issued, agency management should be concerned with identifying why and, at the very least, recognize a strong probability that there is a loss of clients. The agency may be losing them to the competition, to the rising prices of tickets, to inflation, or to a decreasing population (people moving away). There may be many reasons why clients could be lost. The point is, they are lost. That problem needs to be addressed early and it cannot be addressed early if it is not recognized early. Conducting a weekly comparison of tickets issued is probably the best way to identify this type of a problem early enough to take positive steps to overcome it.

Average Ticket Price. Another part of the weekly report is the *average ticket price.* The average ticket price for tickets issued during the week is determined by dividing the number of tickets issued by the total amount of sales of air tickets. If the average ticket price for the tickets issued last week is compared with the average ticket price for tickets issued during the same week last year and the average ticket price for the same week each year for the last five years, management will get a good idea as to how the agency is doing as compared with last year and with the past five years. In some cases the average ticket price is not the result of anything the agency does. In other cases it is. It may be the result of a concerted effort on the part of management to push better sales. Trying to push more first-class ticket sales, suggesting business class seats on international flights (rather than discounted or economy), and other such tactics may result in an agency-designed increase in average ticket price. Other approaches are specialization in some high-ticket sales area or selling more long-distance flights.

But in many cases, an increase in the average ticket price will be due to air carriers raising their fares for the types of tickets the agency normally issues (or for all tickets). It also will reflect something of the types of clients the agency has. If the agency has predominantly business clients, one can expect that the agency will probably have a higher average ticket price than if it were predominantly leisure-travel oriented. Many people who purchase tickets for leisure or vacation purposes are people who will try to meet all the requirements, restrictions specified by the air carriers to get the cheapest fare. Business people often will not be able to do that and in some cases it would be a disservice to them if they did try to meet all the requirements specified by the air carriers to get the least expensive fare. If they had to change planes a number of times or had to take a flight that left at a different time of the day in order to save money, they might miss business appointments or arrive so tired that they would ineffectively conduct the business that they were sent to do in the first place. Therefore, the agency will have a higher average ticket price if it specializes in business rather than leisure or vacation travel. As a result and to some degree, if an increase in average ticket price is noted as a weekly pattern, it might mean a change in client type as well as all other potential explanations identified earlier.

Refunds. Another part of the weekly financial report addresses the number of *refunds* that were processed during the week. The reason the agency cares about the number of refunds is that they affect the profit or loss for the week. If there is a large amount of sales, but an accompanying large amount of refunds, there may not be a profit for the agency. The agency gets no commission on tickets that have been refunded. However, agents spend twice the amount of time (sometimes more) on these tickets.

Another factor shown by a large or increasing number of refunds is that the agency may be serving one or more accounts that may be detrimental for the agency. It is a clue to the fact that the agency may be better off no longer handling those accounts. Perhaps the expense of handling the account(s) should be discussed with the account(s) involved. If the account is not willing to change whatever practices result in refunds (which in turn results in the agency losing money), it is usually better to drop the account and no longer provide service for it. Some agencies will charge the account a service fee and then will be in a position to continue serving such an account profitably. The high cost of continually processing tickets and refunds, when no commissions are received for doing so, must be recouped from somewhere.

A recent case highlights the point. This is a company which experienced an average of six changes for each ticket actually used. Over two-thirds of the changes resulted in refunds. An initial review of the account led all executives at the agency to strongly consider dropping the account. However, further analysis showed that the actual tickets used were almost all either long-distance (coast to coast) flights within the United States or international travel. Nevertheless, it was very hard for the agency to handle the account profitably. By working with the travelers and executives at the company, the agency was able to structure its internal arrangements in such a way that what had been a marginally-profitable-at-times account and a losing account at other times became a consistently profitable account. So one thing a weekly analysis of refunds tells management is that there might be a problem and management might want to initiate an investigation to determine why. This will probably lead to a recognition that one or more of the agency's accounts may be unprofitable. These will normally be corporate accounts. However, they could be incentive travel accounts. It may apply to F.I.T. clients or to any number of other client groups as well.

Weekly Debit Notices. Still another part of the weekly financial report deals with *debit notices.* The number of debit notices can be revealing. A debit notice is a report back from individual airlines or the Airline Reporting Corporation saying that there was a mistake or an error and that money is owed to the air carrier(s) for one reason or another. Receiving a large number of debit notices gives an agency an indication of two potential problems. One is that the agency may have employees who are not accurate in their work. They are making a large number of mistakes. This can apply to one or more than one employee. Mistakes can be expensive, because the agency must go back and rectify each debit notice with the airline, the client, or both. A second indication is a potential for theft. Debit notices point out areas where, in some cases, there has been theft. Therefore, many agency managers want to have a complete report on the status of debit notices received each week. Often management will go beyond just a request for the level of weekly debit notices and will ask for a comparison with the level of debit notices for the same week last year.

Weekly Dollar Commission Earned Level. The next part of the weekly financial report deals with the amount of *commission earned* on airline tickets. Normally, for the weekly report, the travel agency does not expect to have an exact amount, but it is rounded off on an average of 10 percent. This gives management a pretty good idea of where the agency stands this year versus last year. As noted, for the weekly report this figure is usually obtained by rounding off. There is a monthly report that provides exact figures. The weekly report is usually calculated by taking the total airline ticket sales level and multiplying it by 10 percent. If management compares this with the same data for the same week last year, it gives the agency a good sense of where it is financially in regard to actual money coming in with which to run the business.

Override Commissions Received. An item that sometimes appears on the weekly financial report, but normally does not, is the *override commission* received during the week. This should be reported in dollar amounts, not on a percentage of sales basis. Some agencies, however, do ask for both the dollar amount and the percentage of sales for the vendor providing the override. Again, this is compared to the override commissions received last year. Usually this is reported as a comparison of override commissions received year-to-date last year with override commissions received year-to-date this year.

Non-ARC Sales. Although most agencies find that the sale of airline tickets as reported through the weekly ARC Report constitutes the bulk of all sales made by the agency each week, there are several product sales that are not included on the ARC Report. Therefore, the next section of the weekly financial report deals with sales other than those reported on the ARC Report. For example, the agency receives checks from hotels paying hotel commissions. This may not be reflected on the ARC Report, but it is an income for the agency. Or the agency may sell two or three cruises. These are usually not reported through the Airline Reporting Corporation. The deposit or full-payment monies are sent directly to the cruise lines. Car rental commission receipts are also usually included in this section of the report. These constitute other sales for the travel agency that are not normally reflected as ARC ticket sales.

Dollar Commissions Earned on Non-ARC Sales. The dollar commissions earned on the sale of travel products not reflected on the ARC Report are normally recorded on the weekly financial report as a separate line-item to the report. Some travel agencies break this down into dollar commissions earned as a result of hotel commissions received, car rental commission checks received, sales of their own tours, the sale of F.I.T.s not reflected on the ARC Report, and so forth.

Commissions from Non-Travel Product/Service Sales. Any other income that the travel agency may have received for the sale of anything other than travel products or services will be reported separately. Some travel agencies, for example, take passport pictures and charge $10 for a set. It is not a commissionable item; it is a fee levied by the agency. Some agencies also sell travel books, flight bags, and other products or services not normally considered traditional travel agency products or services.

Total Weekly Estimated Income. All areas of income are added up and a total estimated weekly income is calculated. This is estimated both because the commissions on airline tickets are usually estimated (in terms of dollar figures) and some of the reports themselves purport to be (and are) estimates rather than calculated exact dollar amounts. This total estimated weekly income figure is one of the most important figures the agency generates because this figure is compared with the figure from last year to determine where the agency stands versus last year. Many factors may be up and down, but one of the most important factors is how much actual money has been brought in as compared with last year during the same week.

Percentage of Weekly Salaries Compared to Weekly Income. Another important factor for a travel agency is what the employees are paid. As noted before, in the majority of profitable travel agencies, salaries and benefits constitute between 48 and 52 percent of total expenses. Therefore, if the agency finds that what the employees were paid during the past week is more money than the agency took in (in terms of all sales commissions and all other income), the agency has a problem. But if the agency finds that what was taken in (in terms of commission income and all other income that stays with the agency—interest, etc.) was about 50 percent of what employees were paid, the agency will possibly break even. Since 50 percent of expenses will be employee costs, this is a pretty good indicator of where the agency is relative to overall break-even capability.

However, if employee compensation constitutes 25 percent of the money that is brought in in terms of operating capital, the statistics suggest that the travel agency should be making a profit. For example, if the travel agency brought in $100,000 on $1,000,000 of sales last week and agency employees are paid $25,000 (including benefits and employee taxes), the agency has about $75,000 to pay all other costs. After paying its bills, any balance will be profits, and it is probable under this scenario that profits would be substantial. Therefore, if employee compensation is calculated as a percentage of total income to the agency, agency management will have a good feel for where the agency stands. Keep in mind, however, that this is not a comparison to total sales. It is comparing salaries, benefits, and employee taxes to total income for the travel agency. This is the money the travel agency gets to operate with. This is the income from commissions earned, override checks, passport photo sales, and everything else that the travel agency gets money from. Most owners and managers want the type of rough determination of the agency's status that comes from this comparison.

OTHER MONTHLY, QUARTERLY, AND ANNUAL REPORTS

Each of the following reports is also needed on a monthly, quarterly, and/or annual basis for budgeting purposes. These are summarized here since they are discussed in detail in other sections of the book.

The most basic is the Receipts and Disbursements Statement. It is called by different names, one of the more popular being "Income Statement."

Another report is a Balance Sheet. Like the Receipts and Disbursements Statement, the Balance Sheet is prepared on a monthly basis.

There are a wide range of productivity and profitability reports to be considered. Three of them are especially important: the Commercial Account Profitability Analysis, the Product Profitability Report, and the Personnel Return-on-Investment Analysis.

A marketing cost versus return-on-investment report is a monthly status report that is exactly the same as the weekly marketing cost vs. R.O.I. report.

On a quarterly basis it is important to have productivity reports and tax reports. On an annual basis Receipts and Disbursements (Income) Statements and Balance Sheets are most important.

This is a considerable amount of material to have before considering or starting the budgeting process. However, it is most beneficial to have all of these reports and documents, and to digest them thoroughly before starting the budgeting process.

SUMMARY

Before starting to develop the travel agency's annual budget, it is recommended that reports and data be gathered and studied. If the raw data and the timely reports have been developed on a regular basis and have been kept accurately, the steps in preparing the annual budget can be followed systematically and a good annual budget can be developed.

The raw data consists primarily of tickets, invoices, receipts, deposit slips, ticket logs, and ledgers. It is especially important that deposit slips and invoice/receipts be filled out completely, providing all needed data on clients and individual transactions. This accuracy and completeness will assist the agency in many aspects of financial management, not just in developing the annual budget.

By developing a system that is recorded in a policy and procedures manual and by following that system, the agency is assured of having data recorded in the same way consistently and in a timely manner. The security of accountable documents, money, and checks is increased. The system and procedure should be monitored and changed when changes are called for, with special emphasis on making certain that security is maintained. One should not wait until after a theft to recognize that tickets and money need to be kept locked away, cash drawers need to be kept out of sight and in secure locations, and safes need to be kept locked when not actually in use.

Reports can be broken down by type and frequency of preparation. There are daily reports, weekly reports, monthly reports, quarterly reports, and annual reports. Daily reports consist of the bank deposit, a daily sales balance, and a daily employee time log. Weekly financial reports consist of the weekly ARC Report, a weekly source analysis report, a weekly petty cash report, a weekly cash balance report, and, for many agencies, a weekly status report.

The weekly status report identifies the total amount of ticket sales during the week, the number of tickets issued during the week, the weekly average ticket price, the number and the amount of refunds for the week, the number and the amount of debit notices received and processed during the week, the weekly dollar commissions earned level, the override commissions received during the week, the non-ARC amount of sales for the week and the commissions received on non-ARC sales, the commissions or profits earned from non-travel product/service sales, total weekly estimated income, and the percentage of weekly salaries compared to weekly income. For many travel agencies the weekly status report is considered to be almost as important as the weekly ARC Report. Agency management often depends on the financial data contained in the weekly status report in making both major and minor management decisions. Well prepared weekly status reports can answer most of management's questions about the finances of the company even before the questions come up.

The daily and the weekly reports contribute to the development and preparation of monthly, quarterly, and annual reports. The preparation of these reports is discussed in other parts of this book and therefore, information on how to prepare them is not provided in this chapter. However, it is important to understand which monthly, quarterly, and annual reports are utilized in preparing the annual budget. The income statement (also referred to as the Receipts and Disbursements Statement) and the balance sheet are the two major monthly reports. These are prepared to show not only financial activity during the month for which they are prepared, but also to show financial activity on a year-to-date basis. Sometimes on a monthly basis, but often on a quarterly basis, productivity and profitability reports are prepared as well. Some of these include the Commercial Account Profitability Analysis, the Product Profitability Report, and the Personnel Return-on-Investment Analysis. Many agencies will prepare a monthly marketing cost versus return-on-investment report, as well.

Tax reports, summaries of the income statements and balance sheets, and productivity reports are frequently prepared on a quarterly basis. Primary end-of-year reports are the income statement and the balance sheet. In many travel agencies these two end-of-year reports are prepared by outside accountants, and in an increasing number of cases they are either prepared by or audited by certified public accountants. Having these documents prepared by CPAs can be most beneficial in documenting the financial history of the travel agency if and when agency stock or the entire agency is offered for sale.

❑ DISCUSSION QUESTIONS

1. What reports are prepared on a weekly basis?
2. What are the components of the weekly status report and why is each component considered to be important?
3. What information should be recorded on deposit slips and when should deposit slips be completed and bank deposits made?
4. Why are ticket logs important?
5. What are some of the systems and security procedures that can be adopted to help minimize the possibility of loss of accountable documents and money and to make theft harder?
6. What figures and data are balanced in preparing the daily sales balance?
7. What is included on the source analysis report and why is this report important?
8. Why is expense forecasting important and what data/reports can be helpful in preparing expense forecasts?
9. How is the weekly average ticket price calculated and what data is needed in order to accurately determine that price?
10. Why is a determination of weekly salaries compared to weekly income important and what steps should be taken to calculate the percentage of weekly salaries compared to weekly income?

❑ ROLE-PLAYING EXERCISE

Two students may participate in this role-playing exercise either as an out-of-class or in-class fun way to review the process of preparing the weekly status report. One student plays the travel agency's bookkeeper who has just returned from vacation. The other plays a senior agent who filled in for the bookkeeper. Please read the script and then pick up the conversation in your own words.

Senior Agent: I'm glad you are back from vacation and I hope you enjoyed it. Completing the weekly ARC Report for you was no problem after you briefed me so well. However, I made a mess of the weekly status report.

Agency Bookkeeper: It is a time consuming report to prepare, but the steps taken to prepare it are pretty clear-cut.

Senior Agent: They may be clear-cut to you. I followed the procedures manual, but it seemed like I had questions at every turn. Tell me, exactly what is included on the weekly status report. How is it prepared? What points do I need to consider in order to flag any potential problems?

Agency Bookkeeper: I'll answer all of those questions. Let's start with the reasons for the report in the first place. Probably the major reason is. . .

CONTINUE ON YOUR OWN

❑ CHAPTER TWELVE EXERCISE

INSTRUCTIONS: Utilizing the information below, complete the blank weekly status report on the last two pages in this chapter. Identify any potential problems you feel might be indicated from the data gathered for the report and that management may want to consider watching.

DATA FROM THE PAST WEEK'S ACTIVITIES TO BE USED IN PREPARING THE WEEKLY STATUS REPORT

1. The source data information compiled by agents when they obtained bookings indicates that 34 percent of the business last week came from repeat clients. One percent was from the telemarketing of package tours. The full-time sales person accounted for 29 percent of all bookings. Seven percent of the bookings came from the yellow page advertisements. Outside sales persons generated 21 percent of last week's bookings. There was no record indicating the source of the balance of the bookings from last week.

2. Override commission payments were received from only one vendor last week. This was from AABC Hotels. The amount of their override check was $76.29.
3. The petty cash report indicates that the agency started the week with $100.00 in petty cash; the amount in petty cash at the end of the week was $21.19.
4. In looking at the ARC Report for last week, it is found that the reported credit card amount was $13,520.56 and the reported cash amount was $11,171.56.
5. The bookings report indicates that the total bookings for last week was $31,612.
6. Hotel commissions received last week, according to the hotel commission log, were $1,003.90.
7. The salaries report compared to the income report for last week shows that salary expense constituted an expense of 54 percent of the income received last week.
8. Package tour sales for last week amounted to $3,722.29.
9. The commissions report shows the following commissions earned last week for the following amounts: Package tours - $383.40; cruises - $481.27; rail sales - $62.05; and air sales - $2,765.51.
10. Total sales for the past week included rail sales in the amount of $620.54 and cruise sales in the amount of $4,765.00. In addition, $425.76 was received for car rental commissions that were from previous weeks' business, dating back as much as eight months ago.
11. Comparative studies indicate that the commissions earned and actual monies received for past week activities during the same week last year was $5,423.30. It was $5,610.78 for the same week for an average of the past five years.
12. Other comparative studies for previous years indicates that the total sales for the same week last year were $36,431.16 and the total sales for the same week for an average of the past five years was $38,091.64. In addition, 86 transactions were handled during the same week last year and 87.2 transactions were handled on average during the same week for the past five years. This compares with 84 transactions handled last week.
13. Other comparison studies dealt with a wide variety of data and found that: 1) nineteen debit notices were received for the same week last year and an average of sixteen debit notices were received during the same week during the last five years; 2) four refunds were made the same week last year and an average of seven refunds were made for each of the same weeks during the last five years; 3) the average ticket price for this same week last year was $364.10, while $303.76 was the average ticket price for each of the same weeks during the last five years; and 4) total expenditures for the same week last year amounted to $3,065.13, but the total expenditures average for the same week each year for the past five years was $3,042.84.
14. This comparison data can be compared with actual data for last week, which includes information on total expenditures, average ticket price, the number of refunds made, and the number of debit notices received. This data shows that expenditures totaled $3,103.02 last week. The average ticket price last week was $390.66. Twelve refunds were made last week and twenty-two debit notices were received last week.

WEEKLY STATUS REPORT

FOR THE WEEK OF

____________ 19__

1) ARC Report Total Sales $____________
2) ARC Report Total Cash Sales $____________
3) ARC Report Total Credit Card Sales $____________
4) Non-ARC Report Sales — Cruises $____________
5) Non-ARC Report Sales — Own Tours $____________
6) Non-ARC Report Sales — Rail $____________
7) Non-ARC Report Sales — Package Tours $____________
8) Non-ARC Report Sales — F.I.T. $____________
9) Non-ARC Report Sales — Other: ____________ $____________
10) Commissions Earned from past week air sales $____________
11) Commissions Earned from past week cruise sales $____________
12) Commissions Earned from past week own tours $____________
13) Commissions Earned from past week rail sales $____________
14) Commissions Earned from past week Pkg tours $____________
15) Commissions Earned from past week F.I.T. sales $____________
16) Commissions Earned from past week other sales $____________
17) Total Sales for past week $____________
18) Total Commissions Earned from past week $____________
19) Monies received in past week Hotel Commissions $____________
20) Monies received in past week Car Rental Commissions $____________
21) Any other income during past week $____________
Specify source of income: ____________
22) Total Commissions Earned & Monies Rcvd Past Week $____________
23) Total Comm. Earned & Monies Rcvd Same Week L.Y. $____________
24) Total Comm. Earned & Monies Rcvd Avg Past 5 Yrs $____________
25) Total Sales Past Week $____________
26) Total Sales Same Week Last Year $____________
27) Total Sales Same Week Average Past 5 Years $____________
28) Total transactions handled last week ____________
29) Average commission per transaction last week $____________
30) Average commission per transaction past 5 Yrs $____________
31) Average sale value per transaction last week $____________
32) Average sale value per transaction past 5 Yrs $____________
33) Total transactions handled same week last year ____________
34) Average transactions handled same week past 5 Yrs ____________

Figure 12–1

35) Source Analysis Data for Bookings Last Week
(Rank by percent of total bookings and show percentage after the source of bookings)

Source ____________________ % Booking $ Total $______________
Source ____________________ % Booking $ Total $______________
Source ____________________ % Booking $ Total $______________
Source ____________________ % Booking $ Total $______________
Source ____________________ % Booking $ Total $______________
Source ____________________ % Booking $ Total $______________

36) Petty Cash beginning balance last week $______________
37) Petty Cash ending balance last week $______________
38) Amount of money spent from petty cash last week $______________
39) Total Expenditures last week $______________
40) Total Expenditures same week last year $______________
41) Total Expenditures same week average last 5 years $______________
42) Average ticket price last week $______________
43) Average ticket price same week last year $______________
44) Average ticket price same week average last 5 years $______________
45) Number of refunds made last week ______________
46) Number of refunds made same week last year ______________
47) Average number of refunds same week last 5 years ______________
48) Number of debit notices rcvd last week ______________
49) Number of debit notices rcvd same week last year ______________
50) Avg number of debit notices rcvd same wk last 5 yrs _____
51) Override Commission payments received last week

Vendor ____________________________________ Amt $______________
Vendor ____________________________________ Amt $______________
Vendor ____________________________________ Amt $______________
Vendor ____________________________________ Amt $______________

52) Total Estimated Income from last week $______________
53) Percentage of weekly salaries to weekly Income
Salaries constituted _____% of the income rcvd. last week
54) Based on the above, use the rest of this page to identify problems and/or trends to be concerned with and/or any projections that may be appropriate.

Figure 12–1 (Continued)

13

PRODUCTIVITY AND PROFITABILITY ANALYSES

OBJECTIVES

Upon completion of this chapter, the student will be able to:

- ❑ Justify an employee's salary increase request when the employee's return-on-investment analysis data is made available and to do this based upon a student-completed personnel return-on-investment analysis
- ❑ Analyze vendor override proposals utilizing data that is provided for the product profitability report and based upon a student-completed product profitability report
- ❑ Compare the profitability of two or more commercial accounts by completing a commercial account profitability analysis when the report data has been provided
- ❑ Identify the similarities between the commercial account profitability analysis, the product profitability report, and the personnel return-on-investment analysis form

INTRODUCTION

For travel agencies to make money, costs must be watched carefully. In addition, an effort must be made to obtain the greatest possible amount of dollar commissions or income from each sale. In the dual effort to decrease costs and increase income, both productivity of staff and maximization of profits from vendors are needed. The other half of the profitability formula is reduction of costs. Therefore, still another aspect of productivity/profitability is a recognition of costs versus income in handling each corporate account.

In this chapter, three productivity/profitability analyses will be discussed. The first of these relates to the profitability of specific product lines. This is called the *Product Profitability Report.* This report allows agency management to identify those particular products that generate the greatest percentage and the greatest dollar amount of commissions. The report is especially beneficial in identifying the range of products which agency management should consider emphasizing.

The second productivity/profitability analysis discusses the productivity of personnel. This is the *Personnel Return-on-Investment Analysis.* This analysis allows agency management to evaluate the productivity and profitability of each inside sales person. In addition, agency management may compare the productivity/profitability of each agent with every other agent. This is especially beneficial in identifying agents who may be either underpaid or overpaid so that appropriate action may be taken.

The third productivity/profitability analysis discussed is the *Commercial Account Profitability Analysis.* This analysis allows agency management to identify those corporate or business accounts that provide the greatest degree of return on investment. In other words, it lets agency management understand which accounts provide an excellent commission/profit for the agency and which ones do not. Because there are variables involved in handling corporate or business accounts, it is sometimes possible for agency management to change an account from one on which there is either marginal or no profit to one on which the profit is reasonable or even good.

THE PRODUCT PROFITABILITY REPORT

The Product Profitability Report is developed to try to determine which item of the agency's total product range is producing the best profits or return on investment. This is done by measuring the actual amount of sales of each product on a monthly, quarterly, or annual basis. Some agencies take this measure even on a weekly basis, especially very large travel agencies that have the process totally computerized. But for most travel agencies, it is quarterly and annually. Once the agency has identified the total sales in each product area, the agency next identifies what the commissions are for the particular period being considered for each product area. By looking at the product commissions for the period and the total sales, the agency can determine a figure, which is *Commissions as a Percentage of Bookings* for the period. That figure gives the agency an indication of what the most profitable product is.

The Product Profitability Report Form

Review the blank Product Profitability Report form in figure 13–1. At the top is the title of the report. Then comes the month or quarter for which the report is being prepared. This would normally be the last month of the

PRODUCT PROFITABILITY REPORT

FOR MONTH ________________ 19 ____

This Month	Air	Hotel	Car Rental	Cruise	Rail	Package Tours	Other ______	Other ______	Other ______	Total
Dollar Value of Bookings	$	$	$	$	$	$	$	$	$	$
Commissions in Dollars	$	$	$	$	$	$	$	$	$	$
Commissions as a Percent of Bookings This Month	%	%	%	%	%	%	%	%	%	%
Year-to-Date										
Dollar Value of Bookings	$	$	$	$	$	$	$	$	$	$
Commissions in Dollars	$	$	$	$	$	$	$	$	$	$
Commissions as a Percent of Bookings Year-to-Date	%	%	%	%	%	%	%	%	%	%

Figure 13–1

quarter, but some agencies will complete the analysis every month. Then the particular products sold by the travel agency are broken down. Bookings for the particular period are always shown here as a dollar figure. Start with air. Hotels come next. Then car rentals and cruises are shown. Rail is next and finally package tours are listed. If there are enough of them, F.I.T.s and D.I.T.s, can be listed in one or more of the "other" columns. Finally, the total is shown on the far right.

The next line calls for commissions. This is the dollar figure for actual commissions received for each category during the month or quarter being considered.

The final section is "Commissions As A Percent of the Booking" for each of the individual categories. The same information is provided for "Year-to-Date." By looking at, for example, the package tour commissions level as a percentage of bookings for the period and comparing that with the year-to-date "Commissions as a Percentage of Bookings Year-to-Date" for package tours, the travel agency has an idea as to whether or not it is a skewed period, i.e., how well this particular period fits into the overall sales pattern for each product sold.

This does not have much meaning until one considers a Product Line Commissions Report form that has been completed. Therefore, review figure 13-2. This is XYZ Travel. It is for the month of March, but it also reflects the activity for the first quarter of the year. Note that bookings for domestic air total $189,756.98 for March. The commissions amount to $19,162.56. This gives XYZ Travel an air commission level of 10.1 percent.

There is a 10.3 percent average commission for hotels. This is very good for hotels. To be able to get this average commission figure, XYZ would have to be collecting almost all of its outstanding hotel commissions (many travel agencies are not able to do this well). XYZ Travel would also have to have some override commission agreements which are based on higher than 10 percent commissions being paid per booking. The standard hotel commission is only 10 percent.

Car rental commissions for the month are slightly lower than might be expected. However, year-to-date commissions are very high. This suggests that one or more large lump-sum override commission(s) were received in either January or February.

With cruises a similar pattern is seen. The average commission for the quarter is 10.4 percent while the year-to-date figure is 10.6 percent. This is unusual. Most cruise booking averages will reflect a considerably higher average commission than 10.4 percent. For this kind of volume it should be higher. Again, this indicates that XYZ Travel is not working with favored-vendor status cruise lines. The agency staff is probably selling any cruise that the individual agent might like or perhaps any cruise whose brochure happens to be on or near the agent's desk.

PRODUCT PROFITABILITY REPORT

FOR MONTH *MARCH* 19 ____

This Month	Air	Hotel	Car Rental	Cruise	Rail	Package Tours	Other F.I.T./D.I.T.	Other ____	Other ____	Total
Dollar Value of Bookings	*$189,756.98*	$ *8,481.13*	$ *10,474.79*	$ *36,512.08*	$ *5,237.39*	$ *54,718.36*	$ *9,019.87*	$	$	*$314.200.60*
Commissions in Dollars	$ *19,162.56*	$ *869.49*	$ *990.41*	$ *3,799.59*	$ *495.21*	$ *5,566.11*	$ *1,898.06*	$	$	$ *32,781.43*
Commissions as a Percent of Bookings This Month	*10.1%*	*10.3%*	*9.5%*	*10.4%*	*9.5%*	*10.2%*	*21%*	%	%	*10.4%*
Year-to-Date										
Dollar Value of Bookings	*$537,209.83*	$ *22,334.40*	$ *20,321.16*	$ *98,649.35*	$ *20,810.05*	*$176,164.19*	$ *21,668.27*	$	$	*$897,157.25*
Commissions in Dollars	$ *54,065.02*	$ *2,638.78*	$ *2,719.18*	$ *10,540.69*	$ *1,286.00*	$ *18,006.23*	$ *3,014.33*	$	$	$ *92,270.23*
Commissions as a Percent of Bookings Year-to-Date	*10.1%*	*11.8%*	*13.4%*	*10.6%*	*6.2%*	*10.2%*	*13.9%*	%	%	*10.3%*

Figure 13–2

Rail commissions are good for the month, but low for the quarter. This suggests a lack of collection on rail bookings made in January or February.

The package tour level is low. This indicates that probably there are not a lot of override commissions. Quite likely, there are none. This is an area that XYZ Travel should work on, because they probably can reach an average level of something well in excess of 10 percent. This conclusion is reinforced when one considers the year-to-date level that is identical in its percentage.

When considering F.I.T.s, one can see that not a large number of F.I.T.s have been sold. The volume of sales is respectable compared to hotel and car rental sales. But the commission level is very good in terms of dollars and extremely good as it relates to overall commissions as a percentage of bookings this month. It is 21 percent. This is about twice what the other categories reflect in terms of income. It suggests that XYZ Travel may want to concentrate on F.I.T.s and make an effort to sell more since this would appear to be its most profitable product area (and XYZ Travel is not selling many F.I.T.s).

However, when looking at the year-to-date F.I.T. figure, one finds a very different, and a somewhat less impressive figure. The agency is now down to 13.9 percent. This would indicate that there may be a pricing difference or a skew of some type for the month of March. This is something the management of XYZ Travel may want to review and consider. Obviously, if XYZ Travel's management can bring the annual F.I.T. commission as a percentage of bookings to the level of 21 percent on a consistent basis, then it is something that the agency will probably want to specialize in. If it consistently stays around the level of 14 percent (it's current year-to-date level), it will still be considerably better than most other income areas and the justification may be there to concentrate on F.I.T.s. However, costs will need to be considered carefully also. Whatever the case, more effort in selling F.I.T.s is probably called for.

Looking at the overall commissions as a percentage of bookings for this period versus year-to-date, one finds that they are almost identical, i.e., 10.4 percent versus 10.3 percent. This is slightly below the norm for travel agencies. It is fairly good. It is not something XYZ Travel should be overly concerned about, but it does suggest that there may be ways in which the travel agency can make more money.

EXERCISE #1

Exercise #1 is based on this type of analysis. XYZ Travel will be analyzed for this period. Three basic questions are asked. The questions get a little harder each time. The first question reviews what has already been discussed. It asks which products are bringing in the greatest amount of commissions. Answering this question should be easy.

Question 2, however, is a little harder. A potential override offer from a vendor is presented. The analysis must determine: 1) what the financial ramifications are, considering what the override offer is in terms of real dollar figures based upon history; and 2) where the agency currently stands in terms of the same product. The analysis will help identify which option will be better. There are two override commission offers to consider. Both of these offers need to be weighed against each other, but they also need to be weighed against what XYZ Travel currently has. It may be that XYZ Travel will not want to accept either of the override commission offers that have been extended. It may be that XYZ Travel will want to adopt both offers. Maybe neither offer should be accepted. Therefore, both options need to be considered and compared with what the current status is.

Question 3 also deals with a special kind of situation. It introduces additional computerization that theoretically can bring in more revenues. Here the management of XYZ Travel needs to consider how much more in revenues will come in versus what additional costs there will be. One needs to consider costs any time one starts identifying anything additional to be done in terms of collection efforts for commissions.

In completing this exercise, play the role of XYZ Travel's bookkeeper or accountant who will be making a recommendation to the agency's manager.

CHAPTER 13 — EXERCISE #1
XYZ TRAVEL
PRODUCT PROFITABILITY REPORT ANALYSIS

INSTRUCTIONS: For this exercise study the XYZ TRAVEL PRODUCT PROFITABILITY REPORT — MARCH 19__ AND YEAR-TO-DATE. Analyze the figures and answer the following questions. Explain your reasons for each answer provided.

1. XYZ Travel holds weekly meetings for all staff members. The manager of the agency wishes to increase commission dollars during the next fiscal quarter. He/she wants to encourage sales agents to push the product that has the potential of bringing in the largest dollar increase based on commission dollars. What product do you suggest the manager of the agency concentrate on stressing at the next weekly meetings? Why? (Be specific.)

2. The manager of XYZ Travel has been approached by the SLUMMBERBETTER HOTELS chain with an override commission offer. If XYZ will sell a minimum of one-third of its annual hotel sales utilizing SLUMMBERBETTER HOTELS, the chain will provide the agency with a $500 override commission for every $5,000 of sales after the first $30,000 of annual bookings. In addition, the standard commission will increase to 10.1 percent on all bookings

after the first $10,000 of bookings. Meanwhile, EZ INNS has offered the agency a continuation of its standard 10 percent commissions up to the first $500 of annual bookings for next year with an increase of one-tenth of one percent paid retroactively for every additional $500 of annual bookings. Which offer should the manager of XYZ Travel take and why? Should the manager take both offers? Why? Should the manager take neither offer? Why?

3. The manager of XYZ Travel has been concerned for some time about the inability of the agency's manual tracking system to result in the collection of all car rental commissions due to the agency. He/she estimates that the agency is receiving only between 75 and 85 percent of earned commissions even though overrides for car rental bookings are being paid at an acceptable level. A sales representative from COMPUCARENT was in the office yesterday and offered to place XYZ Travel online with their new tracking system. Using this sytem, COMPUCARENT guarantees a collection percentage of at least 95 percent of all car rental commissions on in-country car rentals from national company franchisees. The quarterly cost is only $200 and the agency only has to sign a two-year contract. Based upon the data available to you, would you recommend that the agency manager sign the COMPUCARENT contract? Explain your answer in detail.

Exercise Analysis

It is not the single answer to the questions presented in these exercises that is as important as the process that is used in completing the exercises. The travel agency must project data that usually is not easy to project. It is based on the history of XYZ Travel itself.

Answering Exercise #1, Question 1. Question 1 was easy and fairly simple. It asks for an identification of the single product that has the potential of bringing in the largest dollar increase based on commission sales. As discussed earlier in this chapter, for this agency that is F.I.T.s. During March F.I.T.s accounted for a 21 percent commission as a percentage of bookings. It is only 13.9 percent for the three-month period of the year, but even at 13.9 percent, the F.I.T. figure is higher than the figure for all of the other products for the year to date. But if XYZ Travel continues to do even a part of what is was doing for the last three months, XYZ Travel will be able to get a much better dollar commission level for every dollar of F.I.T.s sold than for any other product the agency sells.

Answering Exercise #1, Question 2. Question 2, however, is a little harder to work with. Question 2 asks agency management to presuppose some data that is not provided. One of the things an executive needs to do if he/she wishes to identify what one is able to do with somewhat better hotels is to identify what the sales level will be. When one looks at what the three-month figure is for hotels, one can see that the total bookings for the three-month period is $22,334. If that is projected into total bookings for the year, XYZ Travel will be considerably over the $30,000 level. Since we all know that no agency has every one of its clients staying at the same hotel, however, XYZ Travel should not automatically assume that it will reach that first $30,000 level that is needed to get the $500 initial override commission. However, there is a realistic chance that with directive selling, it will. So, although XYZ Travel may sign a contract with SLUMMBERBETTER HOTELS, realistically speaking, XYZ Travel should not expect to have any real income from it. The minimum level of sales before overrides start is too high. They are asking for one-third of XYZ Travel's hotel bookings. If XYZ Travel booked at one-third, that is probably $29,771 and not $30,000 (which is XYZ Travel's minimum booking level to start earning override commissions). Therefore, any way one looks at it, the SLUMMBERBETTER HOTELS override commission criteria makes its program one that is probably not going to be particularly beneficial for XYZ Travel. Perhaps a few years later XYZ Travel may benefit by reconsidering the SLUMMBERBETTER override commission program.

When looking at the arrangement for the other hotel chain, EZ INNS, one finds that the requirements are not quite so difficult to meet. Again, XYZ Travel executives will need to start out by looking at what annual hotel sales will be. They calculate this figure by doing a projection of the three-month into a twelve-month figure. This will produce a hotel sales figure of just slightly under $90,000. At a one-tenth of one percent increase for every $500 of sales for EZ INNS, if the travel agency put every client it booked this past year into EZ INNS (and of course XYZ Travel did not do that), it would give XYZ Travel an opportunity to earn 168 override commission levels or 168 times one-tenth of one percent. The decision of XYZ Travel's management then becomes a question of how many EZ INNS room nights XYZ Travel can expect to sell, and what the average room night cost will be. Some would say that XYZ Travel could project putting one out of every four clients into EZ INNS. That probably is unrealistic. It is doubtful that any travel agency will be able to put one out of every four clients into any hotel or hotel chain, no matter how good that property's override commission program is. Perhaps XYZ will project they will put one out of every seven or one out of every eight clients into an EZ INN. For the sake of developing a scenario, one out of every eight clients will be used, although even that is quite high. However, by taking this figure, one can get an understanding as to how the decision to adopt override commission programs is undertaken. With a potential of 168 $500 levels, one divides eight into 168. This produces 21 $500 levels. With each $500 level providing one-tenth of one percent of override commission dollars, this would give XYZ Travel 21/10 of one percent in overrides or an override of 2.1 percent. Since this override commission level is retroactive, the standard 10

SCHEMATIC OF
CALCULATIONS FOR QUESTION 2, EXERCISE #1
CHAPTER 13

DETERMINING POTENTIAL BENEFITS OF THE EZ INNS
OVERRIDE COMMISSION
PREFERRED-VENDOR OFFER

STEP 1: Determine projected twelve-month hotel sales figure. Divide three-month total sales ($22,334.40) by 3 and multiply times 12:

$89,337.60

STEP 2: Determine the maximum number of override units the agency might earn based on estimated sales by dividing the projected twelve-month hotel sales figure of $89,337.60 less $500, or $84,337.60 by the required unit of sales increase amount ($500).

$84,337.60 ÷ $500 = 168 maximum override units

STEP 3: Estimate percentage of clients the agency can put into the preferred vendor's hotels (EZ INNS). This has been arbitrarily set at one out of eight.

1:8

STEP 4: Divide the step three figure (8) into the step two figure (168) to determine the projected realistic number of override units the agency might earn based on its projected hotel sales.

168 ÷ 8 = 21

STEP 5: Multiply the projected number of override units (21) times the percent of override commission per unit (one-tenth of one percent) to determine the projected override level (twenty-one tenths of one percent).

21 × .1 = 2.1 percent

STEP 6: Add the standard commission (10 percent) to the projected override commission (2.1 percent) to determine total commissions (12.1 percent).

10% + 2.1% = 12.1%

Figure 13–3

percent commission plus the 2.1 percent commission would apply. If XYZ Travel did enter into this override commission agreement, XYZ Travel could expect to earn a 12.1 percent overall commission from EZ INNS. In other words, this would provide an additional 2.1 percent commission on EZ INNS bookings. XYZ Travel is not required by EZ INNS to sign a contract for a minimum amount of bookings, and there is no penalty involved for not reaching predetermined booking levels. Therefore, there is nothing XYZ Travel will lose by entering into an override agreement with EZ INNS and there is a possibility that XYZ Travel will obtain as much as a 2.1 percent increase in terms of overall commission level. XYZ Travel will probably go forward with the EZ INNS Override Commission Program proposal.

Answering Exercise #1, Question 3. Now consider the third question. This particular question asks one to identify whether or not it is profitable to install some equipment to increase the sales commission in terms of the monies being brought in for car rentals. As is common knowledge, some car rental franchisees do not send in commissions to travel agencies as readily as others. Therefore, this equipment would help the agency to bill or rebill car rental companies and/or their franchisees.

Ideally, this would help the travel agency collect closer to 100 percent of the car rental commissions due to the agency. It is doubtful that the agency will ever attain 100 percent, although that is a possibility. However, it is easier to project 100 percent. Therefore, that is the figure this chapter will work with, figure 13–4.

Presuming that the sales shown, for example, represent commissions collected for 80 percent of the actual car rental sales, then to project what the agency's twelve-month figure is for actual car rental sales, the accountant could divide the $2,719.18 by .80, divide that figure by 3, and multiply the resulting figure by 12. That final figure will give the accountant approximate commissions for 100 percent of car rental sales for twelve months.

Now that that figure has been calculated, the next step is to consider the difference between the commission earned on 80 percent of commission sales (which is what the agency is collecting currently), and the commission earned on 100 percent of that figure (which is what the agency ideally wants to collect) and determine whether the difference between these two figures is the same as or higher than the cost of the equipment itself. The equipment costs approximately $800 per year. The probability is that the additional commissions that the travel agency will be collecting, even if the agency is able to increase its commission collection level to only 90 or 95 percent, will bring more money into the agency than the $800 annual figure. The ideal situation projects a maximum benefit (total additional collections less additional costs) of $1,919.18 per year.

SCHEMATIC OF
CALCULATIONS FOR QUESTION 3, EXERCISE #1
CHAPTER 13

DETERMINING POTENTIAL FINANCIAL BENEFITS OF COMPUCARENT'S GUARANTEED CAR RENTAL COMMISSION TRACKING/COLLECTION SYSTEM

STEP 1: Divide the five-year average percentage of car rental commissions, 80 percent, into the three-month total of car rental commissions, $2,719.18, to determine 100 percent of the approximate car rental commissions for three months.

$2,719.18 ÷ .80 = $3,398.98

STEP 2: Divide the three-month approximate car rental commissions, $3,398.98 by three and multiply by 12 to determine the projected one-year (annual) car rental commissions.

$3,398.98 ÷ 3 = $1,132.99
$1,132.99 × 12 = $13,595.88

STEP 3: Determine projected commissions on 80 percent of projected annual car rental sales by multiplying 80 percent times $13,595.88.

$13,595.88 × .80 = $10,876.70

STEP 4: Subtract the 80 percent of commission level, $10,876.70, from the 100 percent of commission level, $13,595.88.

$13,595.88 – $10,876.70 = $2,719.18

STEP 5: Compare the difference (additional income) determined in step four, $2,719.18, with the cost of the equipment, $800.00 (annually) to determine whether or not the equipment/system would be cost effective.

$2,719.18 – $800.00 = $1,919.18

Figure 13–4

Penalties

One question that has not been addressed thus far is the question of what happens if a penalty has to be paid for not reaching an override commission agreed-to sales level. In other words, if the agency financial manager says to a vendor that the agency will sell a specific level so that the agency can get an override, agency management needs to concern itself with what the penalties will be if the sales needed to reach the override level are not attained. Penalties frequently are in override commission contracts. Therefore, "penalties" becomes an important additional point to consider when calculating override commissions and override sales quotas.

Override Benefit Combinations

When considering which vendors to sell, therefore, agency executives need to consider which vendor(s) will provide the best combination of benefits for the travel agency and its clients. Certainly favored-vendor status is being sought by an increasing number of vendors and many are offering attractive packages of benefits to entice travel agency executives to select them as preferred vendors. Override commissions constitute the most important ingredients of the benefit packages, but they are only one type of benefit, and there are often sales quotas and penalties associated with override agreements.

PERSONNEL RETURN-ON-INVESTMENT ANALYSIS

When one considers the large amount of money that is paid for personnel costs in a travel agency, the ability to analyze the productivity of each agent becomes especially important. The Personnel Return-on-Investment Analysis form, figure 13–5, gives agency management an opportunity to measure productivity. As will be recalled, there is a salesperson copy of the invoice/receipt. When these copies are retained for each inside travel agent, it is possible to compare the total amount of bookings/commissions with the total number of sales hours worked during a particular period of time (normally a quarter, i.e., three months) to determine a comparison between agent cost and agent productivity. This analysis can be utilized to identify which agents are producing the greatest amount of profit per hour of work and which agents are losing money for the travel agency, i.e., not producing a profit.

It is critical that all productivity of each agent be determined. For example, if an agent has responsibilities beyond sales, the Personnel Return-on-Investment Analysis form will be skewed and will not present an accurate picture. However, variations of the analysis can be constructed for those working in each job in the agency. Because in most travel agencies the largest number of employees are inside sales agents, the Personnel Return-on-Investment Analysis form is directed toward those who are full-time inside sales agents with responsibility for only selling travel.

The Personnel Return-on-Investment Analysis Form

Figure 13–5 shows a blank example of a Personnel Return-on-Investment Analysis form. As with the Product Profitability Report, the first line is the

PERSONNEL RETURN-ON-INVESTMENT ANALYSIS

MONTH ENDING: ____________________

Agent Name	Dollar Bookings for Period (1)	Commissions Earned (2)	Overrides & Vendor Bonuses Paid (3)	Sales Cost (Salary & Benefits) (4)	Contribution 5 = (2) + (3) – 4 (5)	Break Even 2 × (4) = (2) + (3) (6)	Profit (3 or more × (4) = (2) + (3) (7)

Figure 13–5

name of the form. Also the quarter or month ending date line is provided to show a one-month or a three-month period ending. The body of the form starts with a column for the name of the sales agent. Each of the other columns is numbered so that calculations can be identified.

The first numbered column, (1), is "Dollar Bookings for Period." In this column the gross dollar bookings for the period is entered.

The third column from the left, column (2), calls for "Commissions Earned." This is the amount of actual earned commissions on the bookings.

The next column, (3), is "Overrides and Vendor Bonuses Paid." All override payments or portions of override payments earned and paid during the month/quarter for business generated by or sold by the sales agent are shown in this column.

Column (4), which is actually the fifth column from the left, is "Sales Cost." It is here that the salary and benefits paid for the agent/salesperson is entered. Many in the travel agency who prepare the personnel return-on-investment analysis believe that the figure entered into the sales salary column should always be as close as possible to the total of the personnel sales cost, i.e., salary, benefits, contributed tax, educational allowance (if it is provided), bonuses, and other amounts of money paid by the travel agency in order to have this particular person work for the agency. In fact, the difference between sales salary and sales cost can be considerable.

The contribution column is designed to show the dollar amount of "contribution" made to the agency by the inside salesperson. This is the amount agency management retains from sales completed by the agent after paying the agent earned salary and benefits. The "contribution" is based on "net" income, i.e., that money retained by the agency after paying vendors. It is usually only commissions and override/vendor bonus income.

The next column is "Break Even." To determine whether or not the travel agency is potentially breaking even from the work of the sales agent, the total of columns (2) and (3) should be equal to or more than the total of twice the amount of column (4). In other words, the amount of commissions earned and overrides paid to the agency for the work performed by the sales agent during the designated time period should be equal to or more than twice the total sales cost to the agency for employing the sales agent during the same time period.

The last column on the Personnel Return-on-Investment Analysis form is "Profit." Profit will occur only when the total cost of the employee (sales agent) is less than 1/3 of the amount of money brought into the agency by the sales employee. In other words, when the commissions earned and overrides paid on business generated by the sales agent is equal to three times (or more) the total costs of the sales agent (salary, bonuses, employee taxes, etc.), then the travel agency should be making a profit from the work of the sales agent.

Jane Doe Example. To understand how the Personnel Return-on-Investment Analysis form works, study figure 13–6. This is a Personnel Return-on-Investment Analysis for Jane Doe based upon her work during the first three months of the year for XYZ Travel. During January, February, and March, Jane sold a total of $62,500 in travel bookings, column (1). The commissions she received on the sale of the $62,500 was $6,275, column (2). An override payment received compensating for sales Jane made during this period was $75, column (3). The salary paid to Jane during the three-month period was $1,000 per month or a total of $3,000, columm (4).

To determine column (5), Jane's contribution to XYZ Travel, one subtracts her salary ($3,000) from the commissions and overrides she earned ($6,350). This indicates that Jane has contributed $3,350 to the travel agency. Since it is known that approximately 50 percent of a travel agency's expenses are allocated to employee costs, for the travel agency to barely break even, each agent/salesperson must be able to earn commissions and overrides that will be at least twice their cost. If one considers Jane's contribution of $3,350 added to her salary of $3,000, one can calculate the total commissions earned and can readily identify the fact that Jane has provided more than enough contribution for the travel agency to reach break even, i.e., at least as much in contribution as in salary. Although the agency will not make much, if any, profit on $350 of contribution, at least under this scenario Jane is providing enough contribution that the agency appears to be breaking even.

Sales Cost

However, salary is not the only compensation paid by a travel agency to cover the cost of most employees. In addition to salary, employees normally receive benefits that have a cost attached. In addition, the travel agency pays a contribution tax on top of salary deducted tax to the government for each employee. Other benefits are often provided as well. For example, education allowances, FAM trip contributions, and bonuses are not uncommon.

For the example provided in figure 13–6 for Jane Doe, one should consider that in addition to the annual $12,000 salary she makes, the agency pays for other compensation. This includes $2,600 for benefits, $960 for contributed tax, $1,140 for education allowance, and $1,000 for a bonus. The total is $17,700 for the year. Broken down into a quarterly figure, it comes to $4,425. This, then, is the real cost for employing Jane as an agent.

When this cost of $4,425 is entered into column (4), "Sales Cost" (see the lower row of figures in figure 13–6), and when the sales cost of $4,425 is subtracted from the commissions and overrides earned during the first quarter ($6,350), the contribution becomes only $1,925. Looking at the sales cost and determining whether or not the travel agency will at least break even by

PERSONNEL RETURN-ON-INVESTMENT ANALYSIS

QUARTER ENDING: *MARCH* 19____

Agent Name	Dollar Bookings for Period (1)	Commissions Earned (2)	Overrides & Vendor Bonuses Paid (3)	Salary (4)	Contribution (5) = (2) + (3) − 4 (5)	Break Even 2 × (4) = (2) + (3) (6)	Profit 3 or More × (4) = (2) + (3) (7)
Jane Doe	*$62,500*	*$6,275*	*$75*	*$3,000*	*$6,275* *+ 75* *$6,350* *−3,000* *(5) = $3,350*	*$3,000* *× 2* *$6,000*; *$6,275* *+ 75* *$6,350* *Profit is $350*	*No Profit*
Jane Doe				Sales Cost (Salary & Benefits) *$4,425*	*$6,275* *+ 75* *$6,350* *−4,425* *(5) = $1,925*	*No Break Even*	*No Profit*

Salary	*$12,000 per year*
Benefits	*$ 2,600 per year*
Contributed Tax	*$ 960 per year*
Education Allowance	*$ 1,140 per year*
Bonus	*$ 1,000 per year*
	$17,700 per year

$17,700 ÷ 4 = $4,425

Figure 13–6

employing Jane Doe, one now finds that Jane is producing only approximately 25 percent more than her sales salary for the travel agency. Therefore, she is costing the agency money rather than providing profits for the agency. If the agency as a whole is not losing money, then another agent/salesperson is "carrying" Jane by contributing more than the contribution needed from her to create a break-even point.

Agency managers, under these circumstances, should seriously consider either working with Jane to make certain that her bookings and commissions are increased; reducing the cost of Jane to the agency by reducing benefits, allowances, bonuses and/or salary; or terminating Jane and bringing in a less expensive agent to handle the business currently handled by Jane.

EXERCISE #2

Exercise #2 relates to Jane Austin's desire to justify a salary increase request. This exercise shows how both management and employees can utilize the Personnel Return-on-Investment Analysis to manage compensation in a travel agency so that a reasonable amount of profits results and so that employees are fairly compensated. Utilize the Personnel Return-on-Investment Analysis form, figure 13–7, to identify on the first line what the agent in this case is expected to sell, (use 1/4 of this figure for the bookings figure for the quarter), and what the agent would receive in commissions if the commissions were an average 10 percent. On line two of the Personnel Return-on-Investment Analysis form compare this with what the agent actually does sell (based on the quarter of a year figure) and 10 percent of these commissions. This comparison will provide the information needed to answer the questions.

CHAPTER 13 — EXERCISE #2
TRAVEL AGENT
SALARY INCREASE JUSTIFICATION ANAYLSIS #1

INSTRUCTIONS: Jane Austin, a travel agent, has a quota to sell $500,000 in travel during a year, but in reality sells $1 million in travel. She is being paid a salary and benefits totaling $20,000 per year. How might Jane back up a request for an increase in salary and what salary level could she realistically expect to receive? Base your answers on a statistical analysis and show your calculations on figure 13–8.

PERSONNEL RETURN-ON-INVESTMENT ANALYSIS

QUARTER ENDING: *MARCH* 19____

Agent Name	Dollar Bookings for Period (1)	Commissions Earned (2)	Overrides & Vendor Bonuses Paid (3)	Sales Cost (Salary & Benefits) (4)	Contribution (5) = (2) + (3) – 4 (5)	Break Even 2 × (4) = (2) + (3) (6)	Profit 3 or More × (4) = (2) + (3) (7)
Jane Austin							
Sales Expectations	*$125,000*	*$12,500*		*$5,000*	*$7,500*		
Actual Sales	*$250,000*	*$25,000*		*$5,000*	*$20,000*		

Figure 13–7

Override Commission Considerations

"Sales cost" is frequently considered to be a good figure to use in column (5) of the Personnel Return-on-Investment Analysis, since it reflects the actual compensation paid by the agency to have the employee work for the agency. At the same time, "contributions" should consider not just commissions earned on the bookings sold by an agent, but also override commissions earned by the agency as a result of the agent selling preferred vendors. Therefore, column (3) stresses the inclusion of override commissions and vendor-paid bonuses.

To see how override commissions affect the contribution formula, study exercise #3, Salary Increase Justification Analysis #2, and calculate the figures. Compare your figures, calculations, and arguments with the "Travel Agent Salary Increase Data Example" information provided.

CHAPTER 13 — EXERCISE #3
TRAVEL AGENT
SALARY INCREASE JUSTIFICATION ANAYLSIS #2

EXERCISE #3

INSTRUCTIONS: Jane Austin has reached agreement for a salary increase based upon her annual sales performance. However, during the conversation with the agency owner/manager about her increase, Jane has the opportunity to negotiate further by pointing out her ability to sell preferred vendors and earn override commissions for the agency. She notes that override commissions earned on her sales should be substantial since she is selling favored vendors over 55 percent of the time. She points out that other agents probably sell favored vendors only about 15 percent of the time. Jane receives no compensation for selling favored vendors rather than any other vendors. How might Jane back up an additional income, bonus, or salary increase request based on her ability to sell preferred vendors? What can she realistically expect to receive? Base your answers on a statistical analysis and show your calculations on figure 13–8.

POINT: Jane Austin works for Give Me A Break Travel and is paid a salary of $20,000 per year. She has been given a sales quota of $500,000 in annual bookings and sales. However, she always doubles her quota and for the past two years she has sold slightly in excess of $1 million in annual bookings and sales. Jane has kept exact records and in a meeting with her boss, H.Q. Ufic, Jane points out the following:

1. At an average commission level of approximately 10 percent, her sales should be bringing the agency a commission total of approximately $100,000 per year.

PERSONNEL RETURN-ON-INVESTMENT ANALYSIS

MONTH ENDING: ____________________ 19___

Agent Name	Dollar Bookings for Period (1)	Commissions Earned (2)	Overrides & Vendor Bonuses Paid (3)	Sales Cost (Salary & Benefits) (4)	Contribution $(5) = (2) + (3) - 4$ (5)	Break Even $2 \times (4) = (2) + (3)$ (6)	Profit 3 or More $\times (4) = (2) + (3)$ (7)

Figure 13–8

2. If she only reached her sales quota of $500,000 in sales per year, she would be making the same salary and benefits, but would be bringing into the agency only $50,000 per year in commissions.
3. With no additional income for doing it, she has brought the company $50,000 of operating capital (income) each year for the last two years.
4. Therefore, by providing double the income for the company than that which was expected, she should at least be paid twice the salary and benefits she is earning.
5. Looking at the figures another way, national statistics indicate that 50 percent of all agency costs are spent in the area of personnel.
6. Therefore, if the agent can sell twice her income, she should be producing enough or almost enough to cover the agency's operating cost—her part of it, at least.
7. However, Jane is selling five times her income. She is therefore covering not only her cost, but the cost of other personnel as well and she should be producing a large profit for the travel agency.

Based upon these statistics, Jane justifies her salary increase. Mr. Ufic agrees with Jane that she has a point, but he notes that with Jane being free to do nothing but sell travel, the agency must employ other people to do what agents in many other agencies must do. Such jobs as outside sales, ticket processing, bookkeeping, ticket delivery, and others constitute a large expense for the company; and the salaries of these people plus the salaries of administrators must come from the income derived from the sales of each agent. Therefore, this agency is not typical. Agents working for Give Me A Break Travel must sell almost three times their salaries and benefits in order to cover real costs. He therefore suggests to Jane that they compromise. He offers to increase her salary by 50 percent, i.e., to $30,000 per year, and to provide $3,000 of additional benefits paid by the company. He points out that if Jane can increase her sales even more — to $1.25 million a year, he will give her a bonus of approximately 30 percent of all commissions earned beyond the $1 million sales level.

Jane, while appreciative of the increase in salary offered, points out that override commissions have been substantial and she is selling favored vendors over 55 percent of the time. Other agents, she states, probably sell favored vendors only about 15 percent of the time. Yet, notes Jane, she is not paid anything more for selling favored vendors. Jane asks for incentive bonuses if she is able to convert bookings to favored vendors in order to obtain override commissions. Ufic responds that the override amounts are really very low. However, if Jane will increase her favored-vendor sales, he will pay her a bonus of one-tenth of one percent on any sales beyond the 55 percent favored-vendor sales level in any and all months in which Jane is able to accomplish such an increase in percentage sales.

Jane accepts this offer and the meeting is terminated.

THE COMMERCIAL ACCOUNT PROFITABILITY ANALYSIS REPORT

The Commercial Account Profitability Analysis report provides agency management with a vehicle for comparing the profitability of corporate accounts against one another. It also provides the ability to manipulate corporate accounts in such a way that marginally profitable or even unprofitable accounts can sometimes be converted into substantially profitable accounts.

The Commercial Account Profitability Analysis Form

The Commercial Account Profitability Analysis form, figure 13–9, is similar to the reports discussed earlier in this chapter. The body of the report consists of ten columns.

The first column is titled "Account." In this column the name of the corporate account being analyzed is entered.

The next column is "Air Bookings." In this column one enters the total gross air bookings for this account during the quarter covered by the report.

The next column is "Air Commissions." In this block one enters the amount of dollars and cents of the actual commissions paid for air bookings made for this account during the period of the report.

The fourth column is for "Other Bookings." In this column one enters the total gross dollar amount of all bookings other than air made for this account during the three-month period of the report. This includes hotel, car rental, and any other bookings.

The commissions earned on the "other bookings" for the account are entered into the next column, which is titled "Other Commissions." As with air commissions, this figure is entered in dollars and cents.

The next column, "Total Commissions," is calculated by adding the amount of the "Air Commissions" and the "Other Commissions." It should be the total dollar amount of all commissions received as a result of sales for the account during the period covered by the report.

The seventh column is titled "Sales Hours." In this column one enters the number of hours taken by agents (presumably dedicated agents) to book and issue tickets for the corporate account being studied. In some agencies time

COMMERCIAL ACCOUNT PROFITABILITY ANALYSIS

Account	Air Bookings	Air Comm	Other Bookings	Other Comm	Total Comm	Sales Hours	Employee Cost per Hr	Avg. Comm. Per Hour	Profit or Loss

Figure 13–9

logs are not kept and the amount of time spent on any particular account is only a guess. However, if one is to be able to accurately evaluate the profitability of any particular account, it will be necessary to keep a time log since, in a very real sense, time is money in a travel agency. Whether employees are paid on an hourly or salary basis, in the long run, they are paid a compensation per hour of working time. Therefore, the amount of time they spend on any particular account is directly relevant to the potential profitability of that account.

Remember in the "Employee Cost Per Hour" column to include all costs of the employee in the calculations, not just the salary. Usually the best way to calculate this is to go back over the time period covered by the report and add up all monies paid to the employee (except reimbursements for things like mileage, stamps purchased, etc.) or for the employee (taxes, educational seminar fees, etc.). Divide this figure by the number of hours worked by the employee during the same time period of the report.

The next column on the form is titled "Average Commission Per Hour." The average commission per hour is calculated by dividing the number of sales hours into the total commission.

The last column on the form is "Profit or Loss." By doubling the employee cost per hour and subtracting the result from the average commission per hour figure, one is able to roughly calculate the amount of the profit (or loss) per hour which the agency receives by handling the account.

Report Outcomes

These are all of the columns on the report form and they provide some basic information. Review figure 13–10 where data for the first quarter of the year is provided for three accounts.

The most important information furnished on the Commercial Account Profitability Analysis is the average commission per sales-hour. By comparing the average commission per sales-hour of each of the accounts, one is able to identify one factor relating to the relative profitability of corporate accounts served. This rapidly points out which accounts have relatively few interactions and/or long-distance, or otherwise high-cost tickets. It also points out which accounts tend to make changes or frequently call the agency for additional information. Finally, it identifies the accounts that may be purchasing only inexpensive tickets or, perhaps, tickets for short-distance flights.

Additionally, when one compares the cost of the agent who is handling the account to the average commission per sales-hour generated by the account, one is able to identify whether or not the account itself has the potential of being profitable for the agency (if it is currently showing a break-even or a loss status). Keeping in mind that for the travel agency to break even, the

COMMERCIAL ACCOUNT PROFITABILITY ANALYSIS									
ACCOUNT	AIR BOOKINGS	AIR COMM	OTHER BOOKINGS	OTHER COMM	TOTAL COMM	SALES HOURS	EMPLOYEE COST PER HR	AVG. COMM. PER HOUR	PROFIT OR LOSS
Klim Enterprises	*$920.00*	*$98.20*	*$308.00*	*$24.18*	*$122.38*	*2.10*	*$8.00*	*$58.28*	*$50.28 per hour or $105.59 Total*
Mighty Midgets Inc.	*$ 190.00*	*$19.00*	*–0–*	*–0–*	*$19.00*	*.25*	*$7.50*	*$76.00*	*$68.50 per hour or $17.13 Total*
Telegraphics Assoc.	*$2,612.00*	*$248.00*	*$973.00*	*$86.50*	*$334.50*	*5.50*	*$8.00*	*$60.82*	*$52.82 per hour or $290.51 Total*

Figure 13–10

employeee cost per hour should be 50 percent or less than the average commission per sales-hour, one can rapidly identify which corporate accounts are being handled at a profit for the travel agency, which are providing the highest profit, which are at break-even, and which accounts are being handled at a loss.

In addition to providing profitability information on accounts, this analysis gives agency management the opportunity to consider moving dedicated agents from one account to another, so that a break-even or a marginally profitable account might become a considerably profitable account, or so that a losing account can be turned into an account on which the agency is making a profit. In some cases, it may be that an employee who is too expensive to handle any of the accounts and who is not making a profit for the agency because of that high cost can either be asked to work at a lower salary or be terminated and replaced by a less expensive employee. Although this may sound harsh, one should keep in mind that the business of the business is to make a profit. If there is no account on which a profit can be earned because the cost of the employee handling the account is too much, the logical answer is to change the employee rather than manipulate the dedicated agents who handle corporate accounts.

CHAPTER 13 — EXERCISE #4
COMMERCIAL ACCOUNT PROFITABILITY COMPARISON ANALYSIS EXERCISE

INSTRUCTIONS: Study the data on the four commercial accounts identified in the Commercial Account Profitability Comparison Analysis, figure 13–11. Use the blank Commercial Account Profitability Analysis form, figure 13–12, to enter data and conduct an analysis of the four accounts. After entering the data and calculating the information to complete each of the columns, answer the following four questions.

1. Which account would you recommend that agency management spend most of its time and effort to develop? Why?
2. Which account provides the best return on investment? Explain?
3. If agency management decides to cut back on accounts, which account(s) would you recommend them to drop? Why?
4. By changing employees who handle accounts, can agency management better utilize the employee staff? How?

COMMERCIAL ACCOUNT PROFITABILITY ANALYSIS

Account:	Somewhat Sickly Hospitals	Account:	Association of Eastern Block Firing Squads
Air Bookings Last Quarter	$1,721	Air Bookings Last Quarter	$13,769
Average Air Commissions Last Quarter	10.2%	Average Air Commissions Last Quarter	9.7%
Other Bookings Last Quarter	$579	Other Bookings Last Quarter	$9,727
Average Other Booking Commissions	9.8%	Average Other Booking Commissions	13.6%
Sales Hours	12.40	Sales Hours	31.50
Employee Cost Per Hour	$6.73	Employee Cost Per Hour	$18.68

Account:	Dew Gooders Inc.	Account:	All Cheat Financial Management
Air Bookings Last Quarter	$7,202	Air Bookings Last Quarter	$32,200
Average Air Commissions Last Quarter	10.05%	Average Air Commissions Last Quarter	8.4%
Other Bookings Last Quarter	$2,007	Other Bookings Last Quarter	$7,201
Average Other Booking Commissions	11%	Average Other Booking Commissions	10.01%
Sales Hours	35.40	Sales Hours	91.60
Employee Cost Per Hour	$14.81	Employee Cost Per Hour	$16.42

Figure 13–11

COMMERCIAL ACCOUNT PROFITABILITY ANALYSIS

Account	Air Bookings	Air Comm	Other Bookings	Other Comm	Total Comm	Sales Hours	Employee Cost per Hr	Avg. Comm. per Hour	Profit or Loss

Figure 13–12

SUMMARY

Productivity and profitability analyses allow travel agency executives to identify areas where costs can be cut, greater profitability can be realized, and the productivity of staff members can be determined. In this chapter, three productivity/profitability analyses have been reviewed: the Product Profitability Report, the Personnel Return-on-Investment Analysis, and the Commercial Account Profitability Analysis.

The Product Profitability Report allows management to identify those specific products on which the greatest amount of sales have been made, as well as those products which account for the greatest amount of profitability. By working with the data produced through this report, agency management can better understand which products should be concentrated on. In addition, the data produced by this report can assist agency management in selecting vendor override offers.

The Personnel Return-on-Investment Analysis allows agency management to determine which inside sales agents are the best salespeople in terms of total volume of sales. It can also provide guidelines to evaluate agent compensation versus agent sales productivity in order to ensure that the agency earns consistent profits as a result of the efforts of each inside agent employee. Agency management must be careful to understand that the total compensation for employees (sales cost) is a more accurate figure (than is sales salary) against which to evaluate the contributions of an employee. At the same time, agency executives need to keep in mind that an employee's ability to sell preferred vendors and produce override commission earnings for the agency should be considered when evaluating the total commissions earned by the inside agent employee.

By working with the Commercial Account Profitability Analysis agency management can determine which corporate accounts provide a good profit for the travel agency, which ones result in a break-even position, and which corporate accounts are too expensive to handle in the way the agency is currently doing. Agency management can also compare the profitability of handling corporate accounts by the agents who are assigned to those accounts. By manipulating agent inside sales assignments, agency management can conceivably turn a break-even corporate account or the losing account into profitable corporate accounts. To be able to effectively evaluate corporate accounts utilizing the Commercial Account Profitability Analysis, agency management must recognize that accurate time logs will need to be kept. In addition, to make certain that profits can result from marginal accounts, agency management must sometimes consider the possibility of hiring less-expensive agents to handle these accounts.

The bookkeeper/accountant in an agency and the agency's management are charged with helping to produce a profit for the business. By consistently working with evaluation instruments and analyzing the data, it is often possible to produce a profit where a loss has been sustained in the past.

❑ DISCUSSION QUESTIONS

1. Why would agency management wish to complete a periodic Product Profitability Report?
2. Why do some travel agencies break out the data relating to their own tour earnings (profits)?
3. Why are penalties an important point to consider when calculating override commissions and override sales quotas?
4. Why is the ability to analyze the productivity of each agent especially important?
5. What factors might skew the Personnel Return-on-Investment Analysis of an individual inside travel agent, resulting in the presentation of an inaccurate picture?
6. Why should the figure entered into the "Sales Salary" column of the Personnel Return-on-Investment Analysis form always include *all* costs incurred in employing the agent?
7. In what way might override commissions earned on the sales generated by inside agents be considered important in calculating compensation packages for these agents?
8. Why is it necessary to keep a time log if one is to accurately evaluate the profitability of any particular account?
9. What report outcomes might one expect to obtain from the completion of the Commercial Account Profitability Analysis form?
10. What comparison columns should be studied on the Commercial Account Profitability Analysis form if one is to identify whether or not the account being considered is currently unprofitable or if it has the potential to be profitable?

❑ ROLE-PLAYING EXERCISE

Two students may participate in this role-playing exercise either as an out-of-class or in-class fun way to review how productivity and profitability analyses can assist travel agencies to increase profits by managing products and corporate accounts and evaluating personnel productivity. One student plays the senior agent who has been offered stock in the travel agency and a position on the Board of Directors in exchange for signing a long-term employment contract. The other plays the travel agency's bookkeeper. Please read the script and then pick up the conversation in your own words.

Senior Agent: Both board members and the agency manager have impressed on me over the years how valuable your productivity and profitability studies have been in financially guiding the agency. They have stressed that our consistent profits are largely a result of these analyses. Which particular analyses have proven to be most beneficial for our company?

Agency Bookkeeper: Three of them are especially beneficial. These are the Product Profitability Report, the Personnel Return-on-Investment Analysis, and the Commercial Account Profitability Analysis.

Senior Agent: I have heard of these and I have completed some of the forms, but I still don't understand them totally. Explain how they benefit the agency and how they work.

Agency Bookkeeper: Let's discuss the benefits first and then I will explain in detail how each analysis works. Probably the most important benefit is. . .

CONTINUE ON YOUR OWN

PROFIT TARGET BUDGETING

OBJECTIVES

Upon completion of this chapter, the student will be able to:

- Prepare a simple travel agency budget based upon having all key figures for the budget available in advance
- Calculate a next-year projected break-even required revenue for a travel agency when the next-year projected total operating expenses and the next-year projected average commission are provided
- Identify the pros and the cons of selling vendors "with a preference" in order to increase the agency's average commission
- Determine the total amount of sales needed by a travel agency to reach its next-year financial goals when the next-year projected total operating expense level has been identified, the next-year projected profit has been identified, and the next-year projected average commission has been identified

INTRODUCTION

Accounting is designed to provide a business with financial controls and to provide a knowledge base for planning. The major financial control planning instrument is a budget. Budgets act as not only financial control mechanisms, however, but they also provide guidelines for both planned expenditures and planned income generation. Budgeting can become so sophisticated that some companies allow the budget to direct almost every management decision. However, in the travel agency there is a wide degree of budgeting sophistication. Many agencies have no budget at all. A very few have detailed, sophisticated, well-thought-out, computerized budgets. Most fall somewhere in between.

THE CASE FOR HAVING A BUDGET

A successful Florida travel agency has operated for a number of years with a cigar box financial system. The process is simple. When the owner/manager receives money from a client or a vendor, she puts the money in a cigar box kept in the agency's safe. When she needs to pay bills, she opens the cigar box and pulls out money to pay the bills. It works. The reason it works is that she has the only travel agency in a very wealthy retirement community. The agency does an excellent job organizing and running expensive group trips for retirees and has built in substantial profits on all trips. The agency owner is happy with the system. Therefore, the system has been in effect for a long time.

There are at least three problems with this type of system: 1) it will not work for most travel agencies; 2) profits are less than they would be with a more sophisticated budgeting system, and; 3) if the agency owner, or someone who may inherit it, wishes to sell the agency, he/she will not be able to get the best possible price for it.

Why will the cigar box system not work for most agencies? The operating margin of most travel agencies is very small. A recent Lou Harris study of travel agencies found that the average agency in the United States was selling $1.1 million of gross sales and that between 48 and 52 percent of agency income was spent on personnel costs. At a 10 percent average commission (and for most agencies the commission average is 9.9 percent), that means the average United States agency had an income level of less than $110,000 and an income after personnel expenses of slightly less than $55,000 annually. This means the income to cover expenses after paying the staff is only about $4,500 per month. After deducting minimum costs of about $1,000 each for rent and computers, the agency has to cover all other expenses (and earn profits) on only $2,500 per month. That would be a challenge for any business and certainly for a business in which the owner is usually also a full-time travel counselor, unable to devote a major part of his/her time to the management functions of running a business.

And why might profits be less with the cigar box system than with a budget? Comparison data studies indicate that planned income generation and planned expenditures have a better chance of reaching planned profits than decisions based on spur-of-the-moment considerations. A simple case illustrates this factor. An agency owner was recently approached by a sales person asking her to buy an advertising program based on having her agency's name printed on the back of bank drive-window cash envelopes. She would have shared that envelope space with eight other advertisers. When she asked the salesman what kind of return-on-investment current travel agency advertisers were receiving from the program, he said it was impossible to measure. It seems several agencies had bought into the program, but none knew what their return-on-investment was. A financial budget does not stop an agency from making bad marketing decisions. However, it does set a limit on marketing purchases and, if structured correctly, it does hold out for planners the consideration of such factors as return-on-investment. On the other hand, with the cigar box system, it is far too easy to just open the box and give the salesman money.

Perhaps the greatest danger to the travel agency with a cigar box system, however, is the reduction in the probability of selling the agency at a true market value. Those wishing to purchase a business expect to see a history of good financial records. Favorable ratios and historical budget plans accompanied by budget outcomes in the form of annual financial reports tend to impress potential buyers in any industry. Indications are that such documentation is even more impressive in the travel industry—simply because it has traditionally been so rare to find.

BUDGETS VERSES PROFITS

Budgets are financial plans. An increasing number of travel agencies prepare budgets for a wide range of reasons, including those discussed above. However, budgets often fall short of adequate or acceptable financial planning. Far too often budgets are unrealistic guesses about what a travel agency owner wishes might happen. These budgets tend to reflect one of three problems. One type of budget tends to overestimate income and underestimate expenses. This makes the owners and stockholders happy and optimistic at the outset and increasingly disappointed as the year progresses. It is a technique used by some managers and/or owners to fool themselves and/or the owners into believing that the agency is much better off than it really is.

A second type of unrealistic budget is the one that is too pessimistic. It underestimates income and overestimates expenses. Although found far less often than the overoptimistic budget, the pessimistic budget can create considerable problems as well. Typically, business is lost because staff and equipment is insufficient to handle incoming business and clients get poor service. The result is a loss in clients that is very difficult to overcome.

Perhaps the most-often-found error in budget planning, however, comes about as a result of striving to break even rather than make a profit. A good, solid budget can result in a break-even situation year after year. This may seem good on the surface, but it results in two major problems. The original investors do not get their money back and do not make money on their investment. In addition, no reserves of capital are set aside to take care of the agency in a bad or an unprofitable year.

The solutions for the first two problems are often fairly simple. By using historical data, looking carefully at industry developments and trends, and careful forecasting, one can usually develop fairly realistic budgets that, when followed diligently, can guide the agency to hitting its financial projections.

Some agency owners have been able to project budgets that err no more than a plus or minus 5 percent in any category. A few have done even better.

However, the task of budgeting for profits is usually much harder. This means setting exact goals (that are high enough to include reasonable profits, but low enough to be realistic), measuring accomplishments, constantly knowing exactly where the agency is in relationship to its goals, evaluating the market, upgrading the client base, and reevaluating when one or more problems continue to occur. Equally important, it means developing a budgeting system that plans for profits, not a system that plans for the business to reach a break-even figure. It is, therefore, the process of going beyond the break-even point that is referred to as profit target budgeting.

A DEFINITION OF TERMS

When using terms like "break-even," "profit," and "return-on-investment," it is important that there is agreement on what each term means. Although these terms may seem to be self-explanatory, there is a degree of common usage in the travel industry that may well be misleading and certainly different from the way in which the same terms are used in other industries. Therefore, a definition of terms is in order.

The term "break-even" should present little confusion. It is the point at which agency earnings (commissions, interest payments, etc.) equal agency expenses. One must be careful not to confuse earnings with sales. When a \$100 airline ticket is sold, and a commission of 10 percent is paid, the \$90 that is sent on to the air carrier cannot be considered a part of the agency's earnings. Only the \$10 commission belongs to the agency and only the \$10 commission can be considered to be an earning of the agency.

The term "return-on-investment" is the money paid back to the travel agency's investors as a payment for the use of their money in starting (capitalizing) the business. This is usually considered to be a percentage rate applied to the amount of money invested in the agency. As an example, if the agency owners invested \$60,000 and received a return-on-investment of 15 percent, the dollars paid back to the investors for their investment in the agency would be \$9,000 each year.

The term "profit" is the term that can result in confusion as it is applied in the travel industry. Many agency executives consider profit to be any money earned in excess of the break-even point, but they do not consider return-on-investment payments to be part of the agency's expenses. Therefore, if any monies are paid back to the original investors for the use of their money to capitalize the agency, i.e., if any return-on-investment money is earned and paid to the agency's owners, this is considered as coming from profits. This definition of profits differs from the traditional definition of profits. The traditional definition considers return-on-investment to be a legitimate, on-going, budgeted expense of the business and includes return-on-investment payments in the money that must come from earnings in order to reach the break-even point.

For purposes of this chapter and this book, the non-traditional, customary agency interpretation of the term "profit" will be used. In other words, return-on-investment payments will be considered as coming from profits rather than before earning profits.

AN EIGHT-STEP, HISTORICALLY-BASED PROFIT TARGETING APPROACH

A number of years ago, Dr. Donald Madden of the University of Kentucky's College of Business Administration developed a formula and an approach designed to assist travel agents in budgeting for profits through profit targeting. Because profit targeting is a beneficial first step in preparing agency budgets, Dr. Madden's approach has been expanded, modified, and simplified in an effort to develop an easy step-by-step process that agency managers can use to design a framework for a budget for the following year. This step-by-step process is detailed in this chapter. The "Profitless Travel Case Study" is presented in appendix A, providing the reader with an opportunity to apply key parts of the step-by-step profit targeting process to a simulated travel agency financial planning situation. Following the presentation of the case is a set of case results and an explanation of how the results were reached. This combination of setting out a step-by-step process, presenting a case, and reviewing the case resolution should provide the student with the knowledge and skill to apply the approach to part or all of an individual agency financial plan.

PROFIT TARGETING ASSUMPTIONS

Before looking at the eight steps of profit target budgeting, it should be recognized that there are two assumptions on which this process is based. The first assumption is that the agency can generate sufficient commission income to cover intended operating costs. In other words, it is assumed that the agency has the ability to at least break even. In many cases agency managers and owners automatically make this assumption. Reason alone should tell one that such an assumption should not be automatic. Yet, emotion can easily become involved—especially when one's hard-earned cash is involved. In far too many cases, agency owners refuse to accept the fact that the circumstances of their agency are such that the business simply does not have the ability to break even. It is far better for an agency owner or manager to take a hard look at the agency's situation and, if there is any doubt that the agency can realistically reach a break-even point, call in an honest, agency-experienced consultant to give a second opinion. If it is determined that it is not possible to break even and if this determination is made early enough, a range of options may be available. However, a profit-target-based budget is no longer one of those options.

The second assumption on which profit target budgeting is based goes beyond the first and assumes that profit is possible, i.e., that it is possible to earn more commission income than that required to cover intended operating costs. For almost all agencies for which reaching a break-even point is possible, reaching a profit is also possible. However, some of these agencies, especially those that have a history of losing money, cannot expect to reach a profit in the initial year of preparing financial plans or budgets. When such a situation is the case, the agency should consider preparing a break-even budget for the first year and moving to a profit target budget the next year. This can be done by following the first four steps outlined below. By stopping at the point at which profits are targeted, the result will be a break-even budget.

The Three Variables

In addition to the two assumptions, there are three variables that comprise the profit target budgeting model: 1) operating revenues, 2) average commission income, and 3) operating expenses.

Operating revenues are the monies taken into the agency as income for the agency. The bulk of these are commissions. In most travel agencies, over half of operating revenues come from the commissions earned on air sales. However, commissions are also received for the sale of cruises, rail tickets, tours, insurance, F.I.T.s, and other products and services.

The average commission income is often referred to by travel agency accountants as *agency mix*. This is the average percentage level of the commissions earned. The starting point is normally the average commission earned during the previous year. An average commission income can be determined for each product or service sold. There can be an average air sales income, an average domestic versus an average international air sales income, and an average air sales income for each carrier sold. Generallly speaking, the average commission income used for the initial profit target budget is based on the average commission received from selling all travel products and services. This is determined by dividing the total commission earnings into the total gross sales of all travel products and services for the year.

Operating expenses are all the expenses incurred in running the travel agency throughout the year. Although personnel costs normally constitute about half of all operating expenses, there are also administrative costs and sales and marketing costs that constitute part of the total operating expenses.

Step 1: Determining Last Year's Break-Even Point

To determine the historical importance of each income and each expenditure area, it is important to find out what the break-even point would have been for last year's financial activity. This is done by taking last year's end-of-year financial statement figures and plugging them into the following formula:

Total Operating Expenses Divided by Average Commission

By dividing the total amount of operating expenses incurred last year by the average commission, one can determine the necessary operating revenue needed last year to cover all expenses, i.e., the break-even point, figure 14–1. For example, if last year's total operating expenses were $169,000 and last year's average commission was 9.9 percent (a recent average), divide 9.9 percent into $169,000. This determines that the necessary operating revenue (total sales) for last year would need to have been $1,707,071 for the travel agency to break even. This formula can now be used for profit target budget setting and the break-even data can now be used to determine what changes are needed to develop or improve profits as a foundation for developing next year's profit plan (budget).

$$\frac{\text{Last year's Operating Expenses} \quad \$169{,}000}{\text{Last year's Average Commission} \quad 9.9\%} = \text{Last year's Break-even Point} = \$1{,}707{,}071$$

Figure 14–1 Step 1

Step 2: Projecting Next Year's Operating Costs

Step 2 calls for projecting the travel agency's operating costs for the next fiscal year. To do this, it is necessary to go back to last year's end-of-fiscal-year financial statements and to review each line in the expense chart of accounts on an item-by-item basis. Each expense is analyzed to determine changes and project realistic costs for the next fiscal year. For example, occupancy costs may be increasing because the rent is going up. Office equipment costs may be increasing because of the planned purchase of new furniture. By looking at each expense item and projecting next year's operating costs, one can determine next year's projected total operating expenses, figure 14–2. In doing this, however, be careful to keep in mind the formulas and considerations discussed in earlier chapters. Ideally, the personnel productivity formulas will apply to the resulting profit target budget; the average product-line commission level will increase; the resulting chart of accounts will be more finely tuned to reflect an accurate allocation of each expenditure; and the return-on-investment of each capital, marketing, and personnel expenditure will be higher. This should all be tied together and reflected in the realistic development of a cost budget for the next fiscal year. The careful development of the several mini-budgets discussed in the following appendixes will aid substantially in fine tuning an overall cost budget.

Step 3: Projecting Next Year's Average Commission

Step 3 requires projecting next year's average commission. In this era of deregulation, close analysis of the products sold allows agencies to increase their average commission level and sometimes to do so on a substantial basis. There are pros and cons to selling one vendor over another with prejudice. There are those who believe this can be harmful to the client and may lose clients for the agency. However, careful selection of vendors, based not only on quality but especially on override arrangements and across-the-board higher commissions, is occuring among travel agencies far more than at any previous time in the history of the United States agency system. If the agency concentrates on the sale of specific carriers, override commission levels of one-half of one percent or one percent can often easily be reached. Very large agencies are claiming substantially higher override commission levels received from domestic air carriers. Even some, though not all, international carriers are paying override commissions now. Hotels and tour operators are also sometimes paying more than the industry standard of 10 percent. In addition, special deals with suppliers can sometimes result in contracted commission levels in the upper teens or even higher. By analyzing what products to sell and by studying both the commissions and overrides associated with those sales, management can project next year's average commission, figure 14–3.

Step 4: Determining Needed Revenue for Break-Even Next Year

Step 4 requires plugging in step 2 and step 3 figures to the break-even formula to determine the revenue needed for breaking even next year. The formula is similar to the one used in step 1, except that the agency's financial

	Jan	Feb	Mar	Apr	May	Jun	Jul	Aug	Sep	Oct	Nov	Dec	Total Year	Projected Next Year
608														
Office Equip & Furn	51.61	189.24	167.98	99.57	284.00	0	223.12	289.68	132.92	0	112.11	0	1550.23	1,250.00
609														
Office Repairs/														
Maintenance	0	0	0	0	0	0	0	94.20	0	43.38	0	0	137.58	120.00
610														
Office Supplies	42.13	95.19	102.81	115.20	83.05	184.14	124.48	222.45	29.68	111.97	55.27	32.00	1198.37	1,294.24
615														
Postage/Express	42.10	83.30	99.76	141.12	52.12	108.75	94.19	79.67	42.76	69.98	71.14	112.89	997.78	1,117.51
Next Year's Projected														
Total Operating														
Expenses														210,620.00

NOTE: The above $210,620.00, "Next Year's Projected Total Operating Expenses," is based on the projections taken from each and every expenditure extension, not just the expenditures shown in the sample above.

Figure 14–2 Step 2

		Jan	Feb	Mar	Oct	Nov	Dec	Average Total Year	Projected Next Year
		Amt %	Amt %	Amt %	Amt %	Amt %	Amt %	Amt %	Amt %
Airline	1	10.0	10.0	10.0	10.0	10.0	10.0	10.00	10.00
	2	8.9	9.2	9.7	9.9	10.2	10.8	9.86	10.60
	3	10.3	10.2	10.2	10.8	10.9	10.8	10.66	10.90
	4	10.0	10.0	9.9	10.0	9.9	10.0	9.95	10.00
Cruise line	1	10.0	10.0	12.8	10.0	13.7	10.0	11.86	12.50
	2	10.0	14.0	10.0	10.0	10.0	10.0	11.78	12.00
	3	10.0	10.0	10.0	10.0	10.0	10.0	10.0	10.00
Tour op.	1	10.7	11.0	11.2	11.6	11.8	12.3	11.32	11.40
	2	10.0	10.0	10.0	10.0	10.0	10.0	10.00	10.00
Hotel chain	1	10.0	10.0	10.0	10.4	10.4	10.5	10.24	10.50
	2	10.0	10.0	10.0	10.0	10.0	10.0	10.00	10.00
other hotels	1	12.0	N/A	N/A	N/A	12.0	N/A	12.00	12.00
	2	N/A	N/A	N/A	14.0	N/A	N/A	14.00	14.00
car rental co.	1	10.0	10.0	10.0	10.0	10.0	10.0	10.00	10.00
	2	10.0	10.0	10.0	10.0	10.0	10.0	10.00	10.00
Other									
Average Commission Last Year								10.59%	
Next Year's Projected Average Commission									10.87%

NOTE: The "Average Commission Last Year" and the "Next Year's Projected Average Commission" figures (shown immediately above) need to be and are averages for all commission-paying vendors and for all months—not just the sample vendors and the sample months shown above.

Figure 14–3 Step 3

planner uses next year's projected figures instead of last year's actual figures. Next year's projected total operating expenses are divided by next year's projected average commission. The result will be next year's break-even required revenue, i.e., the amount of sales necessary to cover the amount of expected expenses.

For example, if next year's projected total operating expenses are set at $210,620 and next year's projected average commission is determined to be 10.87 percent, one divides $210,620 by 10.87 percent. The resulting figure of $1,937,626 is the revenue required if the travel agency is to break even, figure 14–4.

Next Year's Projected Total Operating Expenses	$210,620	=	Sales Required to Reach Next Year's Projected Break-even Point	= $1,937,626
Next Year's Projected Average Commission	10.87%			

Figure 14–4 Step 4

EXERCISE #1: BREAK EVEN EXERCISES

INSTRUCTIONS: Using the information and formula from step 4, provide answers to the following questions.

Note: The abbreviation "NY" stands for "Next Year"

1. NY projected Total Operating Expenses are $185,423.13.
   NY projected Average Commission is 11.2%.
   What is NY Projected Break Even required revenue?
2. NY projected Total Operating Expenses are $242,971.12.
   NY projected Average Commission is 9.3%.
   What is NY Projected Break Even required revenue?
3. NY projected Total Operating Expenses are $461,722.18.
   NY projected Average Commission is 9.9%.
   What is NY Projected Break Even required revenue?
4. NY projected Total Operating Expenses are $169,000.
   NY projected Break Even Point is $1,707,071.
   What is required NY Average Commission?

ANSWERS TO BREAK EVEN EXERCISES

QUESTION 1

NY projected Total Operating Expenses are $185,423.13.
NY projected Average Commission is 11.2%.
What is NY Projected Break Even required revenue?
ANSWER: $1,655,644.00

QUESTION 2

NY projected Total Operating Expenses are $242,971.12.
NY projected Average Commission is 9.3%.
What is NY Projected Break Even required revenue?
ANSWER: $2,612,592.60.

QUESTION 3

NY projected Total Operating Expenses are $461,722.18.
NY projected Average Commission is 9.9%.
What is NY Projected Break Even required revenue?
ANSWER: $4,663,860.40.

QUESTION 4

NY projected Total Operating Expenses are $169,000.
NY projected Break Even Point is $1,707,071.
What is required NY Average Commission?
ANSWER: 9.9%
Calculation: Divide $169,000 by $1,707,071.

Initial Capitalization	$ 60,000
ROI	× .15
Profit Required to Reach ROI	$ 9,000

Figure 14–5 Step 5

Step 5: Establishing a Formal Profit Target

One of the assumptions on which profit target budgeting is based is that the agency can make a profit next year. Step 5 is the process of establishing a formal profit target. Some agency managers or owners arbitrarily choose a profit figure toward which they will work. Others use a percentage of gross or a percentage of net to determine a profit target. Still others consider profit to be return-on-investment and multiply the percentage they expect to receive times the agency's outstanding capitalization, figure 14–5. All of the above are acceptable ways of determining a profit target and each approach can be justified in standard budgeting practices.

Whichever process is used to determine the formal profit target, one of the most important factors to keep in mind is to set the profit target at a reasonable amount. Any number of justifications, all of which may be quite valid, can be found for having a very high profit. The reality of the situation is, however, that the higher the profit, the more impossible the task of accomplishing the profit; and the higher the profit, the more difficult it will be to maintain the amount and the quality of service needed to stay at the established profit level. If the profit target is set at a figure that is unrealistic, the profit target budgeting process and the resulting budget will, at best, be of little value.

For purposes of explanation, we will presume a $60,000 initial agency unrepaid capitalization and an expected return-on-investment of 15 percent. The profit required to reach this return-on-investment, therefore, is $9,000.

Step 6: Adding the Profit and Next Year's Projected Expenses

In step 6 the formal profit target figure is added to (the already determined) next year's projected total operating expenses, figure 14–6. In step 4 it was determined that in our example the projected operating expenses for next year totaled $210,620. By adding $9,000 to $210,620, the new "next year's expected total operating expenses plus profit target" is $219,620.

Next Year's Projected Total Operating Expenses:	$ 210,620
+Projected Formal Profit Target Figure:	+ 9,000
=Next Year's Expected Total Operating Expenses + Profit Target:	$ 219,620

Figure 14–6 Step 6

EXERCISE #2: PROFIT CALCULATION EXERCISES

INSTRUCTIONS: Using the information and formulas from step 6, provide answers to the following questions.

1. Jane Adams, manager of Preferred Profits Travel, had gross sales of $2,141,600 last year and has determined that she wants to have a profit of 2 percent of gross sales. In order to determine her projected gross sales for next year, what dollar amount should be added to projected expenses next year to account for the projected profit?
2. Jane has changed her mind. Instead of basing her projected profits on gross sales, she has decided that basing it on net would be better. Therefore, she has decided to project a total of 5 percent of last year's net sales as her next year's profit. To determine this figure, you need to know that the agency mix (average commission) was 10.2 percent (including override commissions). In order to determine her projected gross sales for next year, what dollar amount should be added to projected expenses next year to account for the projected profit?
3. Jane's accountant has advised her that the profit projected based on 5 percent of net sales is probably unrealistic. He has suggested that she base it on Return-on-Investment. He suggests a conservative figure somewhat around what the current prime rate is. Jane looks in the *Wall Street Journal* and finds that yesterday's quoted prime was 8.6 percent. In order to determine her projected gross sales for next year, what dollar amount should be added to projected expenses next year to account for the projected profit? Her initial investment in the business was $78,000.
4. Jane decides she really can attain a better profit than this, but she knows she should not try to attain too much. She therefore decides to project a profit at one point above prime. If this can be obtained, she reasons, her chances of selling her agency in the near future could be much better. In order to determine her projected gross

sales for next year, what dollar amount should be added to projected expenses next year to account for the projected profit?

ANSWERS TO PROFIT CALCULATION EXERCISES

QUESTION 1

Jane Adams, manager of Preferred Profits Travel, had gross sales of $2,141,600 last year and has determined that she wants to have a profit of 2 percent of gross sales. In order to determine her projected gross sales for next year, what dollar amount should be added to projected expenses next year to account for the projected profit?

ANSWER: $42,832

Calculation: Multiply gross sales ($2,141,600) times 2 percent and the total is $42,832.

QUESTION 2

Jane has changed her mind. Instead of basing her projected profits on gross sales, she has decided that basing it on net would be better. Therefore, she has decided to project a total of 5 percent of last year's net sales as her next year's profit. To determine this figure, you need to know that the agency mix (average commission) was 10.2 percent (including override commissions). In order to determine her projected gross sales for next year, what dollar amount should be added to projected expenses next year to account for the projected profit?

ANSWER: $10,922.16

Calculation: Multiply gross sales ($2,141,600) times Average Commission (10.2 percent) and the result is $218,443.20. This is Last Year's Net Sales. Multiply Last Year's Net Sales ($218,443.20) times the desired percent of last year's net sales (5 percent) and the result is $10,922.16.

QUESTION 3

Jane's accountant has advised her that the profit projected based on a 5 percent of net sales is probably unrealistic. He has suggested that she base it on Return-on-Investment. He suggests a conservative figure somewhat around what the current prime rate is. Jane looks in the *Wall Street Journal* and finds that yesterday's quoted prime was 8.6 percent. In order to determine her projected gross sales for next year, what dollar amount should be added to projected expenses next year to account for the projected profit?

ANSWER: $6,708

Calculation: Multiply the initial investment ($78,000) times the Prime Rate (a lending rate) (8.6 percent) and the result is $6,708. (It is presumed that there have not been any reinvested earnings.)

QUESTION 4

Jane decides she really can attain a better profit than this, but she knows she should not try to attain too much. She therefore decides to project a profit at one point above prime. If this can be obtained, she reasons, her chances of selling her agency in the near future could be much better. In order to determine her projected gross sales for next year, what dollar amount should be added to projected expenses next year to account for the projected profit?

ANSWER: $7,488

Calculation: Add one percentage point to the prime rate (8.6 percent)—1 plus 8.6—and the result is 9.6 percent. Multiply the initial investment ($78,000) times the prime rate plus one percent (9.6 percent) and the result is $7,488. (Again, it is presumed that there have not been any reinvested or retained earnings.)

Step 7: Divide Next Year's Expenses + Profit by Average Commission

Step 7 divides next year's projected total operating expenses plus profit by next year's projected average commission to determine the projected sales income needed to reach next year's projected expenses plus profit.

In the sample, figure 14–7, $219,620 is divided by 10.87 percent. This equals $2,020,423. In this case, the $2,020,423 becomes the gross sales goal that must be attained to cover next year's expected expenses and to reach next year's expected profit.

$219,620 = Next Year's Projected Total Operating Expenses + Profit:
Divided by: 10.87% =
($2,020,423) Next Year's Projected Sales Income

Figure 14–7 Step 7

EXERCISE #3: PROJECTED SALES INCOME

INSTRUCTIONS: Our good friend, Jane Adams, manager of Preferred Profits Travel, wants to set a goal for the amount of sales her company will need to make next year in order to cover her projected total operating expenses and her projected profit for next year. She knows that she will need to know three figures in order to do this, so she has done her homework. She has determined that next year's projected operating expenses, next year's projected profit, and next year's projected average commission will be as follows:

1. N.Y. Projected Total Operating Expenses:	$212,410
2. N.Y. Projected Profit:	$ 7,225
3. N.Y. Projected Average Commission	9.13%

Question: How much in total amount of sales will be needed next year if Preferred Profits Travel is able to exactly reach these goals?

ANSWER TO PROJECTED SALES INCOME EXERCISE

INSTRUCTIONS: Use the information and formula from step 7 and the information from exercise 3 to calculate the following answer.

ANSWER: $2,405,640.70
Calculation: First, add the Next Year Projected Total Operating Expense figure of $212,410 to the Next Year Projected Profit of $7,225 in order to determine the Next Year Projected Total Operating Expenses Plus Profit figure. This will be $219,635.

Then divide the Next Year Projected Total Operating Expenses Plus Profit figure of $219,635 by the Next Year Projected Average Commission of 9.13 percent in order to determine the required amount of Projected Sales Income needed next year for Preferred Profits Travel to cover Next Year's Projected Total Operating Expenses Plus Profit. This will be $2,405,640.70.

PROFIT TARGET BUDGET FRAMEWORK

At this point the framework for the profit target budget has been determined. The agency financial planner (owner, manager, accountant, or consultant) has: 1) a sales goal for next year, $2,020,423; 2) a total expense objective, i.e., an expense level that the agency should not be allowed to exceed, $210,620; 3) a profit target, i.e., a return-on-investment of $9,000 (15 percent of the $60,000 initial agency unrepaid capitalization); and 4) an agency mix, i.e., average commission goal of 10.87 percent. This framework provides the outer limits of the profit target budget. The budget must now be refined if it is to be made workable and if the framework goals are to be attained.

Profit Target Budget Framework

1. THE N.Y. SALES GOAL IS KNOWN $2,020,423
2. THE N.Y. TOTAL EXPENSE LIMIT IS SET $210,620
3. A PROFIT TARGET HAS BEEN SET $9,000
4. AN AGENCY MIX HAS BEEN DETERMINED 10.87%

Step 8: Monthly Cost Breakdown

The first step in budget framework refinement is to break down costs into attainable, workable units. Step 8 breaks down costs into monthly increments to ensure realistic monthly goals and to provide an objective against which sales can be compared.

The easiest way to break down costs is to divide total projected costs for the next year by twelve months and to arbitrarily assign this figure (1/12 of projected expenditures) to each month. The resulting figure becomes the monthly expense limit which sets the outer limits for monthly expenses in every category of cost, figure 14–8.

However, this arbitrary division of expense limits by twelve will provide a highly skewed picture of what the agency should be spending. It arbitrarily sets unrealistic monthly expenditure levels that are the same for each month of the year. However, while there are fixed costs (rent, for example, may remain the same each month), there are also variable costs (the annual ARC fee, for example, is only paid once a year), and these may vary considerably from month to month.

Next Year's Costs Evenly Distributed

Monthly Costs:

JAN	FEB	MAR	APR	MAY	JUN	JULY	AUG	SEPT	OCT	NOV	DEC	TOTAL
$17,552	$17,552	$17,552	$17,552	$17,552	$17,552	$17,552	$17,552	$17,552	$17,552	$17,552	$17,552	$210,624

Figure 14–8 Step 8

A Better Monthly Cost Breakdown. A better alternative approach in breaking down annual expenses into monthly expense caps is to determine the percentage of expenditures incurred each month last year and to apply these percentages (which should total 100 percent) to the next year total operating expenses figure. This will provide a monthly projected total operating expense figure that is historically based, figure 14–9. Because it is a projection

	Monthly Costs	Projected Formal Profit Target	Monthly Operating Expenses Plus Profit Requirement	Next Year's Projected Average Commission	Monthly Projected Sales Break-even Point	Average Weeks Per Month	Weekly Break-even Sales Goal
JAN	$15,797.00	$750.00	$16,547.00	.1087	$152,226.31	4.33	$35,156.19
FEB	$16,218.00	$750.00	$16,968.00	.1087	$156,099.35	4.33	$36,050.66
MAR	$17,060.00	$750.00	$17,810.00	.1087	$163,845.44	4.33	$37,839.59
APR	$19,798.00	$750.00	$20,548.00	.1087	$189,834.83	4.33	$43,656.82
MAY	$21,272.00	$750.00	$22,022.00	.1087	$202,594.29	4.33	$46,788.52
JUN	$19,588.00	$750.00	$20,338.00	.1087	$187,102.11	4.33	$43,210.65
JUL	$19,377.00	$750.00	$20,127.00	.1087	$185,160.99	4.33	$42,762.35
AUG	$16,850.00	$750.00	$17,600.00	.1087	$161,913.52	4.33	$37,393.42
SEP	$14,954.00	$750.00	$15,704.00	.1087	$144,471.02	4.33	$33,363.23
OCT	$16,428.00	$750.00	$17,178.00	.1087	$158,031.27	4.33	$36,496.83
NOV	$16,428.00	$750.00	$17,178.00	.1087	$158,031.27	4.33	$36,496.83
DEC	$16,850.00	$750.00	$17,600.00	.1087	$161,913.52	4.33	$37,393.42
TOTAL	$210,620.00	$9,000.00	$219,620.00	.1087	$2,020,423.10	52	$38,854.29

Figure 14–9

based on the agency's history, it would be far more accurate than an arbitrary division of expenses into twelve equal monthly amounts. After adding $750 (1/12 of the projected formal profit target of $9,000) to the monthly cost figures, one determines monthly operating expenses plus profit requirements. When this approach is used, the financial planner will have a far more precise projection of monthly expenses.

The Best Monthly Cost Breakdown Calculation Alternative. A third alternative, and best of the three, is to break down next year's monthly expenditure figures calculated in the second alternative (above) by chart-of-accounts line-item and to do this for each month of the coming year. Calculate the percentage of expenditure for each line-item during the same month last year and apply the same percentage of expenditure to the monthly budgeted figure for next year. Of course, this needs to be modified to reflect realistic cost increases, budget changes, and fixed costs, but the percentages provide a starting point. The monthly expenditure figures calculated in the second alternative provide an initial expenditure budget cap for each month.

Monthly and Weekly Sales Goal Setting. This eighth step of the profit target setting process allows the financial planner to set the stage for the development of a formal annual budget. By looking at the month-by-month percentage of income earned during the last fiscal year and by breaking down a projected gross sales figure for the next fiscal year into the same percentages, the financial planner is now able to project gross sales for each month of the new fiscal year. The same process can be used to break out gross sales for each week of the year if the manager so desires. Divide the monthly projected sales break-even point by 4.33 (the average number of weeks in a month) to determine weekly break-even sales goals, figure 14–9. By comparing the actual gross sales to budgeted gross sales, the agency financial planner can know on Wednesday morning (after the ARC Report has been filed on Tuesday) whether or not the agency has: 1) met its budget, 2) exceeded its budget, or 3) not reached budgeted goals.

Step 9

1. DIVIDE MONTHLY PROJECTED COSTS BY 4.33 TO GET WEEKLY PROJECTED COSTS.
2. DIVIDE MONTHLY PROJECTED SALES BY 4.33 TO GET WEEKLY PROJECTED SALES.
3. COMPARE WITH ACTUAL WEEKLY COSTS AND SALES.

CONCLUSION

Formal profit targeting, then, can help agency financial planners project and reach a profit. Perhaps more important, however, profit target budgeting can set the stage for ongoing analyses that can sound the alarm immediately if the agency is beginning to get into trouble. The best time to resolve financial problems is right at the beginning, before they become too serious. Profit targeting, therefore, is a process all travel agency financial planners can use. By following the eight-step process, profit target budgeting becomes simplified profit forecasting.

SUMMARY

It is possible to operate without a budget, but few travel agencies are able to do so and remain successful over a period of time. There are strong indications that even those which are successful without a budget would be even more successful with one. They may be much more profitable with a budget. If put on the market, budget-based agencies should sell for a better price.

❑ *DISCUSSION QUESTIONS*

1. Should a travel agency budget to pay investors a return-on-investment during its first year in business?
2. Should a travel agency realistically expect to make a profit in its second or third year or should it budget for just a return-on-investment, planning to take profits from the agency at the time it is sold?
3. To what degree should an agency's financial planner expect to accurately project the agency's variable costs?
4. The term "break-even" can be interpreted differently. What are some interpretations of this term?
5. What are the pros and cons to the "cigar box financial system"?
6. Why might having a budget help to get the best return-on-investment for marketing expenses?
7. Why is a budget considered to be a financial plan?
8. Why won't profit targeting work if the two assumptions on which profit targeting is based are not met?
9. There are three variables listed in this chapter, presented as *the* three variables on which profit target budgeting is based. Aren't there really more than three variables on which profit target budgeting is based?

10. What is meant by the term "agency mix" and why might this term be used by travel agency accountants rather than the term "average commission"?

❑ ROLE-PLAYING EXERCISE

Two students may participate in this role-playing exercise either as an out-of-class fun way to review the management questions raised in profit target budgeting, or as an in-class exercise. One student plays the agency's financial planner. The other plays the Chairman of the Board of Directors of the Profits Above All Travel Agency. Please read the script and then pick up the conversation in your own words.

Chairman: The budgeting meeting is coming up in six weeks. We have been dilly daddling around with minimum returns for our investments in this agency for long enough. Our profits are ridiculous. We could almost make more money by leaving our money in the bank. This coming year I expect you to set a goal that will give us at least 10 percent more return-on-investment and $10,000 more in profits.

Financial Planner: I always try to realistically plan—and we have always been within 5 percent of our budget projections. But a radical difference like this could throw us way off. Of course, I can draw up a budget that will give you the kind of ROI and profit you want, but we can't possibly reach such a drastic change. If we put it on paper and can't reach it, our budget is going to be both useless and frustrating. Would you settle for goals that are a little more conservative?

Chairman: No! The Board is agreed. We must make more money. I had lunch at the club the other day with the President of that new airline, FLY BY NIGHT AIRWAYS. He told me they fly to the same places all the other airlines fly to, but since they are new, they will give us 3 percent more if we quadruple our sales with them and if we always try to book FBN Air. Start doing that now, figure it into the budget, and there is no way we won't hit the goals I have given you. Why didn't you think of doing this on your own?. . .

CONTINUE ON YOUR OWN

APPENDIX

PROFITLESS TRAVEL CASE

INTRODUCTION

Profitless Travel is preparing its budget for next year. Initial capitalization of the agency was $75,000 and the Board of Directors expects an ROI of 18 percent. Last year's sales were $2,012,792 and the average commission level was 10.615 percent. This included a carrier incentive when a big carrier was trying to take business from a smaller competitor. The smaller airline is now out of business, so the average commission level for next year is being projected at 10.48 percent. Last year employee costs were $100,576. It is expected these costs will increase by 7 percent. Non-personnel costs last year totaled $95,207. It is projected that these costs will be increased by 3.4 percent next year.

PROFITLESS TRAVEL CASE ASSIGNMENT

Calculate the answers to questions 1–7 relating to the Profitless Travel Case. To do so, it will be necessary to use the formulas discussed in this chapter. After answering the questions, review the answers and the discussion on how the results were determined. Then read the Percentage Profits Travel Case and answer the questions relating to that case. The answers to the Percentage Profits Travel Case are also provided for you. The Percentage Profits Case also provides some variables that make it slightly harder.

QUESTIONS RELATING TO THE PROFITLESS TRAVEL CASE

1. What is the projected operating cost for the next fiscal year?
   $________________
2. What is next year's projected break-even point?
   $________________
3. What is the dollar amount of the Formal Profit Target?
   $________________
4. What is Next Year's Projected Income needed to reach Next Year's Projected Profit, i.e., the Gross Sales needed to cover next year's expected profit?
   $________________
5. What is next February's projected dollar sales?
   $________________
6. What is next February's projected agency income?
   $________________
7. What is next February's projected expense budget?
   $________________

ANSWERS RELATING TO THE PROFITLESS TRAVEL CASE

QUESTION 1

Question: What is the projected operating cost for the next fiscal year?

Answer: $206,060.36

Calculation: The employee cost last year was $100,576.00. It is projected to increase by 7 percent. Therefore $100,576.00 is multiplied by 7 percent to determine the amount of employee cost increase. The increase is calculated to be $7,040.32. The non-personnel cost last year was $95,207.00. It is projected to increase by 3.4 percent. Therefore, $95,207.00 is multiplied by 3.4 percent to determine the amount of non-personnel cost increase. The increase is calculated to be $3,237.04. By adding the employee cost last year ($100,576.00) to the calculated increase in employee cost for next year ($7,040.32) the total projected employee cost for next year is determined to be $107,616.32. By adding the non-personnel cost last year ($95,207.00) to the calculated increase in non-personnel cost for next year ($3,237.04) the total projected non-personnel cost for next year is determined to be $98,444.04. By adding the projected employee cost for next year ($107,616.32) to the projected non-personnel cost for next year ($98,444.04) the projected operating cost for the next fiscal year is determined to be $206,060.36. Set out in figures the calculation is as follows:

Employee cost last year	$100,576.00
Increase	× .07
Next year dollar increase	$ 7,040.32
Employee cost last year	+ $100,576.00
Projected Employee costs next year	$107,616.32

Non-Personnel Cost last year	$ 95,207.00
Increase	× .034
Next year dollar increase	$ 3,237.04
Non-Personnel Cost last year	+ $ 95,207.00
Projected Non-Personnel Costs next year	$ 98,444.04

Projected Employee Costs Next Year	$107,616.32
Projected Non-Personnel Costs Next Year	+ $ 98,444.04
Projected Operating Costs for the Next Fiscal Year	$206,060.36

QUESTION 2

Question: What is next year's projected break-even point?

Answer: $1,966,224.80

Calculation: To determine the projected break-even point for next year, it is necessary to divide the projected operating cost for the next fiscal year by the projected average commission level for the next fiscal year. Therefore, $206,060.36 (the figure determined in question 1 to be the projected operating cost for the next fiscal year) is divided by 10.48 percent (the average commission level for next year as projected in the case study). The result is $1,966,244.80. Set out in figures the calculation is as follows:

Projected Operating Costs for the next Fiscal Year (divided by) Projected Average Commission Level for the next Fiscal Year	$206,060.36 / .1048	=	$1,966,244.80	Projected Break-Even Point for Next Year

QUESTION 3

Question: What is the dollar amount of the Formal Profit Target?

Answer: $13,500

Calculation: There are several ways to calculate a formal profit target. The method adopted in this chapter is to determine the amount of unrepaid capitalization and to multiply this amount by the expected return-on-investment. The case indicates initial capitalization of the agency was $75,000 (it is presumed that none has been repaid to the investors) and that the Board of Directors expects to earn a return-on-investment of 18 percent. Therefore, the $75,000 capitalization is multiplied by 18 percent to determine a $13,500 formal profit target. Set out in figures the calculation is as follows:

Unrepaid Capitalization	(times)	Return-on-Investment	(equals)	Profit Target
$75,000	×	.18	=	$13,500

QUESTION 4

Question: What is Next Year's Projected Income needed to reach Next Year's Projected Profit, i.e., the Gross Sales needed to cover next year's expected profit?

Answer: $2,095,041.60

Calculation: To determine the projected income needed to reach next year's projected profit, divide next year's projected expenses plus next year's projected profit by next year's projected average commission. In other words, the first step is to calculate next year's projected expenses plus profit. This is determined by adding $206,060.36 (next year's projected expenses) to $13,500 (next year's projected profit). The total is $219,560.36 (next year's projected expenses plus profit). The next step is to divide next year's projected expenses plus profit ($219,560.36) by next year's projected average commission (10.48 percent, according to the Profitless Travel Case). The result of dividing $219,560.36 by 10.48 percent is $2,095,041.60 (Next Year's Projected Income needed to reach Next Year's Projected Profit). Set out in figures the calculation is as follows:

Next Year's Projected Expenses	$206,060.36		
(plus)			
Next Year's Projected Profit	$ 13,500.00		
	$219,560.36		
(divided by)		= $2,095,041.60	Next Year's Projected Income Needed to Reach Next Year's Projected Profit
Next Year's Projected Average Commission	.1048		

QUESTION 5

Question: What is next February's projected dollar sales?

Answer: $174,586.80

Calculation: Although the best approach toward developing a single month's sales goal is to base it on the percentage of total sales last year (or an average for several years), when such historical data is not available, a simple division of the annual sales goal by twelve will provide a rough, though skewed, monthly projected dollar sales goal. In this case, therefore, $2,095,041.60 (the annual sales goal) is divided by 12 (the number of months) to determine the monthly sales goal of $174,586.80 (February's projected dollar sales). Set out in figures the calculation is as follows:

Projected Sales For Next Year (divided by) Number of Months	$\frac{\$2{,}095{,}041.60}{12}$	= $174,586.80	February of Next Year's Projected Dollar Sales

QUESTION 6

Question: What is next February's projected agency income?

Answer: $18,296.70

Calculation: There are two ways to calculate a rough income for an agency when projecting a budget and both approaches result in the same figure (sometimes slightly different due to a rounding out of cents). One approach is to divide total annual projected income by twelve to obtain a single month's proportional share. A second approach is to multiply the projected monthly gross sales by the amount of the projected average commission. The latter of the two approaches set out in figures is as follows:

Projected Monthly Gross Sales	(times)	Projected Average Commission	(equals)	Monthly (February's) Projected Agency Income
$174,586.80	×	.1048	=	$18,296.70

QUESTION 7

Question: What is next February's projected expense budget?

Answer: $17,171.70

Calculation: Although the best approach toward developing a single month's expense budget is to base it on the percentage of each line-item of expense for each expenditure during the last year (or an average for several years), when such historical data is not available, a simple division of the total annual expenses by twelve will provide a rough, though skewed, monthly projected expense budget. In this case, therefore, $206,060.36 (the projected next year total expense budget) is divided by 12 (the number of months of the budget) to determine the monthly expense budget limit of $17,171.70 (February's projected expense budget). Set out in figures the calculation is as follows:

Projected Expenses for Next Year (divided by) Number of Months	$\frac{\$206,060.36}{12}$	= $17,171.70	February of Next Year's Projected Expense Budget

APPENDIX

PERCENTAGE PROFITS TRAVEL CASE

INTRODUCTION

The financial planner at Percentage Profits Travel is preparing the agency's budget for next year. Initial capitalization of the agency was $80,000 and the Board of Directors bases its expected return-on-investment at three points above the New York Prime Interest Rate on the first day of February each year as published in the *Wall Street Journal* on the second day of February each year. The agency's fiscal year starts on the first day of July each year and runs through the last day of June each year. The budget for the next fiscal year is due to be reviewed at the Board of Directors' annual budget meeting held the first Tuesday in May each year.

To calculate budget figures, the term "last year" is based on the previous twelve months ending the last day of March during the year in which the budget is calculated. The term "next year" is based on the twelve months starting on the first of July in the calendar year during which the budget is being calculated. In other words, if the financial planner was planning the budget for the fiscal year 1 July 1999 through 30 June 2000, the applicable ROI basing interest rate would be the rate for 1 February 1999 and published on 2 February 1999; the "last year" figures would be for 1 April 1998 through 31 March 1999; and the "next year" figures would be for 1 July 1999 through 30 June 2000.

The Board of Directors does not consider profits to be return-on-investment, but expects a minimum of one-quarter of one percent of last year's gross sales to be earned in profit. Last year's sales were $1,795,081 and the average commission level was 10.1 percent. Having just joined a consortium, the financial planner is projecting an increase next year to 10.38 percent average commission. Last year's personnel costs constituted 45 percent of all costs (except ROI and profit payments) and were $76,228. Although the percentage should remain the same next year, the actual dollar costs for personnel are projected to increase by $8,374.

PERCENTAGE PROFITS TRAVEL CASE ASSIGNMENT

Calculate the answers to the questions on the next pages relating to the Percentage Profits Travel Case. To do so, it will be necessary to use and make some modifications in the formulas discussed in chapter fourteen. You will also need to find the applicable interest rate on which the ROI is determined by looking it up in last February's *Wall Street Journal.* Since it may not be available and so that all will have the same answer, use the figure of 10.5 percent. The figures and the percentages given in the case follow. This will allow a class review of the answers. Data on how the answers to the following questions are calculated is also provided.

QUESTIONS RELATING TO THE PERCENTAGE PROFITS TRAVEL CASE

1. What is the dollar amount of the return-on-investment expected by the Board of Directors for the next fiscal year? $________________
2. Based on last year's gross sales ($1,795,081) what is the dollar amount of the profit expected by the Board of Directors for the next fiscal year? $________________
3. What is the projected operating cost for the next fiscal year (do not include ROI or profit)? $________________
4. What is next year's projected break-even point before ROI and profit? $________________
5. What is the dollar amount of the Formal Profit Target (including both ROI and Profit)? $________________
6. What is next year's projected income needed to reach next year's projected profit, i.e., the gross sales needed to cover next year's expected profit (including both ROI and profit)? $________________

7. What is the amount of the dollar sales projected for next November? $__________

8. What is the amount of the dollar sales income projected for next November? $__________

9. What is the amount of the projected expense budget for next November? $__________

10. What is the dollar amount of the additional sales that must be made to produce the expected profit as compared with the amount that must be sold to reach the expected return-on-investment? $__________

ANSWERS RELATING TO THE PERCENTAGE PROFITS TRAVEL CASE

QUESTION 1

Question: What is the dollar amount of the return-on-investment expected by the Board of Directors for the next fiscal year?

Answer: $10,800

Calculation: The Board of Directors bases its expected return-on-investment at three points above the New York Prime Interest Rate on the first day of February each year as published in the *Wall Street Journal* on the second day of February each year. The published New York Prime Interest Rate for the first day of February in 1989 as published in the *Wall Street Journal* on the second day of February 1989 was 10.5 percent. Therefore, adding three points to this figure, the return-on-investment expected by the Board of Directors will be 13.5 percent.

The return-on-investment formula is to multiply the percentage of return-on-investment times the capitalization. If one multiplies 13.5 percent times $80,000, the answer one gets is $10,800.

Percentage Return-on-Investment	(times)	Capitalization	(equals)	The Dollar Amount of the Return-on-Investment
.135	×	$80,000	=	$10,800

QUESTION 2

Question: Based on last year's gross sales ($1,795,081), what is the dollar amount of the profit expected by the Board of Directors for the next fiscal year?

Answer: $4,487.70

Calculation: The Board of Directors expects a minimum of one-quarter of one percent of last year's gross sales to be earned in profit. Last year's gross sales were $1,795,081. To determine profit one must multiply one-quarter of one percent (.0025) times last year's gross sales ($1,795,081).

Last Year's Gross Sales	(times)	Minimum Percentage	(equals)	Projected Profit
$1,795,081	×	.0025	=	$4,487.70

QUESTION 3

Question: What is the projected operating cost for the next fiscal year (do not include ROI or profit)?

Answer: $188,004.44

Calculation: Last year's personnel costs constituted 45 percent of all costs (except ROI and profit payments) and were $76,228. Although the percentage should remain the same next year, the actual dollar costs for personnel are projected to increase by $8,374. To calculate the actual total dollar costs for personnel for next year, therefore, last year's personnel cost of $76,228 needs to be added to the projected increase in personnel cost for next year, i.e., $8,374. The total is $84,602.

However, this is only the personnel cost projection for next year. Since personnel costs last year constituted 45 percent of all costs, it stands to reason that non-personnel costs last year constituted 55 percent of all costs since the only costs a business might have are personnel costs and non-personnel costs. And, since ". . .the percentage (of costs are projected to) remain the same next year," it can be presumed that non-personnel costs for next year will also constitute 55 percent of all costs.

Since personnel costs for next year have now been projected at $84,602, and since this constitutes 45 percent of all next year's costs, divide

$84,602 by .45 to determine that all costs projected for next year will be $188,004.44.

QUESTION 4

Question: What is next year's projected break-even point before ROI and profit?

Answer: $1,811,218.10

Calculation: The formula for determining next year's break-even point before ROI and profit is to divide next year's total operating expenses by next year's projected average commission. Since it has been determined that next year's total operating expenses are projected to be $188,004.44 (not including ROI or profit), and since it has been stated in the case situation that ". . .the financial planner is projecting an increase next year to 10.38 percent average commission," to calculate next year's break-even point before ROI and profit, divide $188,004.44 by .1038. Next year's break-even point before ROI and profits is $1,811,218.10.

QUESTION 5

Question: What is the dollar amount of the Formal Profit Target (including both ROI and Profit)?

Answer: $15,287.70

Calculation: To determine the formal profit target, one must calculate the total of both the return-on-investment and the profit. In question 1 it was found that the projected return-on-investment for next year is $10,800.00. In question 2 it was found that the projected profit for next year is $4,487.70. By adding the projected return-on-investment ($10,800.00) to the projected profit ($4,487.70), one determines that the formal profit target is $15,287.70.

QUESTION 6

Question: What is next year's projected income needed to reach next year's projected profit, i.e., the gross sales needed to cover next year's expected profit (including both ROI and profit)?

Answer: $1,958,498.40

Calculation: Step 7 of the budgeting formula is used. This is dividing next year's projected total operating expenses plus profit (and in this case, plus ROI) by next year's projected average commission in order to get next year's projected gross sales income (i.e., the income needed to reach next year's projected profit and ROI). Therefore, the first step is to find the total of next year's projected total operating expenses ($188,004.44) and next year's projected ROI and profit ($15,287.70). Adding both together, one finds that the total of next year's projected operating expenses, ROI, and profit is $203,292.14.

The next step is to divide next year's projected operating expenses, ROI, and profit ($203,292.14) by next year's projected average commission (10.38 percent). The result is next year's projected income needed to reach next year's projected profit (including ROI and profit), i.e., $1,958,498.40.

QUESTION 7

Question: What is the amount of the dollar sales projected for next November?

Answer: $163,208.20

Calculation: Since exact figures are not available on a month-by-month basis for either total monthly sales or for categories of sales, for this exercise the financial planner is forced to calculate monthly projected sales by dividing the total of all projected sales for the year ($1,958,498.40) by 12 (months). The result is $163,208.20, which is the amount of the dollar sales projected for November of next year, as well as for any other month of next year.

QUESTION 8

Question: What is the amount of the dollar sales income projected for next November?

Answer: $16,941.01

Calculation: Since projected income for a travel agency is calculated by multiplying the amount of projected sales ($163,208.20 for November of next year) times the amount of the projected average commission (10.38 percent), the projected dollar sales income for November of next year is $16,941.01.

QUESTION 9

Question: What is the amount of the projected expense budget for next November?

Answer: $15,667.04

Calculation: In question number 3 it was determined that the projected operating cost for the next fiscal year, not including ROI and profit, is $188,004.44. Since the financial planner does not have exact figures available for last year's expenses on either a month-by-month basis or on a line-item chart-of-accounts basis when calculating the answer to this question, for this exercise the financial planner is forced to calculate monthly projected expenses by dividing the total of all projected expenses, not including ROI and profit, ($188,004.44) by 12 (months). The result is $15,667.04, which is the amount of the projected expense budget for November of next year, as well as for any other month of the year.

QUESTION 10

Question: What is the dollar amount of the additional sales that must be made to produce the expected profit as compared with the amount that must be sold to reach the expected return-on-investment?

Answer: The dollar amount of the additional sales that must be made to produce the expected profit is $43,234.10. The dollar amount of the additional sales that must be made to produce the expected return-on-investment is $104,046.24. Therefore, the sales required to produce the projected profit is somewhat less than half the dollar amount of sales required to meet the projected return-on-investment.

Calculation: To determine the amount of sales needed to produce (or cover) any cost-item, divide the projected cost-item by the projected average commission.

In this case, it was determined in question 2 that the amount of projected profit for next year is $4,487.70. Therefore, to determine the amount of sales needed to produce this profit, the financial planner must divide the projected profit for next year ($4,487.70) by the projected average commission for next year (10.38 percent). The result is $43,234.10.

It was also determined in question 1 that the amount of projected return-on-investment for next year is $10,800. Therefore, to determine the amount of sales needed to produce this return-on-investment, the financial planner must divide the projected return-on-investment for next year ($10,800.00) by the projected average commission for next year (10.38 percent). The result is $104,046.24.

Therefore, the dollar amount of the additional sales that must be made to produce the expected profit is $43,234.10. This compares to the amount of additional sales that must be made to produce the expected return-on-investment ($104,046.24). So the sales required to produce the projected profit is somewhat less than half the dollar amount of sales required to meet the projected return-on-investment.

INDEX